THE SECOND REFORMATION:

Baptists in Colonial America

By Bruce Snavely, Ph.D.

To our friends Norm + Denise
whose home is like an
oasis in a warning world
may God truly bless you both

Bruce

The Second Reformation: Baptists in Colonial America
By Bruce Snavely, Ph.D.

ISBN: 978-1-935986-52-2

LIBERTY UNIVERSITY | PRESS

Lynchburg, Va.
www.Liberty.edu/LibertyUniversityPress

Acknowledgements

To Grace…our children…and grandchildren.

Table of Contents

Foreword

Acknowledgments

Abbreviations

Introduction

Section I - Personalities and Perspective

Chapter 1
Isaac Backus and the Second Reformation in America

Chapter 2
New England Baptists in Historical Perspective

Section II - Origins and Orthodoxy

Chapter 3
The Early Development of the SBBM

Chapter 4
Puritan Orthodoxy and the Development of the SBBM

Section III - Movement and Maturation

Chapter 5
Separate-Baptists: From Revival to Disestablishment

Chapter 6
Tracing the Baptists into the Nineteenth Century

Literary Abbreviations

APRL An Appeal To the Public For Religious Liberty. Boston, 1773

ASBC An Address To The Second Baptist Church in Middleborough, Concerning the Importance of Gospel Discipline. Middleborough, 1787

CA The Charleston Association, 1751

DBF A Short Description Of the Difference between the Bond-woman and the Free, 1756

DCM A Discourse, Concerning The Materials, the Manner of Building, and Power of Organizing of the Church of Christ. Boston, 1773

DPE The Doctrine of Particular Election and Final Perseverance. Boston, 1789

FCN A Fish Caught In His Own Net, Boston, 1768

GLD Government and Liberty Described. Boston, 1778

GWA   The Gospel Worthy of All Acceptation. (Printed in *The Works of the Rev. Andrew Fuller* (8 vols; London: B.J. Holdsworth, 1824)

LBL   A Letter To the Reverend Mr. Benjamin Lord. Providence, 1764

NHC   The New Hampshire Confession of Faith, 1833

PBA   The Philadelphia Baptist Association, 1707

PBC   The Philadelphia Baptist Confession, 1742

SBBM   The Separate-Baptist-Backus Movement, 1756

SCA   The Sandy Creek Association, 1758

SC   The Schleitheim Confession, 1527

TTW   The Testimony of Two Witnesses. Providence, 1786

WBA   The Warren Baptist Association, 1767

Old and New Testament Abbreviations

OLD TESTAMENT

Gen	Genesis	Is	Isaiah
Ex	Exodus	Jer	Jeremiah
Lev	Leviticus	Lam	Lamentations
Num	Numbers	Ezek	Ezekiel
Deut	Deuteronomy	Dan	Daniel
Josh	Joshua	Hos	Hosea
Judg	Judges	Joel	Joel
Ru	Ruth	Am	Amos
1, 2 Sam	1, 2 Samuel	Obad	Obadiah
1, 2 Ki	1, 2 Kings	Jon	Jonah
1, 2 Chron	1, 2 Chronicles	Mic	Micah
Ezra	Ezra	Nah	Nahum
Neh	Nehemiah	Hab	Habakkuk
Est	Esther	Zeph	Zephaniah
Job	Job	Hag	Haggai
Ps (Pss)	Psalm(s)	Zech	Zechariah
Prov	Proverbs	Mal	Malachi
Eccl	Ecclesiastes		
Cant	Canticles (Song of Solomon)		

NEW TESTAMENT

Matt	Matt
Mk	Mark
Lk	Luke
Jn	John
Acts	Acts
Rom	Romans
1, 2 Cor	1, 2 Corinthians
Gal	Galatians
Eph	Ephesians
Phil	Philippians
Col	Colossians
1, 2 Thess	1, 2 Thessalonians
1, 2 Tim	1, 2 Timothy
Tit	Titus
Philm	Philemon
Heb	Hebrews
Jas	James
1, 2 Pet	1, 2 Peter
1, 2, 3 Jn	1, 2, 3 John
Jude	Jude
Rev	Revelation

Introduction

The study of Evangelicalism is an ongoing one as evidenced with the most recent analysis of Bebbington's benchmark evangelical study[1] by editors Haykin and Stewart.[2] If the continuation of Luther's reformation is really important in the overall context of Evangelicalism, then following that reformation of the Puritan's pure church ideal to its ultimate conclusion should be vitally important information to the student of church history. This particular study focuses on one of Evangelicalism's sub-themes and traces its path from the first reformation to the American Great Awakening of 1740 and beyond. It is here where the Puritan baton of the so-called *New Reformation*, is taken up again by those wishing to continue ecclesiological change under the banner of on-going revivalism. Ironically, but predictably, God's sense of humor is justified by using the least equipped and least influential group of the early eighteenth century—the Baptists, and the least among them, the Separate-Baptists of colonial New England—to move the Puritan's experiment in the wilderness forward.

Various research efforts have contributed significantly to our understanding of the Separate-Baptist movement in colonial New England and more particularly its primary leader and historian, Isaac Backus. Consequently, a key to understanding the Second Reformation in Colonial America demands an explanation of how Backus and the Separate-Baptist movement developed into the fastest growing Evangelical movement in America.

---

1   David Bebbington's work, *Evangelicalism in Modern Britain*, (Grand Rapids: Baker Book House, 1992), has been for the last twenty years, the quintessential work for understanding the roots of Evangelicalism particularly in its inherent relationship to the Enlightenment. The Enlightenment connection is a dominant concept underlying the author's thesis.

2   The most recent analysis of Bebbington's work is *The Advent of Evangelicalism: Exploring Historical Continuities* (Nashville: B&H Publications, 2008) by editors Haykin and Stewart. It has attempted to narrow this enlightenment relationship and tie Evangelicalism, as a movement, more to prior evangelical awakenings.

SECTION ONE

Personalities and Perspectives

Chapter One

The Isaac Backus Movement and
the Second Reformation

INTRODUCTION

History has clearly shown us that Luther's reformation introduced significant historical, theological, and social upheaval. Consequently, it can be helpful to conceptualize various aspects of its winding course by familiarization with its key terms, personalities, and participants. This chapter will not only serve as a prologue for understanding the Second Reformation as a historical movement, but it will also show the connection of the Separate-Baptist-Backus Movement (SBBM) to previous Puritan reform and how Baptists thought reformation should continue. Furthermore, this chapter will lay out the necessity of understanding the American Puritan/ Separatist movement as an indigenous movement which pursued the pure local-church ideal which Luther's reformation effort purposefully ignored.[3] Unfortunately, some historians tend to attribute the rise and dominance of exclusive local-church positions to the vagaries of mere sectarianism and doctrinal myopia.[4] The view taken here is that the

---

3   Recognizing the Backus movement as continuing Luther's and the Puritan's original efforts, Gaustad noted, "The Reformation was still incomplete; a new separation was required; and Backus, instead of Brewster, could help show the way." See Gaustad's article "*The Backus- Leland Tradition*" in Hudson, *Baptist Concepts of the Church*, (Valley Forge: Judson Press, 1959), 110.
4   This ecclesiological disposition is generally represented by those who hold the Landmark position of the church. This errant position, championed in the nineteenth century by various men, held that Baptists and their churches could be traced successively in some organic connection all the way back to John the Baptist and the Apostles. For an overview of this position and its seminal beliefs, see C. C. Goen, *Revivalism and Separatism in New England, 1740-1800: Strict Congregationalist and Separate-Baptists in the Great Awakening* (New Haven: Yale University Press, 1962), Leon McBeth, *The Baptist Heritage (Nashville, Broadman Press, 1987)* , J.M. Pendleton, *An Old Landmark Re-Set* (Fulton: National Baptist

Backus movement cannot, and should not be arbitrarily classified as such, nor should it be saddled with the burden of being charged with having ignored clearly defined ecclesiological principles at the expense of perceived ecumenical responsibilities as some have suggested.[5]

THE CONTINUING REFORMATION

The Reformation of Martin Luther in 1517 and its subsequent ecclesiological developments[6] were not in and of themselves, a seamless, final story occurring only in Europe. English Puritans[7] had, in effect, "continued the reformation of Martin Luther, John Calvin, and Henry VIII in England in the on-going effort of identifying the elect[8] (genuine believers) within the visible churches under what was

---

Publishing House, 1899), Bob L. Ross, *Old Landmarkism and the Baptists: An Examination of the Theories of Church Authority and Church Succession* (Pasadena: Pilgrim Publications, 1979).

5 This is the view, among others, of the late Stanley Grenz and will be discussed later.

6 The Reformation as a movement was a re-declaration of biblical theology as understood by its founders to be consistent with the original apostolic movement. As a theological movement, it followed the Trinitarian and Christological developments of the fourth and fifth centuries and the soteriological development of the twelfth century with Anselm. The sixteenth century included all of the former movements, but came to focus primarily on the doctrine of the church as it attempted to live out the realities of its doctrinal heritage in the rapidly changing world of the Renaissance tradition.

7 The Puritan movement, originally precipitated in England by Henry VIII and his break with Rome, was a movement which essentially believed that the reformation of Luther had not yet been brought to completion. Believing that the Church of England required further purification, the Puritans' ultimate desire was to cleanse the English Church from every relic of Romanism. For good discussions of the English Reformation see Edwin Hall, *The Puritans and Their Principles* (New York: Baker and Scribner, 1847) and Alan Simpson, *Puritanism in Old and New England* (Chicago: University of Chicago Press, 1955).

8 This effort at *identifying the elect* within the visible church was the on-going effort of purification of the particular/local assembly of Christ. From the beginning of Luther's reform movement to Calvin and the Puritans, this concept grew increasingly important. Although the goal of the Puritans was "making the invisible church more visible" they did not consider the visible church possible of ever being identical with the universal, invisible aspect of the church. The gradual merging of the invisible/mystical church into the local/visible church was a phenomenon associated more with the church concept of the Anabaptists and the offspring of the Separate-Baptists of New England. For an excellent understanding of the Puritan mindset concerning how they viewed the church in its various aspects; as well as their understanding of professing believers and true members, see Edward Hindson, ed., *Introduction to Puritan Theology* (Grand Rapids: Baker Book House, 1976).

commonly referred to as the Second Reformation."[9] The English Puritans recognized, in the story of Luther, Calvin, and Zwingli, that the outline of continued reform of the visible church was necessary for being able to identify genuine believers. This effort resulted in the restricting of membership within the visible church to those who could give evidence of being regenerated, while rejecting those who lived scandalous lives.[10] This resulted in the appearance of another class of Puritans known as Separatists[11] who were not satisfied with the extent

9   McLoughlin, *Soul Liberty: The Baptists' Struggle in New England, 1630-1833*, (Hanover and London: University Press of New England, 1991), 179. The so-called "Second Reformation," is another name given to the on-going effort by the Puritans to reform the Church of England and establish assemblies which more closely reflected the apostolic model. In the New World, Increase Mather referred to the movement as "the new Reformation." See *Cotton Mather: Magnalia Christi Americana*, edited by Kenneth B. Murdock, (1702; Cambridge, 1977), 49, 51, 53, 130, 144. In Colonial New England, the Baptists saw themselves as the final arbiters of the "new Reformation" because they believed New England Puritans had failed to bring many Reformation ideas to their ultimate conclusions, especially the Puritan insistence on retaining infant baptism, which they believed lay at the heart of papal doctrine, calling it the "badge of the whore." Dissenting individuals and groups down through history normally identified this practice as the key to all false doctrine in the Church of Rome. The Anabaptist *Schleitheim Confession* of 1527 called infant baptism "the highest and chief abomination of the Pope." See John Gill, *Infant Baptism: A Part and Pillar of Popery* (Philadelphia: American Baptist Publication Society, 1851), William Latane Lumpkin, *Baptist Confessions of Faith* (Philadelphia: Judson Press, 1959).

10   This pursuit of those pastors and teachers in the Church of England to keep out of their assemblies the flagrantly wicked was a key tenet of English Puritanism. The Puritans applauded the separation of the English Church from Rome under Henry the VIII but denied that the bishops could claim the disciplinary power which belonged, in their minds, to the individual churches and not the civil authority. The Puritans believed that the inability of the churches to remove the ungodly from their ranks prevented the reformation of other evils necessary to having the church composed of the truly regenerate.

11   The first defender of separation from the Church of England was Robert Browne at Norwich in 1580. The Separatists who followed the Browne ideal became an important link in understanding the development of the visible church concept. Geoffrey Nuttall demonstrated the connection between the "Dissenting Brethren" from the Westminster Assembly in 1643 and the original *Brownists*, including John Robinson the pastor of the Separatist community at Leiden. Many from Robinson's congregation were the first settlers in Massachusetts Bay. For a thorough understanding of English Separatism and the contribution of John Robinson to the ongoing reformation ideal, see Timothy George, *John Robinson and the English Separatist Tradition*, ed. Charles Talbert, vol. 1, National Association of Baptist Professors of Religion Dissertation Series (Macon: Mercer University Press, 1982), Geoffrey Fillingham Nuttall, *Visible Saints: The Congregational Way, 1640-1660* (Oxford,: B. Blackwell, 1957), B.R. White, *The English Separatist Tradition* (London: Oxford University Press, 1971).

of Puritan reform within the Church of England.[12] Some Separatists believed that a fresh beginning in the New World was the *only* solution if a true reformation was to continue. They hoped that their renewed efforts could become, in effect, a show-case[13] for having drawn the perfect distance between the *visible* and *invisible* church,[14] something which had been impossible for them in Old England.

Shortly after the beginning of the Massachusetts Bay Colony, dissenting Baptists[15] came to believe that the Puritans were "unwilling

---

12   For a dated, brief, yet insightful work on Puritan reform from the eyes of an Anglican rector, see D. Mountfield, M.A., *The Church and the Puritans* (London: James Clark and Company, 1881).

13   Although he was of the classic Puritan mindset, this is what John Winthrop meant for those on board the *Arbella* bound for Boston in 1630 when he spoke of the establishment of "a city on a hill." This establishment said Perry Miller was "no retreat from Europe; it was a flank attack. We are to be a city set upon a hill, the eyes of all the world upon us; what we succeed in demonstrating, Europe will be bound to imitate, even Rome itself." Quoted from Perry Miller, *The New England Mind: From Colony to Province* (Cambridge,: Harvard University Press, 1953), 5.

14   These terms for differing aspects of the church are commonly used in ecclesiastical literature. The *True Church* is normally understood as that church defined by Augustine in Platonic terms as the universal, invisible body of Christ comprised of all those predetermined by God for salvation. Later, Augustine defined the visible church in universal terms, essentially synonymous with the kingdom idea. Using the parable of the wheat and the tares to demonstrate the all-inclusive nature of the visible church, he made the church a mixture of the regenerate and the un-regenerate. The idea was strongly opposed by the Donatists, who confronted Augustine on the inherent impurity of such a church. The visible church is defined as a local body of believers, wherever situated, who have covenanted together to obey the commands of Christ. The distance between the two churches was considered to be biblically inconsistent. Consequently, the Puritan reform efforts were aimed at reducing the distance between the two by making the visible church, like the proposed invisible one, to be comprised of the elect or regenerate only. The Separate-Baptists saw themselves in New England as those furthering the *second reformation* with this goal in mind, thereby making this stage of reform more *church*-focused than *salvation*-focused.

15   McLoughlin said of the earliest Baptists in Massachusetts that the "movement was essentially an indigenous, parallel movement to that in England and not an offshoot or extension of it. It stemmed from a common source in the theological and ecclesiological principles of the general Puritan movement, and needed no other source or stimulus than the ideas which the Non-Separatist Congregationalists brought to New England." While true of their *doctrinal* moorings, this statement suggests far too much congruity for their respective origins. An exception was John Myles, who came from Swansea, Wales. Baptists generally were part of the greater dissent community, who usually took offense at the forced baptism of their infants. Taken from McLoughlin, *New England Dissent 1630-1833.* 2 vols. (Cambridge: Harvard University Press, 1971), 1: 6. For the author's entire discussion on early New England Baptists see 1:1-25.

in the New World to carry on that reformation to its logical conclusion."[16] Their two primary intentions were aimed at confronting the practice of infant baptism, which they saw as the final vestige of false doctrine, and the twin pillar of state support, which its "nursing fathers" used to defend ecclesiastical doctrine through judicial force.[17] It was not until the appearance of the Great Awakening,[18] with its attendant doctrine of the new birth,[19] that the zeal of these new converts to the revival message caused them to regard the churches of the Standing Order[20] as impure assemblies. Consequently, they

16   McLoughlin, *Soul Liberty: The Baptists' Struggle in New England, 1630-1833*, 179.

17   This idea, implicit in the concept "Nursing Fathers," is used in various ways by Church Fathers, such as Augustine, along with Reformation leaders and various other Protestant churchmen. The concept describes the unique role the civil magistrates played in supporting the State-controlled churches. For the way this relationship unfolded in New England and particularly in Massachusetts, see Ibid., 13-92; Perry Miller, *Orthodoxy in Massachusetts 1630-1650* (Cambridge: Harvard University Press, 1933). For how this term and its related ideas developed in Protestant circles, see J.W. Allen, *The History of Political Thought in the Sixteenth Century* (New York: 1928).

18   The Great Awakening began initially in the Middle Colonies under the Dutch Reformed pastor Theodore Frelinghuyson. The awakening in the Middle Colonies was continued through the efforts of Gilbert Tennent who preached his famous sermon, "The Danger of an Unconverted Ministry" in 1740. This became a great tool helping to foster the revival spirit all the way up the eastern seaboard alerting many to the great decline of personal piety from pulpit to pew in the various churches. The "Great Awakening" in New England was actually a series of highly successful and influential revivals of religion beginning in 1734-35 by Jonathan Edwards in Northampton, Connecticut. These were followed by the extraordinary revival efforts of George Whitefield. Whitefield became the most highly celebrated of all the revivalists, coming to Boston in 1740. In the wake of his New England tour, hundreds of new converts rushed back into the churches, beginning a reformation of piety in America not previously known. See Edwin S. Gaustad, *The Great Awakening in New England* (New York: Harper & Brothers, 1965), Alan Heimert and Perry Miller, *The Great Awakening: Documents Illustrating the Crisis and Its Consequences* (Indianapolis, IN: Bobbs-Merrill, 1967), Charles H. Maxson, *The Great Awakening in the Middle Colonies* (Chicago: University of Chicago Press, 1920).

19   This evangelical doctrine was the primary focus of revival preaching. For an excellent treatment of how this doctrine dominated the preaching of the evangelists during the Great Awakening, see the chapter entitled "The Nature and Necessity of the New Birth" in Alan Heimert and Perry Miller, ed., *Religion and the American Mind: From the Great Awakening to the Revolution* (Cambridge, MA: Harvard University Press, 1966).

20   This term "Standing Order" is prevalent in the historical literature of the Puritan era and describes the controlling ecclesiastical bodies in England and New England. The English Puritans saw doctrinal and practical corruption in the Church of England while those in New England who had experienced the new birth saw similar problems in the Congregational system. To those in the dissenting community whether English or Colonial, the prevailing

separated for the purpose of forming new churches composed solely of those who could testify to having undergone the new birth experience. Unfortunately, these Separate-Congregational[21] converts were then faced with another series of problems revolving around the issues of baptism and church membership. This struggle concerning the issue of baptism, namely baby sprinkling, led to the subsequent story of the Separate-Baptists.[22] Their role in the Second Reformation demands the identification of the key factors in the pursuit of visible church purity, and how their local-church emphasis became the prevailing church model as opposed to the classic Protestantism of Europe.[23]

The account of this movement's evolution can actually be told best from the life of its greatest leader and thinker, Isaac Backus. This Baptist pastor and historian actually personified many of the New

---

ecclesiastical system bore this name. See McLoughlin, *New England Dissent 1630-1833*.

21   The Separate-Congregationalists became a distinct denominational group almost immediately following the New England revivals. Their inability to remain in their churches revolved primarily around two issues: the new birth experience and infant baptism. Many of them who had been baptized (sprinkled) as infants believed that they had never been truly baptized, and therefore as believers needed to be immersed, thus obeying the scriptural command to "believe and be baptized." The recognized leader of the Separate group was Solomon Paine of the Canterbury Separate Church in Connecticut. The best work documenting this movement including that of the Separate-Baptists is Goen, *Revivalism and Separatism in New England, 1740-1800: Strict Congregationalist and Separate-Baptists in the Great Awakening*.

22   The rise of the Separate-Baptists involved the issue of not holding "communion" or church-fellowship with those who practiced infant baptism. Isaac Backus, who had started a Separate Church in Titicut, Massachusetts, struggled with the issue of communion with pedobaptists from 1751 to 1756 when he finally decided that open-communion was impossible to scripturally maintain. At his home on January 2, 1756, Backus sounded the trumpet of a new movement, "I now declared that I firmly believed that as none are the proper subject of baptism but real saints, so every such soul ought to be baptized by immersion before they come to the Lord's Supper." Taken from McLoughlin, *New England Dissent 1630-1833*, 87.

23   All of the Protestant bodies of the reformers were agreed that all baptized persons in any given territory were members of the visible church. They believed the visible church was virtually co-extensive with the state and should be purged of evil by appointed officers and civil magistrates, all without schism. Protestant doctrine was predominantly Calvinistic, holding to the Augustinian idea of the universal-invisible church comprised of the elect or those predetermined by God in eternity past for salvation. For a valuable discussion of Protestant ecclesiastical thought see Williston Walker, *The Creeds and Platforms of Congregationalism* (New York: Charles Scribner's Sons, 1893), 1-17.

England Baptists' core beliefs and helped set the stage for subsequent generations regarding Baptist ecclesiology. But the narrative requires more than just the biographical material of his birth, life, and death. It also requires an understanding of how individuals like Isaac Backus and other Separate-Baptists came to their opinions, and more specifically, how their visible church convictions molded theological opinion within the Baptist denomination at such a critical time in American denominational thought. Admittedly, little has been written about Backus' theological opinions, but even less has been written about his movement, which became the driving ecclesiological force of the Baptists into the nineteenth century.[24] No doubt, some of Backus' anonymity may exist because the America in which he lived was awash in notable personalities and epoch-making events. This is particularly true for both the continuing reformation and the American Revolution, in which he played key roles.[25] He was truly—as one biographer called him—"a child of his age" living in turbulent, changing times, whereof "his age was one of rising tides of political and religious dissent," and wherein "he became a leading dissenter."[26] As a Separate-Baptist,

---

24   Before the mid-point of the nineteenth century, Separate-Baptist thought about the visible church had crystallized into an ecclesiology which virtually ignored any existence of the universal-invisible church. The effort of this present work is focused on both how this occurred and why, particularly by one who professed to be such a stalwart follower of Edwardsean Calvinism. The Backus progeny would eventually choose to ignore the Universal church in their practical theology and leave it entirely out of their most noted doctrinal statement: the New Hampshire Confession.

25   Despite Backus' influential participation in key historical events, his importance has been overlooked by many historians. William McLoughlin, the former professor of Religion and Church History at Brown University, offered three possible reasons for the unfortunate neglect of Isaac Backus and his enormous contribution to both the literature and tenor of his times. The third reason, and perhaps the most important he says, concerning the Baptist movement in colonial New England is that Baptist scholars "wrongly construed his role to have been marginal." See his Introduction in McLoughlin, ed., *Isaac Backus on Church, State, and Calvinism: Pamphlets, 1754-1789*, 1.

26   Maston, *Isaac Backus: Pioneer of Religious Liberty*, 11.

Isaac Backus became one of the most noted thinkers, historians, and spokesmen of one of America's most rapidly changing generations.

COLONIAL BAPTISTS IN A CONGREGATIONAL WORLD

Like many great and enduring leaders, one would have expected Isaac Backus to have been nurtured from childhood upon the ideas which would later form his adult life. For this Baptist pastor however, his post-conversion life ultimately became a living polemic against the system in which he had been raised.

Born in Norwich, Connecticut, on January 20th, 1724, Isaac Backus was a member of one of the wealthiest and most respected Congregational families in the area. His English-born grandfather, William Backus, had moved to Norwich in 1660 from Saybrook, Connecticut. He was one of the original proprietors of the city, and was also a representative of Norwich in the Connecticut Legislature.[27] Because of his stalwart opinions on Congregational polity as a member of the Standing Church, he opposed the Saybrook Platform[28] as others did the Cambridge Platform[29] in Massachusetts.

Conversely, Backus' father Samuel was a quiet farmer who died when Isaac was only sixteen, having been converted late in his life. It is likely that Backus had more in common with his grandfather than

---

27   T.B. Maston's professed effort was one of identifying Backus' "political ethic with its emphasis on liberty of conscience" which Maston tied directly to his parental background and geographical location in New England.

28   The Saybrook Platform was a position established by Congregational Synod on September 9th, 1708 in Saybrook, Connecticut, which united state authority to the consociations and associations of the Standing Order in Connecticut. It was hotly opposed by many churches and individuals, including Isaac Backus' paternal grandfather.

29   The Cambridge Platform of 1648 was the codification of the doctrines and practices of the Massachusetts Congregational system. This became necessary for the Standing Order because uniformity was no longer a foregone conclusion among the populace. As one historian said, "Massachusetts was forced to profess and develop a homogeneity it had assumed but had not possessed. The spontaneity of the new reformation was slowly congealing in New England, and it continued to do so through the ensuing century." Taken from McLoughlin, *Soul Liberty: The Baptists' Struggle in New England, 1630-1833*, 36.

his own father. Whatever the case, the point should not be missed, that Isaac's local-church opinions, evolving later out of Congregational Separatism, had a prior exemplar of dissent in his grandfather's ardent conservatism concerning Congregational church polity in Connecticut. New England Baptists, prior to the birth of Backus and the Great Awakening, were a numerically weak and scattered people.[30] Their history can only be seen as it lay just below the visible surface of the Standing Order with its dominant personalities and social policies. In the Middle Colonies, Baptists were predominantly under the aegis of the Philadelphia Baptist Association,[31] and the influence of its doctrinal exemplar: the Westminster Confession of Faith.[32]

In New England the Baptists were divided, as were the English, among the General Baptists and Particular Baptists[33] with no local doctrinal expression of their own. Consequently, doctrinal

---

30   The most informative history available on the early New England Baptists is that of Isaac Backus. See Isaac Backus, *A History of New England with Particular Reference to the Denomination of Christians Called Baptists*, Three vols. (1777, 1784, 1796; reprint, Second Edition, two volumes. Ed. David Weston. Newton, Mass.1871). Other excellent sources are Heimert and Miller, *The Great Awakening: Documents Illustrating the Crisis and Its Consequences*, Bill J. Leonard, *Baptist Ways: A History* (Valley Forge: Judson Press, 2003), McLoughlin, *New England Dissent 1630-1833*, A.H. Newman, ed., *A Century of Baptist Movement* (Philadelphia: American Baptist Publication Society, 1901), Tull, *Shapers of Baptist Thought*.

31   This association had its beginning in September of 1706, and was the first Baptist Association in America. It was comprised of five Calvinistic (Particular) churches, but was started under the auspices of the Pennepek Baptist Church as noted in its own minutes. See A.D. Gillette, ed., *Minutes of the Philadelphia Baptist Association from A.D 1707 to A.D. 1807; Being the First One-Hundred Years of Its Existence*. (Philadelphia: American Baptist Publication Society, 1851; reprint, Baptist Book Trust).

32   The Westminster Confession of Faith in England was the effort of the Puritan Assembly in 1643 to frame a Confession of Faith for the three kingdoms of England, Scotland, and Ireland as a revision of the thirty-nine articles of the Church of England. Initiated in 1643, it was finished and published in 1646. It was characterized by the dominating influence of predestination and particular election. As Philip Schaff said, "The Westminster Confession, together with the Catechisms, is the fullest and ripest symbolical statement of the Calvinistic system of doctrine." See Philip Schaff, *The Creeds of Christendom*, 3 vols., vol. 3 (New York: Harper and Brothers Publishers, 1877).

33   The General Baptists were those who believed the atonement of Christ was provided for all in general, while the Particular Baptists believed the atonement was provided only for those elected for salvation in eternity past.

distinctions had less significance for Baptists prior to the Great Awakening. In the early colonies up until the turn of the seventeenth century, the basis of corporate unity lay in their mutual rejection of infant baptism. However, there was even some degree of difference among Baptists concerning whether Baptists should permit regenerate adults who refused adult baptism into church membership. When the Great Awakening arrived in 1740, many Baptists remained aloof to the revival because Whitefield was an infant sprinkling, Church of England minister. This intramural disagreement about membership requirements among Baptists was indicative of the doctrinal diversity of the period. For some Baptists, tolerating infant baptism also reflected a latent desire for social standing among the Standing Order. After all, the presence of respected members of the local Congregational parish in one's meetinghouse could prove socially beneficial, as it did with Baptist pastor, John Myles, in Swansea, Massachusetts.[34] Historically, prior to the nineteenth century, Colonial Baptists enjoyed little respect either socially or politically among the ruling classes.

During the politically turbulent seventeenth century in England, Baptists had wisely crafted their doctrinal expressions as closely as possible to the prevailing influence of the Westminster Confession. For the Particular Baptists, this influence was seen in

---

34   John Myles was a Welsh Baptist pastor from Swansea, Wales. He practiced open-communion, rejecting baptism as a membership requirement in the visible church. This position was popularized in England by John Bunyan, the Bedford pastor and writer of *The Pilgrim's Progress*. In the church's explication on a series of rules for church admittance drawn up by Congregationalist pastor Thomas Willet, Myles wrote a doctrinal standard demanding strict obedience in such things as the gospel, the deity of Christ, His resurrection, the Trinity, while adding that "this is not understood of any holding any opinion different from others on many disputable points yet in controversy among the godly learned, the belief of these not essentially necessary to salvation, such as, antipedobaptism, church discipline, or the like; but the minister or ministers of the said town may take their liberty to baptize infants or grown persons as the Lord shall persuade their consciences, and so also the inhabitants to take the liberty to bring their children to baptism or forbear." Taken from McLoughlin, as quoted from the Swansea Town Records, McLoughlin, *New England Dissent 1630-1833*, 1:133.

their strict, Calvinist soteriology; for the General Baptists, it was
seen in their universal Church inclusivism which they assumed made
them *good* Protestants. This kind of expediency played a similar
role in Massachusetts as some Baptists were willing to wink at
open membership with Congregationalists who resisted rebaptism
after conversion. They even began to send some of their young men
to Harvard to get their education, and abandoned proselytizing
Congregationalists.[35] Generally however, Baptists were social
outcasts, and were usually spoken of in the most derogatory of terms
by leaders of the Standing Order.[36] Furthermore, the Baptists in
colonial New England, unlike their English brethren, had insufficient
numbers and influence to offer resistance to persecution by the
Standing Order, particularly in the Bay Colony. English dissent was
shared by Congregationalists, Presbyterians, Baptists, and Quakers,
some of which had political influence, but the Baptists stood fairly
alone as voices of dissent in Massachusetts.[37] During the latter half

---

35   McLoughlin, *Soul Liberty: The Baptists' Struggle in New England, 1630-1833*, 6.
This historian inferred that other Baptist compromise took place. Some Baptists even agreed
not to evangelize among the Congregationalists. Because they had yielded up this ground, they
increasingly became more Arminian, reflecting Harvard's theological drift.
36   Most terms used by Colonial Congregationalists to describe Baptists had their
roots in historic, dissent ideology. For interesting reading on the epithets used to describe
Baptists and others in the dissent community, see Leonard Verduin, *The Reformers and Their
Stepchildren* (Grand Rapids: Baker Book House, 1964).
37   One such exception to the sharing of English dissent was a near case of tragedy
which occurred in Aylesbury in Buckinghamshire where twelve General Baptists were arrested
and convicted in 1663 for conventicling (unlawfully meeting together). Facing the decision to
either conform or suffer exile, these brave Baptists chose neither, and were thereby sentenced
to death. Only a message from Particular Baptist, William Kiffin, to the attention of King
Charles saved them from an impending and certain death. Further English dissent had been
effectively crushed under "The Clarendon Code." This act of Parliament extended from
1661-1665 through a series of Civil Acts passed during that period. The Act of Uniformity
of 1662 drove up to two thousand Puritan clerics out of the State Church. The Corporation
Act removed the possibility of dissenters and Baptists serving in local municipal life. The
Toleration Act of 1689, though it did not repeal the Clarendon Code Acts, provided religious
freedom to dissenters and Baptists from persecution from the Church of England. Baptists
remained unable to hold office in spite of the Toleration Act. For further discussion of English
dissent among the entire dissent community in seventeenth century England see B.R. White,
The English Baptists of the Seventeenth Century, ed. Roger Hayden, 4 vols., vol. 1, *A History of*

of the seventeenth century, the Baptist community had no means of pressuring Congregational leaders other than through appeals to their English sympathizers, who in turn would apply pressure for toleration.[38] The Standing Order and its parish ministries were sustained by taxation of those living within the parish area. Even after 1692, when the Act of Toleration was passed in Massachusetts, it remained difficult for Baptist dissenters to obtain relief.[39] For many that relief would arrive by way of separatism in the wake of revival.

SEPARATISM AND THE STANDING ORDER

Dissent was never far from the surface in Colonial New England. As Baptists made their way to America searching for greater freedom of worship, they were surprised at how much like their Anglican persecutors the Separatist-Puritans had themselves become. Perry Miller quoted Clarke's pamphlet saying, "While Old England is becoming new, New England is become old."[40] The iron-fisted rule exhibited so clearly in New England, particularly in

the English Baptists (Oxford: The Baptist Historical Society, 1983). The story above is found on p.106 in White. For a dated yet helpful source to understanding early English persecution of the Baptists, see Benjamin Evans, *The Early English Baptists*, 2 vols. (J. Heaton and Son, 1864; reprint, The Baptist Standard Bearer, Inc.).

38   This began in the Colonies with John Clark and his pamphlet "*Ill Newes from New England*" wherein he chronicled the persecution being exacted against the Baptists by the Standing Order. His efforts brought a return of much scrutiny and pressure from the mother country to follow England's example of rising toleration for dissenting religious groups.

39   From the 1640s, Baptists and other dissenters sought the disestablishment of the Standing Church in regard to coerced taxation. In a series of laws after 1727, the Massachusetts Baptists, Quakers, and Episcopalians were given relief from paying taxes to support the Congregational Church if they lived within its jurisdiction. However, the "certificate system" devised to exonerate non-Congregationalists was easily used to the advantage of the prevailing State Church. Backus' own mother was jailed in 1752 for failing to pay the "minister's rate," which was the tax collected to pay the Congregational ministers' salary. For insight on the tax issue among the Baptists see Backus, *A History of New England with Particular Reference to the Denomination of Christians Called Baptists*, 95-101; McLoughlin, *Soul Liberty: The Baptists' Struggle in New England, 1630-1833.*, 228-248, and Maston, *Isaac Backus: Pioneer of Religious Liberty*, 77-101.

40   Miller, *Orthodoxy in Massachusetts 1630-1650*, 283.

Massachusetts, set the stage throughout the seventeenth century for challenges from the mother country for Massachusetts authorities to become more tolerant to the voices of dissent. As the colonies moved closer to the war for independence, Baptists were often charged with being loyal to the King, while siding against their own countrymen. This was not necessarily true, but because the Baptists sought a balance of ecclesiastical power in New England, they once rejected participation in a "Christian Union" of colonial churches opposing Church of England plans to send a bishop to Boston.[41] Even after English attempts at colonizing the intolerant Massachusetts Bay Commonwealth, toleration was still spitefully observed by those who had the power to temper it. English efforts at influencing the Bay Colony's political and social policies toward greater toleration occurred throughout the seventeenth century with constant attempts at establishing the right of the Church of England to worship within their bounds. In 1664, an English Commission came to Boston to secure a change in the state's denominational elitism with the reminder to authorities that the foundation of the Massachusetts charter was freedom of conscience. Being rebuffed, in 1684, these same authorities revoked the Massachusetts charter in an effort to bring New England under the ecclesiastical and political control of England. It should be recognized that the English at this time prior to the revolution were not just interested in toleration for all religious groups. Their political aspirations for control in the Colonies dominated their agenda, but

---

41   For a good representation of original documents and correspondence between England and the Colonies in the years leading up to the revolution and prevailing sentiments among the Baptists in America, see William H. Brackney, ed., *Baptist Life and Thought: 1600-1980*. (Valley Forge: Judson Press, 1983), Leon H. McBeth, *A Sourcebook of Baptist Heritage* (Nashville: Broadman Press, 1990).

the ecclesiastical elitism of the Bay Colony exacerbated the tensions greatly.[42]

The Standing Order had suffered from its own internal problems. Church ordinances, once the holy observances of believers only, were now offered to all comers as a sort of spiritual elixir aimed at building up a sagging constituency.[43] The Standing Order, powerless and without piety, desperately needed revival if their efforts at the Second Reformation were to continue. And, had revival depended on the beleaguered Baptists, it would have been an unlikely prospect. Revival concerns and doctrinal strength had been relegated to something below mere survival. Although most groups were divided by the Calvinist and Arminian designations, there were actually several strains of Baptist thought prevalent between 1630 and 1700, unfortunately few of these were focused on spiritual renewal.

However, by 1734, portents of great hope began to appear in the life and ministry a pastor-theologian in Northampton, Massachusetts,

---

42   For further understanding of the social and political development of this period, see William Warren Sweet, *Religion in Colonial America* (New York: Cooper Square Publishers, Inc., 1965).

43   This declining piety within New England Congregationalism is a point of much contention among historians. Obviously, those who were involved in revival efforts believed the spiritual situation to be grave. Most of the debate concerning the state of the churches revolved around measures taken to affect positive change in church attendance and involvement during the seventeenth century. The most noted of these measures was the Half-Way Covenant of 1662. This allowed any person to join a Standing Church by signing the covenant and professing to believe its Calvinist doctrines, and promising to outwardly obey its standards. These persons were allowed to have their children baptized, but they were not allowed to come to the communion table or vote in the church's affairs. Thus, until, if ever, they could give a clear testimony of conversion, they were only "Half-Way" members. This practice was exaggerated further by Solomon Stoddard, a Congregational minister from Northampton, Connecticut, in 1777. He advocated that the communion table should be opened to all upright persons, regenerate or not, and that the ordinance was a "converting ordinance." McLoughlin said that this "confused the gospel of grace with the doctrine of works and transformed the gospel church of visible saints into a national church with a birthright membership." In this sense, the Congregational system in New England had morphed itself into the very kind of system from which they had fled in Old England. See Handlin, ed., *Isaac Backus and the American Pietistic Tradition*, 57-76, Edmund S. Morgan, *Visible Saints: The History of a Puritan Idea* (Ithaca: Cornell University Press, 1963),146-151.

named Jonathan Edwards.[44] In answer to prayer and the preaching of the need for experiencing justification by faith, Edwards' entire church and community experienced a powerful moving of the Spirit with a number of surprising conversions. This event became the theological catalyst for revival and social change among people of faith in Britain and America, but the popular personality used by God as the means of spreading the vocabulary of this new revival spirit was the English evangelist, George Whitefield.[45] The Grand Itinerant, as he would later be called, with the help of William Tennant and James Davenport, was committed to the Calvinism of Edwards, but he preached the new birth as if everyone could be saved and needed to individually respond to the claims of the gospel. As a result, Whitefield and his associates not only suffered under the accusations of Arminianism from the churches of the Standing Order[46] but also as those who advocated dissent and separation. Schism, though an intolerable

---

44   Jonathan Edwards was the great grandson of Solomon Stoddard, and he became the pastor of his grandfather's old church. In 1734 Edwards chronicled the first of the New England revivals in *A Faithful Narrative of the Surprising Work of God in Conversion of many hundred Souls in Northampton and neighboring Towns and Villages*, in a letter to the Rev. Benjamin Coleman of Boston in 1737. Edwards' Calvinism was an "evangelical Calvinism" which staunchly believed in the doctrines of John Calvin, yet believed in the necessity of preaching to reach the elect with the gospel. Edwards' Calvinism would continue to be modified into the nineteenth century and beyond as the doctrine of election met the continuing need of personal revival among the unregenerate masses moving westward.

45   For a thorough understanding of how revival became a transatlantic phenomena characterized by a network of letter writing, published advertisement and social interaction, see Frank Lambert, *Pedlar in Divinity: George Whitefield and the Transatlantic Revivals, 1737-1770* (Princeton, N.J.: Princeton University Press, 1994). This work is not written from a position of supporting the spiritual labors of Whitefield and other revivalists but of exposing the amazing network of communication which enabled the Great Awakening to become such a social, as well as religious, phenomena.

46   Whitefield's preaching style was a social phenomenon in New England. With his preaching of the need for sinners to experience the new birth, along with the sense of urgency with which he presented salvation to his mass audiences, the "Grand Itinerant" was accused of believing in the "universal atonement" of Jacob Arminius, the Dutch theologian. Whitefield responded to such charges primarily through his letter-arguments with John Wesley, whom he had personally installed over his English itinerancy before his first trip to America in 1739. Shortly after Whitefield left Wesley, Wesley came out in clear opposition to Calvinistic theology. Although Whitefield was a staunch Calvinist, his preaching style made him appear to his detractors as believing in free will.

offense to the Congregational system in Massachusetts, became an inevitable response as individuals and churches attempted to adjust to the impact of fresh converts. Those in favor of the revival and its methods were called New Lights, and those who rejected were called Old Lights.[47] Many of these new converts, heated in the cauldron of revival and impassioned by their fresh understanding of God, could no longer tolerate communion with unregenerate ministers and church members. Communion would now be based exclusively upon the spiritual kinship of the new birth and the plain teaching of Scripture, even though these commitments would indirectly challenge the core doctrines of Puritan orthodoxy.[48] Doctrines challenging the practices of infant baptism and the Lord's Table became confrontational issues as these new converts pursued the pure-church ideal in post-Great Awakening New England.

Isaac Backus' transformation to a Separate-Congregationalist and then Separate-Baptist is likely attributable in some ways to the fact that he understood more clearly than his contemporaries the true essence of Puritanism, particularly in its effort to make more visible the invisible church concept of Augustine and the Magisterial

---

47   These distinctions, general in nature, came to describe both a theology and a methodology for ministry. By the end of the eighteenth-century, this cleavage had broken the culture of Colonial New England. Middle ground between the revivalists and its detractors became non-existent. For good discussions of the "New Light-Old Light" factions and their respective social and religious implications see Gaustad, *The Great Awakening in New England.*,126-140; and David Harlen, *The Clergy and the Great Awakening in New England*, ed. Robert Berkover, *Studies in American History and Culture, No. 15* (Ann Arbor: UMI Research Press, 1980).

48   Backus' second pamphlet came in the form of an apologetic defending his rejection of covenant theology. By denying Congregational orthodoxy, including infant baptism, the Middleboro pastor challenged the entire Standing Order, thereby directly challenging the concept of territorial parishes, Congregational tax-support, including the social structure of New England. One historian said by doing this the Separate-Baptists had "guaranteed the existence of pure churches," and consequently, had "cut the Gordian knot once and for all." See William McLoughlin's introduction to "The Bondwomen and the Free" in McLoughlin, ed., *Isaac Backus on Church, State, and Calvinism: Pamphlets, 1754-1789*, 130-132.

Reformers.[49] Backus also clearly understood the failure of the
Reformers in clarifying visible church doctrine,[50] including the awful
mistreatment of their Anabaptist contemporaries. The Middleboro
pastor not only freely used Puritan writers as a means of justifying his
own thought about the visible church, but in doing so, he exposed the
failure of Puritanism to reach the goal of its own pure-church ideal. In
understanding that failure, Backus, as a historian, became intimately
acquainted with Baptist dissent in the early history of New England
Congregationalism and its precedents. This dissent, which Standing
Church ministers said only went back to Munster,[51] was traced by
Backus, among others in the Baptist community, back at least to the
12th century.[52] Backus saw those Anabaptist groups and individuals
who rejected infant baptism as the doctrinal forebears of contemporary

---

49   In 1773, Backus responded to the sermons of Rev. Joseph Fish, pastor of the
Congregational Church in Stonington, Connecticut, articulating his views on the visible church.
These replies, along with Backus' extensive quotations of the views of Puritan divines such
as John Owen and Cotton Mather, were aimed at identifying and defining the visible church,
differentiating it from all other civil and ecclesiastical government, and giving the grounds for
separating from churches who ignored all such differences; those differences being believers'
baptism and baptism preceding the Lord's Table. This work of Backus, constituting the
Separate-Baptist ecclesiological position, was the strongest Baptist polemic written against
the Congregational system at the time. In it, the historian offered very little opinion on the
universal, invisible church, only to say that it "is the same which it always was…but entered
my exception against its being true of the visible church…." See Isaac Backus, *A Discourse,
Concerning the Materials, the Manner of Building, and Power of Organizing the Church of
Christ* (Boston: J. Boyles Publishing, 1773), 15.
50   Because the Reformers maintained the essential "all-inclusive" church of Augustine,
buttressed by the parable of the wheat and the tares, they failed to establish Christian
communities comprised of only the regenerate. Luther, Bucer, Zwingli, and Calvin all courted
the idea at various times, but ultimately rejected the pure-church ideal of their Anabaptist
contemporaries for the state provided protection of the magistrate.
51   From the Reformation all the way to colonial New England, Baptists were often
derogatorily referred to as Munsterites. This term represented a fringe group of fanatical
Anabaptists in Germany between 1524 and 1535 who sought to set up the kingdom of God
through force in the Catholic city of Munster. For a thoroughgoing analysis of Anabaptist
dissent including the Peasant's War and the Munster debacle, see G.H. Williams, *The Radical
Reformation* (Philadelphia: The Westminster Press, 1962).
52   In reality, Backus utilized Tertullian as the most notable historical voice rejecting
infant baptism. But more contemporary examples were noted centuries before the Reformation.
See Backus, *A Discourse, Concerning the Materials, the Manner of Building, and Power of
Organizing the Church of Christ*, 32.

New England Baptists. Any corporate connection lay in the mutual rejection of infant baptism and state-supported churches.[53] Because of Backus' own conception of historical dissent, his conception of the visible church must be seen from the perspective of dissenters who held similar principles. Anabaptist historian Franklin Littell pointed out, "The doctrine of the Church affords the classifying principle of first importance" in understanding them."[54] Historians, Anabaptist and otherwise, have made considerable contributions in the last century to understanding critical distinctions between Reformation and Anabaptist ecclesiology.[55] This classifying principle of the Anabaptists was that their concept of the church was not all-inclusive, but rather sectarian, at least in terms of defining membership. The sect-style church of the Anabaptists, as opposed to the church-style of the Reformers, was recognized as a third church type for this reason. This sect-style church was marked by regenerate membership, symbolic ordinances of baptism and the Lord's Supper, including the rejection of infant baptism. Overarching all of these was the first principle of church discipline.

For the Middleboro pastor, the most notable church concerns involved tensions over similar problems he faced in Massachusetts.

---

53   Backus' key source for rejecting infant baptism and his subsequent view of Baptist history was rooted in
Wall's History of Infant Baptism. Anti-infant sprinkling principles were almost automatically associated with Baptist principles by Backus. See ibid, 32.

54   Franklin Hamlin Littell, *The Anabaptist View of the Church* (Boston: Starr King Press, 1958), 17.

55   For ample discussion of the third church type and related issues, see Paul D.L. Avis, *The Church in the Theology of the Reformers* (Atlanta: John Knox Press, 1981), Backus, *A Discourse, Concerning the Materials, the Manner of Building, and Power of Organizing the Church of Christ,* Peter Y. De Jong, *The Covenant Idea in New England Theology* (Grand Rapids: W.B. Eerdmans Publishing Co., 1945), Littell, *The Anabaptist View of the Church,* McLoughlin, ed., *Isaac Backus on Church, State, and Calvinism: Pamphlets, 1754-1789,* Ernst Troeltsch, *The Social Teaching of the Christian Churches,* trans. Olive Wyon. (New York: The Macmillan Co., 1931), A.C. Underwood, *A History of the English Baptists* (London: The Carey Kingsgate Press Limited, 1947).

Consequently, Backus believed that the New Reformation in Baptist hands involved correcting the ecclesiological mistakes "that our fathers brought to this land."[56] The correction of these mistakes was couched in the question he posed to Rev. Fish.[57] Backus asked, "Is any other visible church-state instituted in the gospel, but a particular one? The seven churches of Asia are spoken to by their great Head, not as one national or provincial church, but as so many distinct churches."[58] Even as the Separate-Baptists sought to establish their first Calvinist association of churches in 1767, this strong local-church emphasis was not noticeably diminished.[59]

The need for associational life became more apparent to Baptist leaders among the Separate-Baptists in New England, especially with those committed to raising up an educational institution designed for educating its local ministers. Backus saw in the endeavor the same potential problems existing in others of its kind, namely challenges

---

56   Backus, *A Discourse, Concerning the Materials, the Manner of Building, and Power of Organizing the Church of Christ*, 17. This mistake, which Backus explains to Rev. Fish, involved the twin pillars of infant baptism and magisterial authority; with the State insuring that rejection of such would be treated as heresy. For the Separate-Baptists in New England, correcting these two primary mistakes were the final steps in bringing the first Reformation to its logical conclusion, something their Puritan fathers were unable, or perhaps unwilling, to accomplish.

57   Reverend Joseph Fish was a Congregational pastor in Stonington, Connecticut, which was an area between Connecticut and Rhode Island known for frequent skirmishes between the Separates and the Standing Churches. Fish, in 1767, claimed that he had lost about two-thirds of his congregation to the Separates and so preached a series of nine sermons to his remaining people about the errors and excesses of the Separate movement. Backus used these sermons to highlight the doctrinal distinctions which he felt characterized the Baptists, and therefore the Second Reformation which he understood as moving forward with the Separate-Baptists. For the Backus response to Rev. Fish's sermons, see the pamphlet "A Fish Caught in His Own Net" (FCN), in McLoughlin, ed., *Isaac Backus on Church, State, and Calvinism: Pamphlets, 1754-1789*.

58   Backus, *A Discourse, Concerning the Materials, the Manner of Building, and Power of Organizing the Church of Christ*, 17.

59   The Warren Association was for Baptists in New England what the Philadelphia Association was for Baptists in the Middle States. This association was characterized by the same ardent local-church emphasis which characterized Isaac Backus. No perceivable activity known to be opposed to a particular-church function was practiced by the Warren Baptist Association. They understood their identity only in terms of assisting the biblical mandate of the particular member churches.

to local-church autonomy. The sort of biblical autonomy which he identified was grounded in the fact that no earthbound entity had any jurisdiction over Christ's churches. Any interference from a church council or civil magistrate was interpreted as contrary to Christ's original intention, and Baptist leaders considered the Congregational system as one which had come out of Rome and, unfortunately, had brought much of it to Massachusetts.[60] For him and his constituency, their view of associational life served as a portent of how their spiritual offspring would come to understand and value, if at all, the relevance of a universal church.

FROM REVIVAL TO A NEW CONFESSION

Ecclesiastical development within the SBBM was, like its original idealist, a product of its times. Key parallels existed between the rise of local-church domination and the decline of the election doctrine, especially in New England.[61] The rejection of the election doctrine was the one primary point of agreement among the majority of the dissent groups from the revolutionary period to about 1782. This rejection is one of the precursors marking the doctrinal shift from the Westminster Confession to other confessions and statements into the nineteenth century.[62] At the center of this shift was the

---

60   For a thorough presentation of the church-state issue, and how Backus perceived the Congregational system as having carried out of Rome many of its own practices, see his pamphlet entitled "A Fish Caught in His Own Net" in McLoughlin, ed., *Isaac Backus on Church, State, and Calvinism: Pamphlets, 1754-1789.*

61   The decline of Calvinism in New England is not traceable to any one source. Key to understanding the social tensions of Calvinism in New England is the advent of revivalism. From this came the Separate movement which focused attention on the baptism issue, and from this came the deliberate and entire rejection of the Congregational system. For related discussions see Keith J. Hardman, *Charles Grandison Finney, 1792-1875: Reformer and Revivalist* (Grand Rapids: Baker, 1987), Joseph Haroutunian, *Piety Versus Moralism: The Passing of the New England Theology* (Hamden, CT: Archon Books, 1964).

62   The most notable confession of the period was the New Hampshire Confession constructed less than thirty years after Backus death. This confession is marked by two clear

commitment to and desire for revival. Revival began to be understood in different terms than it was in the days of Jonathan Edwards and George Whitefield. As revival later reoccurred under different men and in various places,[63] revival, through mass preaching endeavors, was seen in a more utilitarian light as a necessary means for reaching vast numbers of previously unconverted people groups.[64] Despite differences held over the election doctrine by many revival preachers,

distinctions which differentiate it from the previously dominant Westminster Confession which so strongly influenced the Philadelphia Confession of Faith in the Middle Colonies. The first is the clear softening of the election doctrine which is "perfectly consistent with the free agency of man," as it "comprehends all the means in connection with the end." However, a close examination of other doctrinal statements preceding New Hampshire reveals that there were doctrinal tendencies already leaning in this direction. The second distinction is that the local or visible church is spoken of in exclusive terms. This combination strongly suggests that soteriological changes had played a particular role in an ecclesiological shift before, during, and after this period.

63   Historically, the distinction is sometimes spoken of here between revival and revivalism. Revival is normally spoken of as something which is theo-centric, or centered in God's sovereignty. Revivalism is often referred to as anthropocentric, or centered in man's autonomy and subsequently, man's methodology for producing revival. The New England revivals, from 1770-1790, are seldom referred to in the latter vein ironically even when some of them were produced under the ministries of Free-Will Baptist preachers. The various revivals of this period offer tremendous insights into the motivations for revival and how varying sorts of New England Baptists participated in them simultaneously. This revival model, with its softened Calvinism, would later be taken to inordinate extremes by evangelist Charles Finney and the "New Measures" Theology, which played down the effects of original sin and seemed to give the human will unfettered autonomy to choose or reject Christ. Most scholars concur that Finney was an intellectual protégé of Timothy Dwight and Nathanial William Taylor who both taught that man's will was not corrupted by the sin of Adam but was completely qualified of itself to respond for or against God. Therefore, Finney reacted against the Calvinist concept of total inability and that revival could be produced with the use of human means. For a clear understanding of Finney's theology, methods, and influence, see Winfred E. Garrison, "Characteristics of American Organized Religion," *Annals of the American Academy of Political and Social Science*, 256 (March, 1948), McBeth, *The Baptist Heritage*, Sidney E. Mead, *The Lively Experiment: The Shaping of Christianity in America* (New York: Harper and Row Publishers, 1976).

64   Revival toward the last quarter of the eighteenth century gravitated toward reaching large numbers of people who were unaffiliated with any church. The frontier regions of New England, and later, the migrations westward and southward found similar phenomena. As one historian noted, "With 90% of the population outside the churches, the task of organizing religion could not be limited to encouraging 'Christian nurture'…in families, or to ministering to old members as they moved to new places farther west. It had to be directed toward that 90%. What they needed first was not nurture or edification, but radical conversion,…[and since they] followed no chiefs…they had to be brought in one by one." Taken from Mead, *The Lively Experiment: The Shaping of Christianity in America*, 122.

there was marked interaction among them in their common resolve to preach a mass-appealing gospel.[65] This served to demonstrate that in revival, both Calvinist and non-Calvinist men interfaced. As the New England revivals moved south and west after the turn of century, that interaction turned to doctrinal statements reflecting a modified Calvinism evolving out of mutual concerns for the salvation of previously unreached people.

As is the case normally, doctrinal shifts in New England, along with their spiritual and social implications, were usually preceded by much the same in Old England. The hyper-Calvinist doctrines of John Gill[66] had been challenged and tailored by a young theologian named Andrew Fuller.[67] Fuller's modification to the atonement doctrine

---

65   This interaction becomes noticeable only as the revival records are examined. On many occasions, a revival carried on by a Calvinist group would benefit directly from the revival results of a non-Calvinist group, and vice-versa. Although doctrinal peer-pressures kept these groups from openly rejoicing over mutual spiritual victories, this sort of "silent interaction" occurred again and again. In this way, revival became an unspoken, yet cordial connection between the opposing groups, with Calvinist Baptists and Free-will Baptists mutually participating in revivals together.

66   John Gill was an influential Baptist theologian in England from 1730 to 1770. Gill's views on election and predestination, although not unusual, were extreme to the point where exhortations and invitations for sinners to respond to the gospel were considered insults to the Spirit of God, who, according to his view, was the only necessary and able agent in regeneration. Isaac Backus depended heavily on Gill and Benjamin Wallin for his views on infant baptism and its connection to the particular church. Although Backus agreed in general terms with Gill on Calvinism, he identified himself on a more practical level with Whitefield's model of "Evangelistic Calvinism," which even by his death in 1806 was continually softening. Gill's views may be seen in John Gill, *Body of Divinity* (London: J. Briscoe, 1769; reprint, Turner Lassetter, Atlanta, Georgia, 1957), John Gill, *The Dissenter's Reasons for Separating from the Church of England* (London: Wightman and Cramp, n.d.), 528-559, Arthur Henry Kirkby, "The Theology of Andrew Fuller and Its Relation to Calvinism" (Ph.D. diss., University of Edinburgh, 1956), 31-33, Henry Vedder, C., *A Short History of the Baptists* (Valley Forge: Judson Press, 1907), 239-243.

67   Andrew Fuller played a significant role in the theological shift among the English Particular Baptists. His theological insights, although not immediately accepted, eventually spelled the end to the dominance (not existence) of hyper-Calvinism among the Particular Baptists which predominated in the greater London area. For an accurate portrayal of Fuller's Calvinism see J.H.Y. Briggs, *The English Baptists of the Nineteenth Century* (Didcot: Baptist Historical Society, 1994), Earnest F. Clipsham, "Andrew Fuller and Fullerism," *The Baptist Quarterly* 20, no. 6 (April, 1964), Earnest F. Clipsham, "Andrew Fuller and Fullerism (1)," *The Baptist Quarterly* 20, no. 3 (July, 1963), Earnest F. Clipsham, "Andrew Fuller and Fullerism

and the nature of God revolutionized the Particular Baptists[68] and introduced a new age of missionary organizations and expansionism which traversed across Particular/General lines. In New England, other moderating forces were represented largely by the Free-Will Baptist movement under the leadership of Benjamin Randall. Beginning in 1770, Randall's movement was the first of note which directly confronted the election doctrine. His outright opposition to Calvinism struck a note deep within the heart of the SBBM. Although Backus and Randall could both boast of being converted by Whitefield, Randall eventually perceived a breadth in the atonement doctrine that Whitefield and Backus seemed to hint at in their evangelical pathos, yet never admitted. Conversely, Randall testified,

I saw an universal atonement - an universal love - an universal call - and that none would ever perish, only those who refused to accept...O what love too I felt for all mankind, and wanted that they all might share in that all fullness, which I saw so extensive, so free to all...[69]

Randall's open repudiation of the Calvinist bulwark could no longer be summarily argued against and rejected under the assumption that

---

(2)," *The Baptist Quarterly* 20, no. 4 (October, 1963), Earnest F. Clipsham, "Andrew Fuller and Fullerism (3)," *The Baptist Quarterly* 20, no. 5 (January, 1964), Roger Hayden, *English Baptist History and Heritage*, 2nd ed. (Oxfordshire: Nigel Lynn Publishing and Marketing Ltd, 2005), 122-124, Leonard, *Baptist Ways: A History*, 100-102, Peter Naylor, *Calvinism, Communion, and the Baptists*, Studies in Baptist History and Thought, 7 (Nottingham: Paternoster Press, 2003), 205-219.

68   Some distinction needs to be made here of the geographical centers of Gill and Fuller. Gill remained predominant in urban areas, primarily London, while Fuller's modifications became predominant in the outlying counties, particularly in the Midlands. (Wesley was also much more successful here.) A stronger Calvinism persisted much the same in Boston and other urban areas after the death of Isaac Backus, while the rural areas were much more revivalistic in nature.

69   Davidson takes this statement from Buzzell, "Extract," *216; Buzzell, Life of Elder Benjamin Randall, 20,21; "Apostolic Succession," The Morning Star, XXXIV (May 18, 1859), 1.* Quoted in Allen C. Guelzo, "An Heir or Rebel? Charles Grandison Finney and the New England Theology," *The Journal of the Early Republic* 17, no. 1 (Spring 1997): 129.

any social impact could be avoided. Within a decade, several from
the Backus fold migrated to the Randall position on the atonement,
widening the breach in the Calvinist dam.[70]

For some historians, this breach is seen as having existed
within Edwards' theological system all along. In this respect, the real
culprit behind Calvinism's demise was apparently not its enemies but
one of its dearest friends.[71] By the time these ideas inherent within the
revival movement crystallized into the New Hampshire Confession
of Faith,[72] social and political elements could also be identified

---

70   This movement was seen by Backus and the Separate-Baptists as heretical.
Doctrinal orthodoxy was still found in the written exemplars of the period: The Westminster
Confession and the Philadelphia Baptist Confession. When, at the request of his Calvinist
friends in Virginia, Backus wrote his polemic entitled *The Doctrine of Particular Election and
Final Perseverance, Explained and Vindicated* (DPE), he was essentially battling the inroads
of Wesleyan doctrines. This complex of new ideas included the freedom of the will, the denial
of predestination, universal atonement, and the possibility of falling from grace. With the
exception of falling from grace, most Baptists in the nineteenth century were affected to some
degree by the rest of the ideas so vigorously rejected by Backus in this pamphlet. Ironically,
before his death in 1806, he was able to rejoice in the Baptist revival meetings in Kentucky
which identified with most of the doctrines he had formerly opposed. For further comment and
the text of this Calvinist polemic, see McLoughlin, ed., *Isaac Backus on Church, State, and
Calvinism: Pamphlets, 1754-1789*, 448-471.
71   Edwards' *Freedom of the Will* produced arguments for justifying various positions on
both sides of the predestinarian/free-will debate. Most interesting is the fact that many "New
Measures" preachers and theologians claimed to be direct descendants of Jonathan Edwards.
For a fairly recent and extremely important discussion concerning Jonathan Edwards'
distinction between natural ability and moral inability, and how it may have contributed to
the demise of New England Calvinism, see Guelzo, "An Heir or Rebel? Charles Grandison
Finney and the New England Theology." The most recent work on the doctrinal history of New
England from Edwards to the Finney era is Douglas A. Sweeney and Allen C.Guelzo , ed., *The
New England Theology: From Jonathan Edwards to Edwards Amasa Park* (Grand Rapids:
Baker Academic, 2006).
72   For fear of offending the predominant middle class so committed to revival in
New England, the New Hampshire Convention greatly moderated its Calvinist theology. For
a balanced summary of how this Confession evolved, see Isaac Backus, *A Fish Caught in
His Own Net: An Examination of Nine Sermons, from Matt. 16. 18. Published Last Year, by
Mr. Joseph Fish of Stonington: Wherein He Labours to Prove, That Those Called Standing
Churches in New-England, Are Built Upon the Rock, and Upon the Same Principles with the
First Fathers of This Country, and That Separates and Baptists Are Joining with the Gates of
Hell against Them : In Answer to Which, Many of His Mistakes Are Corrected, the Constitution
of Those Churches Opened, the Testimonies of Prophets and Apostles, and Also of Many of
Those Fathers Are Produced, Which as Plainly Condemn His Plan, as Any Separate or Baptist
Can Do* (Boston: Printed by Edes and Gill, in Queen-Street, 1768), Isaac Backus and American
Imprint Collection (Library of Congress), *An Appeal to the Public for Religious Liberty against*

characterizing its doctrinal content. The democratic principle found a complete expression within the context of revival,[73] and in the NHC. Locke's political philosophy,[74] and a new social vocabulary, buttressed by the democratic ideals of revival, became the criteria for eventually transforming Colonial America and disestablishing the Standing Order. Religious toleration had provided the environment for its complete manifestation in the American colonies.[75] In this sense, the NHC is not

---

the Oppressions of the Present Day (Boston: Printed by John Boyle, 1773), J.M. Pendleton, Church Manual, Designed for the Use of Baptist Churches (Philadelphia: The Judson Press, 1867), 360-361.

73   Marsden provides an excellent overview of how revival became embedded in American culture throughout the eighteenth and nineteenth centuries. See George M. Marsden, Religion and American Culture (Orlando: Harcourt Brace Jovanovich College Publishers, 1990). Refer also to Nathan O. Hatch, "The Christian Movement and the Demand for a Theology of the People," The Journal of American History 67, no. 3 (Dec 1980), 561.

74   Isaac Backus' use of John Locke's political theory is prolific. The Lockean theory of government was so dominant during this time that it would have been impossible for Backus to not have been influenced by it. Locke believed in the "Contract" theory or that the authority to govern came directly from the people or the governed. Locke also confined the right of civil government to punish only those who broke the contract or civil covenant. Conversely, church authority was derived only from Christ, through the Word of God, and operative upon the conscience of every believer. Thus, Locke's democratic theory prohibited the civil authorities from exercising any influence over ecclesiastical government. Interestingly, this theory was first articulated by John Wise in 1710 and 1717 and was quoted by Congregational historian H. M. Dexter in a defense of Congregational church government. Backus' paternal grandfather sought counsel from John Wise during his opposition to the Saybrook Platform in Connecticut. For more on Backus' use of Wise and Locke, see the following Backus' pamphlets, Isaac Backus and American Imprint Collection (Library of Congress), Government and Liberty Described; and Ecclesiastical Tyranny Exposed (Boston: Printed by Powers and Willis, and sold by Phillip Freeman, 1778), McLoughlin, ed., Isaac Backus on Church, State, and Calvinism: Pamphlets, 1754-1789. For a good summary discussion of the general subject of political philosophy see Marsden, Religion and American Culture. For an excellent treatment of Wise and Locke, along with their use in Backus literature, see Perry Miller, "The Contribution of the Protestant Churches to Religious Liberty in Colonial America," Church History, no. 4 (March 1935).

75   Most Protestant historians suggest that the religious freedom which came to dominate in America was concomitant to the Reformation at large. Religious liberty, born out of the English Toleration movements, had within a few centuries, altered the course of the Second Reformation. Uniformity of religion could not be maintained in the marketplace of free choice, particularly in the ideology of the Baptists. The eventual democratization of American religion as a corollary movement is a fascinating element of American ecclesiological development. For further discussion see Hatch, "The Christian Movement and the Demand for a Theology of the People", Mead, The Lively Experiment: The Shaping of Christianity in America, 38-72; Harry S. Stout, "Religion, Communications, and the Ideological Origins of the American Revolution," The William and Mary Quarterly 34, no. 4 (Oct 1977).

simply a document categorizing the current religious thought of its day, but actually mirrors over a century of cultural transformation from the rigid Calvinism of Puritanism to the universal atonement message of the revivalist preachers.

In the midst of an emasculated Calvinism, further modifications within a generation of the Backus movement became inevitable. Because revivalism was governed more by the message of individual responsibility to the new birth and voluntarism[76] regarding the visible church, the invisible notion lost both its use in the common vocabulary of the day and its place in practical theology. Without the implicit ideas of election and predestination connecting the elect individual to the concept of a *true* church, this ecclesiological concept slowly became both an unspoken and unnecessary metaphor in religious discourse and written dogma among a significant and influential number of Baptists. The impact of the Backus movement during the nineteenth century and beyond has forced appraisals of the man, his motivations, and his movement oftentimes interpreted solely in the context of his fresh ecclesiological principles. Such reappraisals involve discussion of Backus' complete rejection of the State-Church alliance with the caveat that in today's religious climate Backus would be unable or unwilling to maintain a separation argument.[77] However, this is highly unlikely.

---

76   This concept advanced the idea that religion in general, and churches in particular were to be maintained only by the free-will offerings of their own constituencies and not through forced tithing by the civil magistrate. This issue was not novel to New England Baptists however. In the General Baptist Confession of 1660, article XVI repudiates the practice of "any forced Maintenance" for the ministry. In Massachusetts, Backus fought tirelessly for the voluntary principle of church maintenance and ministerial support. For this principle among the English Baptists, see Backus and American Imprint Collection (Library of Congress), *An Appeal to the Public for Religious Liberty against the Oppressions of the Present Day*, 57; Backus, *A Discourse, Concerning the Materials, the Manner of Building, and Power of Organizing the Church of Christ*, 230. For the Colonial Baptists and voluntarism see Handlin, ed., *Isaac Backus and the American Pietistic Tradition*, Hudson, ed., *Baptist Concepts of the Church*.

77   This is the overall assessment of biographer Stanley Grenz in his work, *Isaac Backus - Puritan and Baptist: His Place in History, His Thought, and Their Implications for Modern*

In relating to churches and their members who rejected the re-baptism of believers in his day, Backus unashamedly supported the separation from those "who will not conform to it."[1]

For Backus and the Separate-Baptists, separation was not a novel idea, nor was it to be considered sectarian or arbitrary. The reasons for it had been discovered in the Scriptures, recognized in the common strain of the dissent community, and leveraged against the original ideals of the Puritan Commonwealth. Despite the fact that Backus the historian would devise intellectual arguments from the Puritans for his own movement, he would ultimately identify himself with the Baptists whom he perceived as the rightful heirs of the Puritan's visible church ideology. This earned him, from Mary Hewitt Mitchell, the title "The Father of American Baptists."[78]

As such, this book endeavors to understand the Backus movement not only through the lens of the Reformation tradition but also through the lens of the historical dissent community preceding it. The principles around which the Separate-Baptists would eventually gather had *long-standing* historical precedents, and Backus was convinced that the continued Reformation had opened an unprecedented opportunity for bringing the reformation to its ultimate conclusion in America.[79] Backus leveraged his visible church views against the Protestant narrative and a continued reform under Puritan management. However, he was personally motivated more by

---

Baptist Theology.

78   Mary Hewitt Mitchell, *The Great Awakening and Other Revivals* (New Haven: Tercentenary Commission of the State of Connecticut, Yale University Press, 1934), 27.

79   Backus was convinced by English Baptist historian Thomas Crosby that the principles of rejecting infant baptism and civil control over the church had historical precedents "derived from a maxim of reformation, which was held by the Waldenses, Petrobrussians, Wickliffites, and Hussites, long before Luther's day...." See Backus, *A History of New England with Particular Reference to the Denomination of Christians Called Baptists*, 2: v-vi.

his desire to win both respect and position for his struggling Baptist denomination than by a Puritan self-image.

This view of the Backus movement has been carefully constructed upon the corpus of Backus' pamphlet literature, Backus' extended Discourse on Church Matters (DCM),[80] Backus' personal diaries,[81] personal letters from the Backus papers,[82] and various ecclesiastical histories which deal with entire history of the era.[83]

SUMMARY

The Backus movement in New England is best understood

---

80   Backus' *A Discourse Concerning the Materials, the Manner of Building, and Power of Organizing of the Church of Christ*, published in 1773, offers the broadest treatment of the Backus corpus on visible church matters, and provides valuable theological insights into how Backus interpreted New Testament church passages.

81   The personal correspondence of Backus was written from 1741-1806, up to the year of Backus' death. The diaries themselves, which compose a significant part of the Backus Papers collection were edited by William McLoughlin and published in a three volume set by the Brown University Press in 1979. The text is an autobiographical compilation of Backus' written accounts taken from the Middleboro church, his travel records, and several other annotated materials. In volume three, McLoughlin included twenty-six appendixes which cover many of Backus' most important autobiographical papers, significant pieces of correspondence concerning church, associational, and government issues, providing rich insights into the daily life of the pastor-farmer up to and beyond the Revolutionary War.

82   The major collection of the Backus Papers is housed at the Andover-Newton Theological Seminary in Newton Centre, Massachusetts. Apart from the aforementioned Backus diary, the Backus Papers also include numerous sermons on the Psalms and the book of Acts, letters from his mother Mrs. Elizabeth Backus, scores of personal letters, and other materials. Several of the letters received and sent by Backus during this period dealt with the issues of baptism and church order among the Separate-Baptists.

83   Understanding the Congregational system from which the Separates and the Separate-Baptists emerged is vital in understanding the trajectory of the Baptists in the post-Great Awakening era. Great insights are provided by Heimert, ed., *Religion and the American Mind: From the Great Awakening to the Revolution*, Miller, *The New England Mind: From Colony to Province*, Perry Miller, *The New England Mind: The Seventeenth Century* (Cambridge, MA: Harvard University Press, 1954), Miller, *Orthodoxy in Massachusetts 1630-1650*, Randolph Crump Miller and Henry Herbert Shires, *Christianity and the Contemporary Scene* (New York: Morehouse-Gorham Co., 1943). The best work on the Congregational-Separates is by Clarence Goen, *Revivalism and Separatism in New England, 1740-1800: Strict Congregationalists and Separate-Baptists in the Great Awakening*. A key work on the effect of the Great Awakening upon the existing Congregational system is Edwin Gaustad, *The Great Awakening in New England*.

as an indigenous and self-propagating spiritual crusade which both justified its existence and its doctrinal fortunes on being heirs of *pre-reformation* dissent groups, as well as the *first* Reformation's ecclesiastical ideal. Consequently, in the aftermath of the Great Awakening, Backus' Congregational background offered three elements to assist him. First, it provided him a vantage point of analyzing the very denomination from which he would ultimately be forced to defend his theological positions. Secondly, it deprived his enemies of being able to dispatch his notions as those of a crackpot dissenter blindly fighting the Standing Order. Finally, it produced the catalyst for establishing the Second Reformation on doctrinal principles implicit in the original Puritan vision, thereby allowing the Separate-Baptists to bring them to their logical conclusions.

In this Congregational world, Backus placed an unrelenting finger on the critical issues facing those who pursued the ideal of a pure-church. After his momentous decision in 1756 to make baptism the basis for local-church membership, and participation at the Lord's Table, his life became a living polemic against a Congregational system he saw as intolerably misguided from their originating values. Backus believed that the two things necessary for his denomination's success were religious toleration for all and maintaining a state of revival.[84] However, these later Baptist developments cannot be historically appreciated apart from their earlier representatives. This requires a brief description of the Baptists prior to the Great Awakening but

---

84   In the minds of most revival-oriented Baptists and evangelical Protestants of the post-revolutionary period, this continued state of revival and missionary activity was the means through which the millennium or golden age would ultimately come to pass. This period would be marked by "great awakenings, the evangelization of the world through missions, and the turning of the nations to Christ," followed by the literal return of Christ to the earth. For further reading see McLoughlin, ed., *Isaac Backus on Church, State, and Calvinism: Pamphlets, 1754-1789*, 60-63; and for a well-formed discussion of the various elements behind the development of American denominationalism, see McBeth, *The Baptist Heritage*, 103-133.

especially the similarity between the Backus movement and the English Baptists.

Chapter Two

New England Baptists in Historical Perspective

THE PRE-AWAKENING BAPTISTS

Baptists of the pre-awakening period bore little resemblance
to those who would later become known as Separate-Baptists. Their
differences demonstrate the factors behind the tremendous expansion
the Separates would experience under the leadership of Backus
and like-minded leaders committed to revival, and the cultivation
of strong, anti- pedobaptist, closed-communion churches. Despite
their doctrinal distinctions, both the pre-awakening Baptists and the
Separates had a mutual desire for legal toleration and a willingness to
endure persecution by the Standing authorities. In the midst of their
mutual likenesses and distinctions, both English Particular Baptists
and colonial Baptists determined that the fight for liberty of conscience
was fought best in the doctrinal cast of Westminster's theological
heritage. When Backus finally adopted the close-communion Baptist
identity in 1756, he set off on the task of bringing the pre-awakening
Baptists into the Calvinist mold of the Philadelphia Baptist Association
(PBA) and its subsequent confession (PBC).[85] Disparate by nature and

---

85   This activity by Backus was preceded by a similar effort in North Carolina and
Virginia about 1750. The majority of the churches there were largely made up of those whose
lineage was traced to the English General Baptists. Elder Lemuel Burkitt and Jesse Read
based this on "some original papers" connecting them to those "both in London, and several
counties in England," This likely refers to the General Confession of 1660 which said it was
"presented to King Charles the second." See this notation in Joseph Biggs, *A Concise History
of the Kehukee Association* (Tarborough: George Howard: Office of the Tarborough (N.C.)
Free Press, 1834), 28. Lumpkin reported that the earliest known reference to a confession
was in 1724 when the Philadelphia Baptist Association referred to "the Confession of Faith,
set forth by the elders and brethren met in London, 1689, and owned by us." See Lumpkin,
Baptist Confessions of Faith, 349. This confession of the London Baptists was based upon
the Westminster exemplar and found its way to America in the form of the so-called Keach

rooted in a general atonement view, the majority of these churches were galvanized by the Middleboro pastor into a unified group of Calvinist-oriented churches at least for the first generation. This process was significantly helped by the founding of two institutions: the Rhode Island College (later becoming Brown University) in 1764, and the Warren Baptist Association (WBA) in 1767. The former provided the Baptists with a basis for gaining some measured respect in the Massachusetts Commonwealth, while the latter provided them with a means for conducting a united campaign for religious equality in New England throughout the rest of the century.[86] Their earlier development stands in stark contrast to the Baptist cause at the close of the seventeenth century. As the century turned, the Baptists in New England, and Massachusetts in particular, were few in number and extremely vulnerable. McBeth observed,

They entered that century with a handful of churches, divided in doctrine, dispirited by persecution, and despised by most observers. They had formed no associations, sponsored no mission efforts, and launched no schools. By 1800 they were a different people with a different spirit.... Without doubt, the event which did most

---

Confession. This was a condensed form of the 1689 edition which came to America through his son Elias Keach. This confession became the basis of the new confession written and printed in Philadelphia in 1742 by Benjamin Franklin. Although a few other local confessions pre-dated the Philadelphia model of 1742, the movement of so many General Baptist churches to the Calvinistic position by 1750 made it the most widely accepted doctrinal standard of the period until the advent of the New Hampshire Confession of Faith.

86   McLoughlin, ed., *Isaac Backus on Church, State, and Calvinism: Pamphlets, 1754-1789*, 11. This introduction by the Brown University historian is the best summation available on the life of Backus within the context of the Separate-Baptist movement. However, after mentioning the decline of Calvinism toward the end of the century, he chooses to ignore, in this decline, the implications of the frontier revivals beginning early in the nineteenth century. For the Separate-Baptists in New England, the frontier revival movements in Tennessee and Kentucky likely continued the reduction of the election doctrine and consequently, its Universal church corollary which found ultimate expression in the New Hampshire Confession of Faith.

to transform the Baptists was the First Great Awakening.[87]

In the previous fifty years, their numbers had increased, but social stigma still kept most sympathizers from public acknowledgement and dissent. Many of the pre-Awakening Baptist churches in the Massachusetts colony did not share in the fervor of the Awakening. The primary factor which limited their involvement surrounded the major character of the revival, George Whitefield. As a Church of England priest and a strong, Calvinist-oriented pedobaptist, he appeared an extremely unlikely candidate for introducing spiritual revival to the stodgy Baptists of New England. Even though many Baptists during this period were concerned more about economic and social survival than doctrinal exactness, many of the Baptist churches refused to support Whitefield because of his theological background.. Many of the Regular Baptists[88] disparaged the revivals as "enthusiastic", while many, who were to become Separate-Congregationalists or New Lights, encouraged the proclamation of the new birth doctrine, and Whitefieldian style revival.[89] By 1790 in New England, these descriptions began to become obscured as the Baptist denomination continued in rapid growth to the western frontiers with the strong, local-church tendencies of the Separates having gained the ascendancy.[90]

McLoughlin lists a total of 10 Baptist churches in New England by the end of the seventeenth century. He mentions six Baptist churches in Rhode Island: three in the Plymouth Colony, and one

---

87   McBeth, *The Baptist Heritage*, 251.
88   This distinction was used to qualify Particular-Baptists who valued an educated clergy, normally subscribed to the Reformed-like Philadelphia Baptist Confession, and valued the Philadelphia model of association which the Separate-Baptists feared would undermine local-church autonomy.
89   Vedder, *A Short History of the Baptists*, 309.
90   Leonard, *Baptist Ways: A History*, 123.

in Boston[91]—Backus included only nine in New England by 1700
and five more elsewhere in America.[92] Backus may have omitted
the second church in Swansea, Massachusetts which started in 1693
under the leadership of Thomas Barnes who served under founding
pastor John Myles.[93] This second church began as a result of a fire
during King Philips' War[94] requiring an alternate location for a rebuilt
meetinghouse in 1693. Several members remained attached to the
old site and eventually started a second church. The first church in
the Plymouth colony with a *continuous* existence was in Rehoboth,
where Myles originally settled in 1663. However, the first recorded
effort at establishing a Baptist church in the Plymouth colony, as well
as the Massachusetts Bay Colony, was likely by Obadiah Holmes in
1649.[95] Backus recorded that Holmes, after being dismissed from the
Salem church around 1645, joined the Standing Church in Seekonk,

---

91   William G. McLoughlin, *The Rise of Antipedobaptists in New England, 1630-1655*,
21, Everett C. Goodwin, ed., *Baptists in the Balance* (Valley Forge: Judson Press, 1997), 80.

92   These were located in the Middle colonies. Religious toleration drew a larger
number of Baptists primarily to the Philadelphia area of Pennsylvania. This resulted in the
founding of the Philadelphia Baptist Association in 1707.

93   Backus, *A History of New England with Particular Reference to the Denomination of
Christians Called Baptists*, 2: 434.

94   This approximately one-year war was a series of Indian attacks which nearly
decimated the colonies from 1675-1676. It was considered by most of the most serious Puritan
divines to be a part of God's judgment on the colonies for their spiritual decline. About ten
percent of all the towns in the Plymouth and Massachusetts colonies were destroyed. About
one-tenth of all military aged men were killed in the conflicts. This does not include the great
numbers of women and children who lost their lives usually in brutal fashion. See Nathaniel
Philbrick, *Mayflower* (New York: Viking Press, 2006), xiv-xvii, Walker, *The Creeds and
Platforms of Congregationalism*, 412-415, and Robert G. Pope, *The Half-Way Covenant:
Church Membership in Puritan New England* (Princeton: Princeton University Press, 1969),
186-187.

95   Baptist historians give little recognition to Holmes' church planting efforts in
Rehoboth between 1649 and 1650. Leonard only says he moved there in 1643, choosing to
ignore his baptism in 1649 and his effort at planting a church that year until the fall of 1650
when he was forced to abandon the effort by the authorities in Taunton. See Leonard, *Baptist
Ways: A History*, 79. McBeth chooses to ignore any reference to Holmes' church planting
effort by saying, "In 1649 Obadiah Holmes and Mark Lukar were baptizing converts by
immersion at Seekonk, but apparently no organized church resulted." He then states that the
earliest Baptist church was planted near Swansea (it was actually Rehoboth) in 1663. McBeth,
The Baptist Heritage, 141.

Massachusetts, the same year.[96] He reported this membership lasted for approximately four years, culminating in a hostile separation in 1649. Holmes and about a half dozen individuals immediately began to hold a separate meeting. Becoming convinced of Baptist principles, they were likely baptized by John Clarke upon arrangement that following summer in 1649.[97] They continued their meeting for nearly a year until four petitions were received in October by the Plymouth General Court from all the Standing ministers in Plymouth, the Seekonk church, the Taunton church, and one from the General Court in Boston, each demanding the suppression of this new church in the Plymouth Colony.[98] McLoughlin refers to it as an "abortive Baptist church," apparently dismissing it because none of the former members were there in 1665 with John Myles.[99] This seems odd because the Brown professor recognized that the church under Holmes' leadership had no choice but to disband and leave the colony after the General Court decision in 1650. This disbanding must be related to the fact that the court's "Grand Inquest" mentioned in Backus' history shows at least nine adults meeting together during the previous year in private homes.[100] Disbanding likely suggests the existence of some organizational structure which confounded the authorities. Baptists never considered length of operation to determine the validity of a church's original existence. The court session was dated June, 1650,

---

96   Backus, *A History of New England with Particular Reference to the Denomination of Christians Called Baptists*, 1: 176.

97   This baptism may relate to the group involving the inquest for this trial listed by Backus from the Plymouth Records indicating a written list of nine persons being indicted. The list was signed by Thomas Robinson and Henry Tomson. Beside Tomson's name he adds "&c., to the number of 14." This evidently represents the total of possible indictments in this particular Court session. This may correspond to McLoughlin's note of Clarke who baptized thirteen or fourteen that previous summer "including Holmes."

98   For further insight on this Baptist effort, see the full citation listed in McLoughlin, *New England Dissent, 1630-1833*, 1:128-129.

99   McLoughlin, *New England Dissent, 1630-1833*, 1: 128.

100   Backus, *A History of New England with Particular Reference to the Denomination of Christians Called Baptists*, 1: 177.

one full year from the time Clarke had immersed the original members. The resultant determination of the Court in 1650, which prohibited new churches from starting without government consent, eventually brought Holmes and his friends to Newport where they joined John Clarke's church.[101] It would then appear that the court's decision strongly admits that the bona-fide existence of a new and autonomous church, operating without the sanction of the court, precipitated the court's final decision.

The Swansea story began with Myles, who, after fleeing potential persecution in Wales under the Uniformity Act of 1662,[102] arrived in Boston in 1663 and settled within the Plymouth colony in the city of Rehoboth. He immediately began an open-communion Baptist church, even offering membership to some influential members of the Standing (Congregational) Church. His open policy concerning sprinkling infants had strong local support.[103] Unfortunately, the Plymouth Court of Assistants had no such sympathies and summarily fined him and his helper (Brown). The Court included a caveat however. If Myles would agree to move the church out of the jurisdiction of Rehoboth, the court would possibly allow them certain

---

101   Leonard's chronology of these events makes no mention of the Holmes group between 1649 and 1650, and mistakenly places Holmes' baptism in 1650 rather than 1649. Then by 1650, he simply says, "Soon after, the Massachusetts establishment took action against him." This runs counter to the official court record which was dated June of 1650, not some undisclosed time after that year. See Leonard, *Baptist Ways: A History*, 79.
102   Isaac Backus, *Church History of New England from 1620 to 1804: Containing a View of the Principles and Practice, Declensions and Revivals, Oppression and Liberty of the Churches, and a Chronological Table. With a Memoir of the Author* (Philadelphia: American Baptist Publ. and S.S. Society, 1844), 93.
103   The Rehoboth town record shows that when Rev. Zachariah Symes became too ill to serve the Rehoboth church, relations were congenial enough with Rev. Myles that he was asked to "preach once a fortnight on ye week day & once on ye Sabbath day." The citizens reaffirmed this request with a town vote in August, but by this time the authorities had realized Myles was also holding Baptist meetings in Rehoboth and considered him to be a danger to the peace of the community as well as a threat to the Standing Church who had sought his services. McLoughlin includes the words "voted to be a lecturer viz....," but the word *lecturer* is extremely difficult to determine and partially torn on the page edge. Rehoboth Town Records, I, 168-169, Rehoboth Town Clerk's Office.

liberties for future existence. Within three months, Myles and the majority of his church moved to Swansea (Swanzey). The Plymouth General Court so named it at Myles' request (his native town in Wales was Swansea), and incorporated it as a haven for Baptist sympathizers.

The First Baptist Church in Boston began in Charlestown in 1665 as a result of Thomas Gould refusing to bring his infant child to baptism in the Standing Church there. Gould and Thomas Osborne separated from the Charlestown church in May of 1665, and, together with Edward Drinker and John George, were baptized. They joined with "Richard Goodall, William Turner, Robert Lambert, Mary Goodall, and Mary Newel"[104] in a solemn church covenant. Goodall had come to Boston with recommendations from Kiffin's closed-communion church in London. Turner and Lambert had come from a Baptist church in Dartmouth. All three had been faithful Christian believers before their arrival in the colonies.[105] Outside of the Commonwealth, yet before the turn of the century, a Baptist congregation was organized in Kittery, Maine, by William Screven in 1682, having been sent out by the First Baptist Church in Charlestown. Because of severe harassment from the authorities, he and his entire flock eventually fled south and settled in Charleston, South Carolina, where he started the first Baptist church in the state.[106]

McLoughlin affirmed that between the years of 1693-1731, no new Baptist churches were formed in the Commonwealth. A diminished Calvinism, which was considerably less stringent than John Gill's or Benjamin Wallin's prevailed among the majority of them,[107]

---

104   Backus, *A History of New England with Particular Reference to the Denomination of Christians Called Baptists*, 1: 288.
105   Ibid.
106   William Cathart, ed., *The Baptist Encyclopedia* (Philadelphia: Louis H. Everts, 1881; reprint, 1988 The Baptist Standard Bearer), 1036.
107   These two English-born Particular Baptists held great theological influence. This influence was passed on to Rhode Island College through mutual contact with James Manning and Isaac Backus. Both left sizable contributions to the university upon their deaths. See their

and there seemed to be little desire for distinguishing doctrinal beliefs to any significant degree. However, perhaps as a portent of what was to come for the rest of the century:

> *Between 1731 and 1740 five Baptist churches were formed in the province, at Rehoboth (1731), Sutton (1733), South Brimfield (1736), Bellingham (1737), and Leicester (1738). Between 1740 and the founding of Backus' church four more... but they still lacked the fervor, the leadership, and the dynamic spirit which animated the New Light Separate churches.[108]*

The verve that was destined to animate the Baptist movement in colonial New England would have to wait for more than a generation to arrive. Little did these lowly Baptists anticipate that they would eventually embrace the reformation baton first held by their Congregational detractors.

BAPTISTS, COMMUNION, AND INFANT BAPTISM

The ancient disagreement of dissenters, and now the Baptists, focused on the practice of infant baptism in the established church. However, the longstanding intramural debate among the majority of Baptists involved the doctrine of the atonement and the doctrine of election. John Comer, pastor of the First Baptist Church of Newport, Rhode Island, divided all of the New England churches into two categories: those holding to general redemption (General Baptists) and those who held to a limited atonement (Particular Baptists). Even in his pastorate at Second Baptist Church, Newport, Comer took the

---

respective biographical sketches in Ibid.
108   William G. McLoughlin, *Isaac Backus and the American Pietistic Tradition* (Boston: Little, Brown and Company, 1967), 90.

church knowing it was of the General Baptist persuasion, while he himself preached a limited atonement.[109] Of the twenty-two Baptist churches in Rhode Island, most were six-principle Baptists[110] which belonged to a General Association. They opposed particular election, but surprisingly, church fellowship did exist between the General and Particular Baptists of the period as evidenced by the free flow of ministers between both groups with apparent minimal conflict. McLoughlin pointed out that because of this tendency:

Membership could be transferred wherever there was fellowship, and that individual churches themselves changed points of view from year to year, indicates that the same fluidity or inconsistency existed within the persuasion as existed between the Baptists and the Congregationalists in regard to open-communion.[111]

This condition, after Backus' doctrinal transformation, would radically change as these Baptist churches inadvertently accepted new converts among their memberships who held some Biblical doctrines with greater regard than they themselves. This fervency touched off by the new birth experience brought consternation to many over their former baptism. By the middle of the 18th century there were at least two conflicting positions taken by the Baptists on how they were to deal with the baptism issue in relation to the Standing Order.

Not surprisingly, a hundred years earlier, the Particular Baptists were less willing to maintain fellowship with the General Baptists than they were with the Congregationalists.[112] This spirit

109   McLoughlin, *New England Dissent 1630-1833*, 1: 307.
110   This group believed in universal atonement along with a sixth principle known as "the laying on of hands upon all believers" as a requirement for holding church membership.
111   McLoughlin, *New England Dissent 1630-1833*, 1: 306.
112   This is not an unusual behavior among either group during this period, especially in London. Peter Naylor demonstrated that although Particular and General Baptists commonly

was manifested by John Watt, who succeeded Keach as minister of his church in 1692. While preaching for Keach in Philadelphia, Watt was pleased to see that some Presbyterians in the town felt quite comfortable in joining with the Baptists to worship for about three years. When the Presbyterians later hired their own minister, they promptly decided against Baptist fellowship.[113] This first and most pervasive Baptist position sought to occupy an open-communion stance[114] to accommodate the Puritans. Like John Myles had done in Swansea, this involved fostering the spirit of co-existence as opposed to mutual separation. Actually this produced greater confusion in the Standing Churches than an outright separation would have produced. The Congregational system could not allow equal protection to a system which openly challenged the critical issue of ecclesiastical perpetuity. It also created opportunity for Baptist expansion, particularly in places like Swansea, with leaders like John Myles, who followed Bunyan's open-communion position, allowing him to make significant connections with the Standing Church populace right under their noses.

However, open-communion did not insulate those Baptists from charges of schism and separation from the Standing Churches. During the trial of 1668, the Standing Church authorities demanded an explanation over the matter of the *separation* of Gould, Farnum, Osborne, and company from the Standing Church "to set up an

---

rejected infant baptism, neither group would consider "that a common renunciation of infant baptism could unite believers who disagreed concerning predestination and election." See Naylor, *Calvinism, Communion, and the Baptists*, 16.

113   Winthrop Still Hudson, "The Ecumenical Spirit of English Baptists," *The Review and Expositor* 55, no. 2 (1958): 190.

114   This position allowed the Baptists to suggest to their Standing Order accusers and friends that they really shared far fewer differences among themselves than popularly thought. However, most Congregational pastors and leaders rejected such ideas and considered Baptists to be socially inferior. Consequently, toleration would not occur under any theological construct or agreement.

assembly here in the way of Anabaptism...."[115] Obviously, since schism was considered an intolerable offence to the New England Way, the authority's view of Gould and his group's actions were considered worthy of punishment.

In reality, Baptists needed to cast their position to the Standing Church in Massachusetts as the Puritans had cast themselves to the established church in England; namely, that they did not desire separation from the established church but rather separation from perceived corruptions. For these Baptists, neither infant baptism nor immersion was such that demanded mutual separation or schism. The authorities on the other hand accused them of being "underminers" of the churches, to which they replied, "we never designed, neither do... any such thing, but heartily desire and daily pray for the well being, flourishing, and Prosperity of all the Churches of Christ, that the Lord would more and more appear among them...."[116] The irony to which the Baptists pointed was that although the established church had denied church communion to Gould during the "7or 8 years" of his estrangement from them, Gould had prayed for his persecutor's blessing and prosperity. Unfortunately, like many of their Anabaptist predecessors, these efforts at moderation did little more than usher Gould and his friends back to prison, despite Gould's willingness to tolerate the sprinkling of infants. The Massachusetts General Court, acting as the nursing fathers of the church, would not permit this sort of deliberate rebellion. McLoughlin further noted,

> *That Gould, Drinker, and Thrumble were not alone in taking this approach and that in fact it was probably the prevailing attitude among the Baptists of Massachusetts at this time is testified*

115   McLoughlin, *Soul Liberty: The Baptists' Struggle in New England, 1630-1833*, 46.
116   Ibid.

to by the efforts of many anti-pedobaptists to remain within
their parish churches as communicants despite the opposition
of their ministers and most of their former brethren.[117]

Even though Russell's *Brief Narrative* was written over a
decade after the event, and nearly five years after Gould's death, their
fundamental argument had gained additional adherents from the onset
of the 1668 debate. For example, Thomas Pierce, who had been raised
under the covenant of the Woburn Congregational Church, began
attending Gould's church in 1671 and was subsequently fined and
admonished by church authorities. Six years later he was converted
and baptized by John Myles while Myles was filling the Boston pulpit.
However, Pierce—while embracing Baptist principles, yet desiring
to worship with his family—applied for membership in the Woburn
church by petition but was denied. Interestingly, the petition had been
drawn up by several Standing ministers who refused to have their own
names written in the document, clearly demonstrating that the desire
for open-communion with the Baptists at this time was desired by
some ministers on both sides.[118]

---

117   McLoughlin, *Soul Liberty: The Baptists' Struggle in New England, 1630-1833*, 46.
118   McLoughlin's data appears in a confusing manner concerning the petition
Thomas Pierce presented to the Woburn Standing Church in 1672. According to his
own chronology of events, Pierce was converted and baptized by Myles six years
from the time he first attended Gould's church in 1671 which would appear to be
1677. The pastor of the Woburn church had refused Pierce the chance to appear
before the church as a member indicating that Pierce had been converted and was
no longer a Half-Way member. As a result of this refusal, a council was called by
Matt Johnson in 1672 to be attended by several of the aggrieved members along with
several other Standing Church ministers. However, this petition and its subsequent
refusal by the Pastor and the vote of the Standing ministers was based on the
unauthorized re-baptism of Pierce by an unrecognized authority which by the author's
own account had occurred in or around 1677, and not in 1672. Based on the time of
the original petition in 1672, it doesn't appear from the given data that Pierce was yet
converted and baptized.

*The fact that Gould's Baptist church in Boston and Clarke's
and Holme's in Newport had close and friendly relations
with Myles and his church indicates again how ill-defined the
tenants of the denomination were at this time. Obviously while
Myles was preaching at the Boston Church from 1676-1679
he must have encouraged its open-communion policies.[119]*

The demonstrable lack of conviction concerning certain Baptist
opinions may well have had a generational effect for Myles. His son
Samuel—the first son of a Baptist to attend Harvard, graduating
in 1684—ended up becoming an Anglican rector. He joined King's
Chapel in 1688 and never returned to Swansea to assist his father in
the Baptist fold. The perception generated by men from both sides
was that the Standing Churches and the Baptists were, in effect,
parallel Puritan movements demonstrating that "they were remarkably
similar in all doctrines except baptism."[120] The spirit of this era was
captured in the words of Baptist pastor Joseph Allyn saying that "their
different sentiments about baptism, were no more to him than their
different complexion or stature, or the color of their clothes...."[121]
When John Comer, the Newport Baptist pastor was first immersed,
his Congregational pastor advised him against it, but John was
bolstered by the reminder that it would not affect his standing with the
Congregational church. Despite the official view of the Standing Order,
peaceful co-existence was being pursued with determined efforts, yet
it produced few actual results. "Council after council, and conference

119   McLoughlin, *New England Dissent 1630-1833*, 1: 130.
120   McBeth, *The Baptist Heritage*, 205.
121   Backus, *A History of New England with Particular Reference to the Denomination of
Christians Called Baptists*, 2: 442.

after conference recommended it, and there seemed to be no voice against it, and yet it failed."[122]

As would be the case, open-communion would not be permitted in Massachusetts Bay (Boston) for another forty years, despite notable populist sympathies. McBeth reasoned why incompatibility was impossible, particularly for the Standing authorities:

> *First, the inherent incompatibility of infant baptism and believers' baptism could not be forever concealed or papered over. Second, the evangelistic zeal of those who preferred immersion drew multitudes to their position; in some cases the Congregationalists had to withdraw for self-preservation. Third, the adherents of alternate forms often differed in worship styles, an area which proved more divisive than doctrine.[123]*

Although Gould and Myles represented the mainstream of Baptist thought during this period, there were others who were much less willing to accommodate themselves with the Standing Order. This group represented the early exemplars of the Separate-Baptists who emerged out from the Great Awakening. There were two extremes among these conservatives but both differ from the Gould-Myles mindset of non-separation which came to dominate Baptist thought during this period. The less vocal of this extreme position is seen in men such as John Johnson and William Turner. Johnson was from Woburn and had participated in services with Gould in Boston but disdained open-communion with those who sprinkled. Johnson considered infant baptism was best left to the individual whims of parents[124] but believed that the only consistent option was complete

---

122   Ibid.
123   McBeth, *The Baptist Heritage*, 205.
124   McLoughlin, *Soul Liberty: The Baptists' Struggle in New England, 1630-1833*, 47.

separation from the Standing Order. Those who held this view may have desired, like McLoughlin surmised, to be seen as a competing version of Puritanism minus infant baptism, but that seems to be too simplistic even for Baptist tastes at the time. Admittedly, the Baptists had not yet thought through their arguments for soul liberty, freedom of conscience, and the right to exclusively support their own ministers, but they at least possessed a willingness to support separation, which the Standing Order would not allow.

The other extreme element of the Baptist conservatives is represented by such men as William Witter, Benanual Bowers, John Crandall, and William Turner. They believed the Puritan churches to be so corrupt as to be beyond repair and without merit. This differs little from the typical Anabaptist view during the early sixteenth century that infant baptism was "the badge of the whore" and "great sin of Popery and of the Church of England."[125] Unwilling to bring themselves under the veil of the reformation church of Luther or Calvin, the Anabaptists voiced their opposition to any civil authority over the church, believing they themselves were the true representatives of apostolic Christianity. They included magisterial domination and infant baptism as evidences of the reformer's continued alignment with the corruptions of Rome. Witter, although not involved with the debate in 1668, stands shoulder to shoulder with Bowers and Crandall in their mutual repudiation of the Standing Church. When offering testimony during the proceedings, Bowers said that the Standing Churches "have only a form of godliness." Crandall countered, "I do look upon myself as having separated from you all, and I am willing to give you my reasons."[126] Although Crandall was not

---

125   McLoughlin, *New England Dissent 1630-1833*, 1: 38.
126   Ibid, 1: 63. Taken from Joseph B. Felt, *The Ecclesiastical History of New England* (Boston: The Congregational Library Association and the Congregational Board of Publication, 1862), 2: 516.

allowed to testify because he was from Rhode Island, William Turner went on to answer, "Three things I separate from you for: 1. Baptizing infants. 2. Denying prophecy to the brethren. 3. A spirit of persecution of those that differ from you."[127] Almost a century and a half earlier, Anabaptist Michael Satler had summed up similar separatist arguments in the SC urging that

> *He calls upon us to be separate from the evil and thus he will be our God and we shall be His sons and daughters. He further admonishes us to withdraw from Babylon and the earthly Egypt that we may not be partakers of the pain and suffering which the Lord will bring upon them. From this we should learn that everything that is not united with our God and Christ cannot be other than an abomination which we should shun and flee from.*[128]

Despite this, separation over infant baptism was not high on the Baptist agenda. McLoughlin noted that only four pieces of polemical literature against the practice were penned by Baptists between 1692 and 1738, despite the fact that the Baptists had a number of men capable of making a good argument against the Congregationalists.[129] It was not until the Great Awakening, beginning in 1740, that pedobaptism would emerge as the key factor behind nearly every example of separation and finally as a pre-requisite to the Lord's Table.

However, the ongoing battle over pedobaptism and open-communion efforts must be understood within the larger context of the social and political concerns of the period, particularly after the Great Awakening. In a fashion similar to that of the Baptists of England who

---

127   McLoughlin, *New England Dissent 1630-1833* 1: 67.
128   John Albert Broadus, *Baptist Confessions, Covenants, and Catechisms*, ed. Timothy and Denise George (Nashville: Broadman and Holman Publishers, 1996), 25.
129   McLoughlin, *New England Dissent 1630-1833*, 1: 312.

found it necessary to identify themselves as closely as possible with all Protestants during the unstable religious environment of the mid to late seventeenth century, so Backus and the Separate-Baptists found immense value in casting themselves within the doctrinal image of early Congregational idealists. These factors underscore the fact that Baptists on both Continents struggled for existence under intolerant conditions requiring their doctrinal expressions to reflect to some degree the dominant theological constructs of Reformed thinking, particularly in regard to election and the invisible church model. This is a pattern which Backus utilized as a means of identifying his growing denomination with a continuing reformation tradition he considered abandoned by the first planters. By this he hoped to rope himself and the Baptists to the ongoing Reformation in the New World.

PROTESTANT GROUP THINK

English Baptists saw no danger in accommodating what many considered doctrinal non-essentials for the purpose of avoiding persecution. This spirit may be observed as consistent within the non-Separatist Independency in England at the time. The Particular Baptists consistently appealed to the writings of the major non-separatist divines—William Ames, Thomas Goodwin, Thomas Hooker, and John Owen—as identifying the point of view they represented.[130] Backus frequently quoted from Owen and Robinson to bolster the perception of his own visible church views.[131] The Middleboro pastor understood, perhaps better than others, that this use of Owen in defending his church ideology did not mean that Owen had any

---

130   Hudson, "The Ecumenical Spirit of English Baptists," 190.
131   Backus' use of Owen in defending his ecclesiological opinions should be understood in the same context in which the Puritans used Orthodox Church of England divines such as Ames, Goodwin, and Hooker. The use of such men offered credibility in sustaining their arguments and identified them within the Second Reformation tradition.

sympathy with his emerging Baptist views. Backus knew that the English divine had stood with the Standing Order in Boston while Owen plead for toleration of "persons that dissent from you," assuring the Boston leaders that "You know our judgment and practice to be contrary unto theirs, even as yours; wherein (God assisting) we shall continue to the end."[132] Gaustad admitted here that there "might have been powerful motives for his quoting verbatim and at length from John Robinson of Amsterdam," and that "it may have been a bid for sympathy from those then persecuting the Baptists, as they realized that not too long ago they themselves were the persecuted and oppressed."[133]

We gain a clearer perspective of the Backus movement when checked against the historical patterns of its English contemporaries. By the time of the colonial revolution, the American situation had reached a boiling point for the Separate-Baptists. Unable to determine whether they had more to fear from the rising perception of English imperialism or the intolerable Puritans at home, the Baptists finally realized their search for religious liberty was tied to their own political liberty and that of their Congregational neighbors.[134] As English Baptists had feared the political over-lording of the State Church, Backus and his pietistic Baptists feared this same parliament "could establish an Anglican episcopate, institute tithing and ecclesiastical courts, and enact a Clarendon Code for colonial non-conformists."[135] By 1775, this was a greater affront to the colonial Baptists' hope for

---

132   Backus, *A History of New England with Particular Reference to the Denomination of Christians Called Baptists*, 1:314. Owen's sympathies were stated in a letter to the Massachusetts Governor on March 25th, 1669, requesting the court to suspend its proceedings and judgments against Thomas Gould and other church members for unlawfully meeting together and conscientiously refusing to attend the parish church on the Lord's Day. The letter was signed by Drs. Goodwin, Owen, and eleven other Puritan ministers in London.
133   Hudson, *Baptist Concepts of the Church*, 109.
134   McLoughlin, *Soul Liberty: The Baptists' Struggle in New England, 1630-1833*, 188.
135   Ibid, 189.

religious liberty than was the intolerant Congregational system. These similar political and social dilemmas demonstrate at least four mutual concerns for the Baptists on both sides of the Atlantic.

The most notable problem with which the English Baptists wrestled was that of identity. All English Baptists, whether Particular or General in their respective atonement views, had to labor under the social and political disadvantage of a soiled history. Underwood said that "it was difficult for the ordinary Englishman to disassociate these English Anabaptists, as he called them, from the fanatical Anabaptists of Munster."[136] Losing the connection with Munster was nearly an impossible feat. This was the most noteworthy event to which Baptists could be connected by their enemies, and they were "anxious to prove to their many critics that they were not revolutionaries like the fanatical Anabaptists of Munster."[137] Consequently, the Particular Baptist Confession of 1644 borrowed *key* ideas from the non-Baptist Separatist Confession of 1596 in order to secure protection from this common Munster slander. When the Particular Baptists began to experience growth among the Standing Order in London, opposition came in the form of scurrilous publications such as "A Short History of the Anabaptists of High and Low Germany 1642," along with another work entitled "A Warning for England." To these was added one other, written in 1644, called "A Confutation of the Anabaptists and of All others who affect not civil Government."[138] These works were clearly aimed at giving all Baptists a sordid reputation for the purpose of isolating them, and presumably negating their numerical and social

---

136   Underwood, *A History of the English Baptists*, 51.
137   Ibid, 53.
138   Lumpkin, *Baptist Confessions of Faith*, 145.

influence. All of this indirectly led to the formation of the 1644 London Baptist Confession.

Backus and the earlier colonial Baptists shared similar tensions with their Congregational brethren. After the Warren Association had been formed in 1767, the Grievance committee sent Backus as their agent to record Baptist complaints against the Standing Order for persecution. This committee then sought restitution either through the courts or by petition to the State Legislature. The claim that colonial Baptists were the first to renounce infant baptism often earned them the title of the "madmen of Munster," which Backus said was "as absolute a falsehood as ever was uttered by man."[139] To this their English brethren could readily concur. In response, Baptists attempted to discredit this social persona foisted upon them by demonstrating that, despite their views on baptism, they had far more in common with their Protestant brethren than usually admitted by their enemies. It's important to recognize that colonial Baptist efforts to win a measure of political and social acceptance were not unique to them.

The English Particular Baptists openly identified themselves with the doctrinal expressions of the Westminster Confession, while the General Baptists discreetly desired to minimize differences with Calvinists in *The Orthodox Creed or a Protestant Confession of Faith*.[140] Significant effort by the Particular Baptists was made to disassociate themselves from Christological heresy and to demonstrate how they identified with the doctrine of election. The General Baptists made election to reside solely in Christ, and the writers carefully affirmed that the basis of such election was not out of "any foreseen holiness" in Christ's human nature but of "mere grace," as "are all

---

139   McLoughlin, ed., *Isaac Backus on Church, State, and Calvinism: Pamphlets, 1754-1789*, 337.
140   Lumpkin, *Baptist Confessions of Faith*, 296.

the members of His mystical body."[141] Unfortunately, tolerating such *compromised* language was considered by some in the Presbyterian majority in the Westminster assembly to be the seed of their own destruction. Therefore, independent thought in religious matters could not be permitted. Newman observed:

It was the avowed aim of the assembly to enforce uniformity throughout England, Scotland, and Ireland. No regard being had to the consciences of Episcopalians, Roman Catholics, Independents, or Baptists. Toleration was denounced by leading members of the assembly as the "last and strongest hold of Satan."[142]

This resulted in most Baptist leaders purposefully aligning themselves with the Protestant majority in order to avoid either persecution or banishment. The Particular Baptists made significant efforts at making their 1644 language more consistent with Westminster by 1688. Lumpkin commented:

The very document which would be the best proof of this agreement of essential matters was at hand, the Westminster Confession...the Particular Baptists of London and vicinity determined, therefore, to show their agreement with the Presbyterians and Congregationalists by making the Westminster Confession the basis of a new confession of their own.[143]

---

141   This article IX coincides with article XXIX which confirms the "one holy catholic church, consisting of, or made up of the whole number of the elect...." Definite effort was taken here by the General Baptists to connect the elect with the universal-invisible church. See Ibid, 302, 318.

142   A.H. Newman, *A Manual of Church History*, 2 vols. (Valley Forge: Judson Press, 1902), 2: 286-287.

143   Lumpkin, *Baptist Confessions of Faith*, 236.

It is important to remember that the more orthodox Particulars were keenly sensitive to doctrinal exactness in order to avoid accusations which could discredit them. Morris West made a similar observation by suggesting that the authors of the early Anabaptist confessions,

> *were accused, for example, so they said, of believing in free-will and of denying original sin. They complained further that the effect of these false reports has both alienated the godly and encouraged the ungodly to 'get together in clusters and stone us'. Thus the leaders of the congregations decided to publish this confession to establish their Calvinistic orthodoxy.*[144]

This resulted in 1644 with the Particular Baptists producing the first London Confession. The confession is noted for a moderate but firm Calvinism, including clear statements on the universal church and election and is remarkably similar in wording to the Aberdeen Confession of 1616.[145] In 1644, the clarity and soberness of the first London Confession had created such a positive stir that a former Westminster assemblyman, Daniel Featley, opposed it in his book *The Dippers dipt. or, The Anabaptists duck't and plunged Over Head and Eares, at a Disputation in Southwark* (1645). Featley exposed six articles of the fifty-three with which he took exception. Featley was intensely critical of Baptist practices and even criticized Baptists as being unable to comprehend complex theological issues.[146] Consistent with their desire for social and political affirmation, this second edition was presented in 1646 to Parliament for its approval. Lumpkin noted,

---

144   W.M.S. West, *Baptists and Statements of Faith, Foundation Documents of the Faith* (Edinburgh: T and T Clark, Limited, 1987), 84-85.
145   Lumpkin, *Baptist Confessions of Faith*, 145.
146   Leonard, *Baptist Ways: A History*, 51.

The revision was carefully and thoroughly made, so thoroughly indeed, that much of the distinctively Baptist emphasis was removed from some of the articles.... At length, on March 4, 1647, Parliament seems to have given a favorable reply to the appeal of the Baptists; legal toleration was granted.[147]

However, in the midst of the persecutions against dissenters like those fostered through the Clarendon Code of 1661-1665, which included the Conventicle Acts of 1662 and 1664, and the Act of Uniformity of 1662,[148] Baptists needed more than a defense against Munsterism and apparent sympathy with Westminster. By 1661, they also needed to be disassociated from Thomas Venner's uprising against Charles, which resulted in failure, along with the collapse of the Fifth Monarchy movement. This association of Baptists with forced millenarianism only furthered the contention that Baptists were men of violent social disorder.[149] They needed a doctrinal affinity which would identify them as true Protestants, part of a doctrinal stream which tied them to a developing national conscience. This, as West observed, was so-called "Calvinistic orthodoxy."[150] However, Torbet suggested that this conscience was being increasingly driven not just by a jaundiced Parliamentarian desire for orthodoxy but by public prejudice.[151] The common population had become willing to accept toleration as the hopeful price of social peace and order. This required Baptists to find identity within the theological perimeters of the Calvinist-Arminian debate and, more particularly, the Westminster Confession.[152]

---

147   Lumpkin, *Baptist Confessions of Faith*, 148-149.
148   For a useful synopsis of the period, see Lumpkin, *Baptist Confessions of Faith*, 235-236; Schaff, *The Creeds of Christendom*, 720-724.
149   Robert G. Torbet, *A History of the Baptists*, 3rd ed. (Valley Forge: Judson Press, 1950), 50.
150   West, *Baptists and Statements of Faith*. 85.
151   Torbet, *A History of the Baptists*, 51.
152   Because agreement with these positions was impossible for the General Baptists

Moreover, persecution advancing from King Charles forced Baptists, along with other dissenters, to align themselves as closely as possible with a Protestant majority. This connection was further strengthened by the Presbyterian rejection of the Conventicle Act which finally resulted in the ejection of the Puritans from the church in 1662. For the Baptists, this culminated in the Particular Baptists putting out a revision to the 1644 document with the Confession of 1677 which was then reaffirmed in 1688. Concerning this 1677 revision, Underwood observed,

> *They admitted that that they had based it on the Westminster Confession of 1648 and the revision thereof put out by the Congregationalists in 1658. The Confession of 1677 differs in scope and tone from the earlier Confession of 1644. Its Calvinism is more rigid....*[153]

Any doubt of the spirit in which this revision was undertaken—and the doctrinal sympathies its writers wished to suggest to an ardently Calvinist Parliament—is removed by the introductory remarks of the documents. Speaking of their professed doctrinal agreement with "protestants in diverse nations and cities," the writers affirmed,

> *we did in like manner conclude it best to follow their example, in making use of the very same words with them both, in all the fundamental articles of the Christian religion as also with many others whose orthodox confessions have been published to the world....*[154]

---

with reference to the election doctrine, they found other ways to identify themselves within the Protestant majority. Though sometimes means were tenuous, uniformity in any fashion was considered better than none at all.

153   Underwood, *A History of the English Baptists*, 105.

154   Lumpkin, *Baptist Confessions of Faith*, 245..

Those other orthodox confessions would include the Savoy Declaration of 1658, which as a Congregational Confession, was stridently Calvinistic. Schaff reported that in the Baptist Confession of 1677, the sections from the Westminster Confession on the church "Censuses...and of Synods and Councils," including the sacraments, were omitted. However, they showed great similarity in most of the sections, including chapter twenty-nine, which was an insertion of the Savoy Declaration chapter entitled "Of the Gospel and The Extent of Grace thereof."[155] The differences between the London Baptist Confession of 1644 and the 2nd London Confession of 1689 are that the writers of the latter were consumed by identifying with the terminology of Westminster rather than its former exemplar.[156]

After the accession of William and Mary in 1689 and the subsequent Act of Toleration, the dominant doctrinal statement for the Particular Baptists would become known as the Baptist Catechism, commonly called the Keach Confession written in 1693. This confession was largely a down-sized version of the second edition of the 1677 Confession reissued in 1688. New editions were again offered in "1693, 1699, 1719, 1720, 1791, 1809, among other years."[157] A sixteen page appendix on discipline entitled "The Glory and Ornament of a True Gospel-constituted Church" was added later which included a strong attack against infant baptism. Lumpkin notes that the document also demonstrates tension concerning the practice of close-communion, and that difference of opinion was allowed in the General Assembly. Underscoring such tension, neither Rippon nor Crosby

---

155   Schaff, *The Creeds of Christendom*, 1: 856.
156   Kenneth H. Good, *Are Baptists Reformed?* (Lorain: Regular Baptist Heritage Fellowship, 1986), 377.
157   Lumpkin, *Baptist Confessions of Faith*, 239.

included this appendix in their respective copies, and Rippon did not even include it in his narrative of the General Assembly proceedings.[158]

In a similar fashion, the SBBM reflected a pattern of general agreement with prevailing Puritan doctrine in Massachusetts but ultimately appealed more to their earliest historical ideal. Backus identified himself and the Baptists with the doctrinal statement of Robinson (minus infant baptism) and the articles of faith of the Standing Order in order to justify their claims of being the true pioneers of the Second Reformation.[159] Backus' personal use of John Owen is another clear example of this effort to agree in order to establish doctrinal affinities with the Standing Order while at the same time demanding toleration for the prevailing Baptist view on baptism. It is here that Backus is recognized by some as a greater patriot for religious liberty than theological acuity.[160] Leonard, typical of authors who rightly offer this label to the Middleboro pastor, connects his fight for religious liberty only to freedom from compulsory religious taxation rather than his repudiation of infant baptism.[161] On another level, Backus used the example of the English Baptists to demonstrate the inability of the Massachusetts Standing Order to offer the same toleration to colonial Baptists they demanded of the Church of England before embarking for the New World. The Middleboro pastor pointed to a tract printed by Dr. Mather called "The Divine Right to Infant

---

158   Ibid., 240.
159   Backus justified the Separate-Baptist movement on the doctrinal ideals of John Robinson and the first planters in Massachusetts. The first thirty-five pages of his history draw directly from this Separatist pastor. Concerning his own narrative of the New World Baptists, Backus said, "Here therefore are a great number of particulars with good vouchers to support them; which shew that oppression on religious accounts was not of the first principles of New England, but was an intruder that came in afterward." See Backus, *A History of New England with Particular Reference to the Denomination of Christians Called Baptists*, 1: viii.
160   Leonard, *Baptist Ways: A History*, 124.
161   McLoughlin said that "Backus looked forward to the day, when Baptist ministers and evangelists would convert all Americans to antipedobaptism." See McLoughlin, *Soul Liberty: The Baptists' Struggle in New England, 1630-1833*, 259.

Baptism" which was answered by Russell, a local Baptist, and sent to London where "messrs. William Kiffin, Daniel Dyke, William Collins, Hanserd Knollys, John Harris and Nehemiah Cox, noted Baptist ministers, wrote a preface to it...." In it, Minister Russell argued,

As for our brethren of the Congregational way in old England, both their principles and practice do equally plead for our liberties as for their own; and it seems strange that such of the same way in New England...for one Protestant congregation to persecute another... seems much more unreasonable than the cruelties of the church of Rome towards them that depart from their superstitions....[162]

Like their English forebears, Backus and the Separate-Baptists would eventually argue for toleration and respect from the Standing Order in the face of persecution and social stigmatization related to their baptismal convictions.

THE ENGLISH BAPTISTS AND BAPTISM

When the Middleboro pastor took his official step of re-baptism and closed church membership as a Baptist in 1756, he was ostensibly seen as having thrown down the gauntlet against the entire Congregational establishment in Massachusetts. Baptism became the seminal issue in the struggle for New England Baptists as it had among the English Baptists but even more for those who demanded close-communion churches. Not unlike his Baptist predecessors and contemporaries, Backus had rejected infant baptism on the same biblical grounds as his English forebears over a century earlier. As a Calvinist and close-communion churchman, he occupied a position

---

162   Backus, *A History of New England with Particular Reference to the Denomination of Christians Called Baptists*, 1: 391, emphasis added.

among colonial Baptists in the mid-eighteenth century which William Kiffin, Hanserd Knollys, and several others had earlier occupied among seventeenth century English Baptists. Kiffin was one of a number of Particular Baptist leaders "who were concerned for the unity of the churches, cooperation between congregations, and the spread of Calvinistic, closed membership, closed-communion Baptist churches across the country."[163] This view of the Lord's Table would have likely allowed visiting Baptist church members to partake in communion while visiting a sister church. However, a typical closed-communion view only permits members of the practicing church to partake. This was not exclusively practiced by English Baptists like Kiffin. Many would have practiced a close-communion position where the partaker had to be a baptized member but not necessarily of that particular church body. Similarly, Backus attempted to convert all of the General Baptist churches in Massachusetts and Rhode Island to his Calvinist persuasion and his close-communion stance after his conversion to Baptist principles in 1756. Their close-communion position was not politically expedient with either the Congregationalists, or their open-communion Baptist brethren.

Conversely, on the open-communion side, English and Particular Baptist Henry Jessey,

believed and published his views that believer's baptism was the baptism the Bible taught but there is no doubt that he was interested in keeping close links with the Independents while seeking to draw together, in particular, the 'mixed' communion churches.[164]

---

163   Hayden, *English Baptist History and Heritage*, 78.
164   Geoffrey Fillingham Nuttall, *Reformation, Conformity, and Dissent* (London: Epworth Press, 1977), 138.

Jessey's influence in the matter of mixed-communion has been noted in the pastorate of Bristol's John Canne of Broadmead. Canne, in becoming a Baptist after leading a Brownist church in Amsterdam, never made believers' baptism requisite for membership. In his work noted above, Geoffrey Nuttall attributed this influence to Jessey, pastor of the Southwark Church. Apparently, in the heated political climate of the mid seventeenth century, Jessey was one of a number of Particular Baptists who willingly passed over the implications of his own movement's principles for the greater interest of showing solidarity with the Standing Order.

During the Protectorate between 1649 and 1658, Cromwell facilitated less friction among the religious classes and tightened the moral laxity among the clergy. By appointing a board of thirty-eight examiners among the Presbyterian, Independent, and Baptist bodies, Cromwell intended to test the character, piety, and zeal of pastoral candidates filling vacant churches in the Commonwealth. Among this group, four[165] Baptists were appointed: John Tombes, D. Dyke, H. Jessey,[166] and Colonel William Packer, all likely open-communion sympathizers at the time.[167] The open-communion Particulars were perceived as being more conciliatory and less prone to schism than Kiffin and the other Particulars. This becomes noteworthy because the closed-communion position of Kiffin was more commonly held among the General and Particular Baptists than the open position.[168] Kiffin,

---

165   Underwood recorded six Triers including William Goff and Edward Cresset. See Underwood, *A History of the English Baptists*, 80. Vedder included John Myles in that number representing one of the sub-commissions in the district of Wales. See Vedder, *A Short History of the Baptists*, 269.
166   Evans, *The Early English Baptists*, 196.
167   E.A. Payne and N. S. Moon, *Baptists and 1662* (London: The Carey Kingsgate Press Limited, 1962), 13-15. This record does admit the fact that Daniel Dyke became co-pastor of the Baptist meeting house in Devonshire Square, Bishopsgate with William Kiffin in 1668. Kiffin was a well-known closed-communion Particular Baptist. It is therefore likely that Dyke was closed-communion by this time as well.
168   Hayden, *English Baptist History and Heritage*, 86.

like Backus, held baptism to be a prerequisite for admission to the Lord's Table.[169] During this period, this was the predominant Baptist position. Open-communion was considered an "English distortion" of the Baptist position.[170] Wamble suggests correctly that "the best indication of the Baptist conviction" in regard to believers' baptism is the long appendix to the 1677 confession, which was originally intended to show the Particular Baptists' doctrinal agreement with the Presbyterians and Congregationalists.[171] However, the appointments of Baptists would likely not have been possible without a considerably more liberal view concerning the union of church and state as well as open-communion policies existing among Baptists of the day. It appears that this openness was not unique, because other close-communion Baptists like William Kiffin apparently did not vocally oppose it at the time.[172] Howbeit, Kiffin's debates with Bunyan over the issue were well documented, and as Wamble mused, may have been instrumental in Bunyan tightening his baptism views in his second half of Pilgrim's Progress printed in 1784.[173] However, this is debatable because Bunyan never publicly deviated from his open position.

Two of the leading congregations of the early 1650s, the Broadmead Church in Bristol and the Bedford church under Bunyan,

---

169   This view of apostolic baptism understood Galatians 3:26-29 as saying that the unbaptized were not visibly putting on Christ, thus apostolic baptism had been established to show the recipient had experienced the death that the Lord's Table was to show until Christ comes. See McLoughlin, ed., *Isaac Backus on Church, State, and Calvinism: Pamphlets, 1754-1789*, 157.

170   This word was used by Abraham Booth in his 1778 work "An Apology for the Baptists" quoted here from Naylor, *Calvinism, Communion, and the Baptists*, 86. The thesis of Naylor's work was that close-communion was the predominant Baptist position among both the General and Particular Baptists. The election doctrine was not requisite to holding the position.

171   Hugh Wamble, "Early English Baptist Sectarianism," *The Review and Expositor* 55, no. 1 (1958): 67.

172   Wamble demonstrated that Kiffin, who later came out strongly against open-communion, may have been inclined during this period be more tolerant toward the practice because of his affinity to Cromwell, who wanted to unite the independent groups. See Ibid, 65.

173   This idea is broached by Wamble, but he fails to come out and fully support it. It is more probable that although Bunyan appeared to tighten his position ambiguously in this

were decisively committed to maintaining open-communion policies and were considered "predominantly Baptist," even as they continued to maintain the policy of open membership.[174]

The General Baptists' printed position on baptism in the Orthodox Confession saw baptism as preceding real church membership, a priority before admission to the Lord's Table, and a requirement for membership as a foundational principle "of the Church, just as repentance, faith, and holy living."[175] In reality, English Baptists as a whole, excepting the open-communion Baptists, did not compromise baptism or make it a public bartering tool for achieving a Protestant consensus among the Independents.[176] English Particular Baptists were resistant to modifying their baptismal views toward consensus but rather made their emphasis on being in the "election of Grace" by which they meant Calvinistic Protestantism,[177] which Backus emulated a century later in New England's changing social climate.

SOCIAL CHANGE: ROBERT ROBINSON AND ROBERT HALL

The fourth and final concern which both English and American Baptists attempted to exploit was the changing political attitude toward religious toleration. The ongoing non-conformist movement working for toleration in England was not static after 1689. Baptists increasingly used the political process for advancing toleration.

---

second section of his work, he never fully repudiated open views.

174   Wamble, "Early English Baptist Sectarianism", 66.

175   Ibid.

176   Such concerns have continual contemporary applications even today. Paul Fiddes, Principal at Regent's Park College, Oxford, in writing for the Hertfordshire Baptist Association, said "The baptism of believers is a door into a gathered community of believers, an act which includes someone who professes Christ within a group of his disciples." He said by not recognizing all baptisms and affirming the ecumenical idea of "a 'common baptism', Baptists appear to be exclusive." See Paul S. Fiddes, *Believers's Baptism: An Act of Inclusion or Exclusion?* (Oxford: Hertfordshire Baptist Association, 1999), 1, 14.

177   Particular Baptist William Kaye made this statement in 1653 in Baptism Without Bason, 36-42. See the quote in Wamble, "Early English Baptist Sectarianism," 68-69.

Similar to the cause for religious freedom which Robinson and Hall carried on in Old England, Backus engaged in New England. Both groups saw strong advantages in being well connected to university life. Education and academic influence would both work together to dismantle the old orders and forge a new enlightened consensus on both continents.

Robinson was the pastor of St. Andrews Street Baptist Church in Cambridge, and his ministry attracted several members of the university faculty and student body. His themes often championed the cause of religious freedom, effectively criticizing the concept of a State-Church.[178] Backus and Robinson had imbibed a deep passion for liberty and freedom of conscience by reading Milton and Locke and both became convinced of a necessary connection between believers' baptism and freedom of conscience[179] In 1778, Robinson published a series of lectures entitled *The Principles of Nonconformity*, which ostensibly argued that the power of all government was vested in its citizens, comprising the core of Lockean social philosophy. Robinson later became a strong advocate for the Republican cause in the American Colonies and worked publicly for the cause of independence.[180] Unlike Backus, however, he opposed Calvinist subscription tests by his own denomination for the use of denominational resources and pursued toleration on broader terms. He was one of a number of ministers who became known as the "Rational dissenters" who stood for "equal liberty and justice for all."[181] Backus, on the other hand, wanted toleration on much stricter terms, particularly as it applied outside the jurisdiction of the local church. The Middleboro pastor, and many other Baptists, disagreed with

---

178   Payne, *Baptists and 1662*, 43.
179   Ibid.
180   Hayden, *English Baptist History and Heritage*, 114.
181   Ibid, 113.

Jefferson and Madison that the right to hold political offices should be extended to "Jews, Mohammedans, deists, atheists, and infidels."[182] As did his Puritan forebears, he thought public laws which proscribed certain moral behaviors were necessary.[183] Because of his far more limited application of Locke's principles and strict Calvinist theology, Backus may have thought that establishing a relationship on such terms with Robinson as unnecessary or non-productive. Just a year before Robinson died in 1790, Backus wrote his pamphlet "Particular Election and Final Perseverance Vindicated" which strongly opposed Wesleyan inroads into the American colonies, something which Robinson did not, with his broad egalitarian views, publicly oppose in England. Backus figured the success of his Baptist denomination to be contingent upon the Edwardsean Calvinism intrinsic to the first Great Awakening along with his selective application of Locke's principles of toleration.[184]

Robert Hall, who too had drunk deeply of Milton along with Locke's voluntarism, had been educated at J.C. Ryland's College in Northampton. He was deeply committed to religious liberty, religious toleration, and "made no secret of his sympathy with the colonists in America, and the revolutionaries in France.[185] Through his respective ministries at Cambridge, Bristol, and Leicester, Hall effectively influenced numbers of university men through his sharp intellect and tremendous oratory. Being the younger contemporary of Robinson, Hall was privileged to see the repealing of the Test and

---

182   McLoughlin, *Soul Liberty: The Baptists' Struggle in New England, 1630-1833*, 267.
183   Backus was in agreement with the old Puritan view against theatre going. On Feb 11, 1798, Backus noted in his diary that the "grand Theatre in Boston was burnt the 2nd instant; as they were preparing to mimock the burning of Sodom in a play; the fire catched in the house near night, and consumed it, and they could not quench it A plain testimony of mocking God!" See William G. McLoughlin, ed., *The Diary of Isaac Backus*, 3 vols. (Providence: Brown University Press, 1979), 3: 1427-1428.
184   McLoughlin, ed., *Isaac Backus on Church, State, and Calvinism: Pamphlets, 1754-1789*, 452.
185   Payne, *Baptists and 1662*, 44.

Corporation Acts just three years before his death in 1831. Though contemporaries in their common efforts for religious toleration and freedom of conscience under Lockean philosophy, Backus apparently had no direct contact with either Robinson or Hall, yet all were key in forging new freedoms born of enlightenment thought at critical periods of national development on both continents.

THE NEW ENGLAND BAPTISTS

Any ambiguity among Baptists concerning open-communion and infant baptism should be interpreted in light of the ongoing desire by Baptists both in England and in the New World to be seen as "Orthodox Protestants" in all points, except baptism. Some of them were determined to carry the Protestant ethic to its doctrinal and ethical conclusions. Backus' emphasis on local-church authority and antipedobaptism, as an attempt to make the invisible church more visible, created an environment where any ambiguity between the concepts became virtually intolerable.[186] Rejecting covenant theology, Backus consistently argued his case from the authority of Scripture alone. Englishman Thomas Grantham earlier conceded that the Protestants' most vital principle was the supremacy of the Scriptures, believing that this would induce them to adopt a Scriptural view of believers' baptism.[187] However, by the time of Backus, John Myles'

---

186   The vast majority of historians infer that the roots of the successionist theory of Landmarkism go back to the Backus movement. Because of the ultimate influence of revivalism and the diminishment of the election doctrine by the time of the New Hampshire Confession of faith, the visible and invisible church concepts began to hold minimal distinction among American Baptists. What Backus had ostensibly wanted made visible had lost all invisibility soon after his death. See Robert Torbet's discussion on Landmarkism in Hudson, ed., *Baptist Concepts of the Church*, 173. See also Tull, *Shapers of Baptist Thought*, 77, Wood, ed., *Baptists and the American Experience*, 269.

187   Cited in Wamble, "Early English Baptist Sectarianism," 68-69. See also his use of sources Henry Denne, *The Doctrine and Conversation of John Baptist*, 1643, 54; cf. Thomas-Atwood Rotherham, *A Den of Theeves Discovered*, 1643, 11-15; Thomas Grantham, *Truth and Peace*, 1689, 47f; Mar. Nedham, *Interest will not Lie*, 1659, 17-19.

open position was being rejected on biblical grounds by the majority of Separate-Baptists. His church in Swansea justified accepting believers solely in terms of personal salvation based on his former Welsh covenant.[188] Its celebrated open-communion passage read:

> *Indeed, further declaring in that as union in Christ is the sole ground of our communion with all such by judgment of charity we conceive to be fellow members with us in our Head, Christ Jesus, though differing from us in such controversial points as are not absolutely and essentially necessary to salvation.*[189]

Like the Swansea church, most Baptist churches during this period used covenants at their founding as a means of formalizing church behavior norms and practices. Exceptions to this rule were the churches formed at Providence and Newport in the 1630s and 1640s, respectively.[190] The most influential of church covenants was that written by Backus for the Middleboro church beginning in 1756. This covenant found use in Massachusetts, Vermont, Maine, and even as far south as Pennsylvania. Between 1832 and 1878, it was copied or partially used by several Baptist associations in Atlantic Canada and Ontario.[191] The Middleboro pastor also concentrated on refuting the prevalent covenant ideas normally connected to Old Testament circumcision. When defining the essence of what true covenants were, he observed that the confounding of the Old Testament covenant idea with New Testament baptism was the source of "so much darkness" that confusion was the only possible result. He believed the Baptist

---

188   This is the oldest known covenant in North America brought here by John Myles in 1662 and installed in the Swansea church in 1663.

189   Charles W. Deweese, *Baptist Church Covenants* (Nashville: Broadman Press, 1990), 132-133.

190   Ibid, 40.

191   Ibid, 45.

idea of covenant was that people could not be brought into it without giving their personal consent, and that the covenant cannot bind any person or community to act anything contrary to the revealed will of covenant, further establishing the Baptists' rejection of any covenant extending to infants. It was this inability of infants to respond to local-church covenant obligations or salvation which created a theoretical rift between the visible and the invisible church. If, in fact, the particular church is simply making visible that which was formerly invisible, the doctrine of the elect belonging to a universal body of Christ by virtue of a sovereign, unseen act of God appears imbalanced against the doctrine of personal voluntarism. Voluntarism demanded an individual response for salvation, baptism, and the conscious adoption of the covenant for establishing an individual's membership in the visible church.

However, Backus never admitted any disparity between these universal and particular/visible concepts of the church. His rejection of covenant theology and infant baptism brought him to entirely reassess the magisterial church but never to suggest that the different points of entry posited incongruity between the two church concepts. In DCC, Backus rejected Rev. Fish's notion that the church always remains the same. Fish claimed, "That Jesus Christ has but one church in the world, and that is the same which it always was." Backus agreed that the "invisible church is so, but entered my exception against its being true of the visible church."[192] That was as far as he would go.[193] Referring to the Half-way covenant in his discussion with

---

192   Backus, *A Discourse, Concerning the Materials, the Manner of Building, and Power of Organizing the Church of Christ*, 15.

193   Later Baptist observers would not be content with such qualifications between the two ecclesiastical concepts. See William Crowell, *The Church Member's Manual* (Boston: Gould, Kendall, & Lincoln, 1847), 112-116. Norman Maring exposes a similar tendency in the thought of Francis Wayland in his article "The Individualism of Francis Wayland" in Hudson, ed., *Baptist Concepts of the Church*, 136. These tendencies culminated in a full-blown rejection of the universal-invisible concept on Biblical/theological grounds. See Jesse B. Thomas, *The

Fish, Backus argued that this covenant idea of the magisterial church in Massachusetts was foreign to the entire spirit and teaching of the New Testament because it virtually admitted unbelievers to church membership. Backus asked,

> *How can any souls be fit materials of the church which those*
> *gates shall not prevail against, but such as believe in Christ with*
> *their hearts, and confess him with their mouths?... Is any other*
> *church-state instituted in the gospel, but a particular one? The*
> *church spoken of by our Lord in Mat.18:15-18, is such an one*
> *as a brother can tell his grievance to.... The seven churches of*
> *Asia are spoken to by their great head, not as one national or*
> *provincial church, but as so many distinct churches....*[194]

His view was not only considered to be schismatic by the Congregationalists, but by certain Baptists who thought non-communion with pedobaptists to be sectarian. For example, Jabez Bowen of Providence, critical of perceived divisions within Christendom (i.e., The Separate-Baptist movement) and appealing for unity among the denominations, made the effort to write to Backus in 1802 to convince him of this fact by pointing out that the original Baptists in Swansea (1663) were not narrow-minded zealots as he undoubtedly perceived the SBBM to be at that time.[195] Critical of the Separate-Baptists Bowen opined, "I have been always sorry that Christians should be so totally alienated and estranged from each other, solely by the outward forms and ceremonies of religion...."[196]

Church and the Kingdom (Louisville: Baptist Book Concern, 1914).

194   Backus, *A Discourse, Concerning the Materials, the Manner of Building, and Power of Organizing the Church of Christ.*, 17.

195   Jabez Bowen to Isaac Backus, in *Backus Papers, Andover Newton Theological School* (Providence: 1802), 2.

196   Ibid.

This reveals a healthy tension that flourished between Baptists and other denominations, and this served to recast the Baptists' image as the real Biblicists of the emerging era. Outside of the baptism issue, Bowen's letter appeared to be otherwise reasonable and judicious in responding to the then highly respected New England historian. It appears equally evident that Backus' position, although not openly criticized, did not possess any sympathy with Bowen's open-communion policies long since rejected by the Middleboro clergyman. Some eighteen years earlier in a letter to his former pastor Benjamin Lord of Norwich (LBL), Backus' opposition to the Standing Church was so virulent that he prayed that God would overthrow the Standing Order which he believed, "would not stand if it were not for the support of the civil authority...."[197] Backus and the Separate-Baptists recognized their actions as having brought them into the larger dissent community, yet more particularly, the ancient stream of Baptist witness. By 1802, when this letter was written, the SBBM had no desire to find common ground with those who threatened their right to exist on ecclesiological principles.

Ironically, Baptist inter-communion was noticeable on several other points including election, Sabbath days, the laying on of hands, and the free flow of ministers between churches holding various doctrinal combinations. Not surprising, however, pedobaptism would remain the key point of controversy between the Standing Churches and the majority of Baptists during this period, particularly as the Great Awakening doctrine of the new birth forced it to the forefront of local church discussions. Bunyan's open-communion creed[198] was often cited as justification by a Baptist minority attempting to build

---

197   Isaac Backus, *A Letter to the Reverend Mr. Benjamin Lord, of Norwich* (Providence: William Goddard., 1764), 37.

198   Backus, *A History of New England with Particular Reference to the Denomination of Christians Called Baptists*, 1: 116.

bridges and create the image that they were little more than Puritans who believed in baptism for adult-believers only. Notably, during the struggle for toleration within this tenuous period, terminology demanded a different emphasis by the Baptists. The Standing Order rejected the idea that mutual coexistence was possible with the Baptists concerning alternate baptismal views. Tolerance at this point would upset the theocracy's ability to effectively manage dissent. The Great Awakening had not only introduced the need for immediate conversion into the Congregational system but had conflicted congregations on who actually deserved baptism. This was apparent for two reasons. First, most New Englanders held stronger convictions about the necessity of conversion for membership than did their ministers.[199] Secondly, as Congregational families began to be affected by the new birth, baptismal confusion among converts multiplied. For instance, many in Ezra Stiles' Second Congregational church in New Haven had declined baptism for their children because of Baptist and Quaker influence.[200] Backus would raise the issue of infant baptism to another level in 1756 with his formation of the First Baptist Church of Middleboro, clarifying at that time the incongruity between the opposing factions and providing a biblical basis for his fresh understanding of the baptism issue. Recognizing this, Backus drew an exact comparison between his movement and the first Awakening as to historic separatist principles asking,

How much have papists used this argument against protestants, and episcopalians against puritans and dissenters? And is not the same now used against us?...but it is quite as injurious to lay the blame thereof to the main principles or chief leaders of our separation,

199   Edmund S. Morgan, *The Gentle Puritan: A Life of Ezra Stiles 1727-1795* (New York: W.W. Norton and Company, 1962), 188.
200   Ibid.

as it would be to the chief instruments of the revival of religion in
1741...therefore it appeared needful thus to trace matters up to their
original, and set principles and facts in as clear light as might be....[201]

The problem, he suggests, is not the chief leaders who marshaled the general population during these historic periods of spiritual upheaval and reform. The impartial observer must recognize the "principles and facts" which undergirded these pietist reform movements. Backus was clearly suggesting that 'Separatism" from the Standing Order over ecclesiological disagreements was not just local *reactionism*, but consistent biblical *reform* in the same spirit that the original principles of the Puritans motivated them against the Standing Order in England.

SUMMARY

The vulnerable Baptists grew slowly through the closing decades of seventeenth century New England. Of the approximately ten churches in New England at the turn of the century, their collective efforts in Colonial America, particularly Massachusetts, were aimed primarily at political and social survival. Their English predecessors point out the fact that Particular and General Baptists had obtained some political and social deliverance by articulating their doctrines through the vernacular of prevailing Protestant doctrine. Baptists, who had long been tied to the Munster debacle, thought they needed to demonstrate their *Calvinist Orthodoxy* within a developing Protestant heritage. For Calvinist-leaning Baptists, orthodoxy had to be expressed

---

201   Backus, *A Discourse, Concerning the Materials, the Manner of Building, and Power of Organizing the Church of Christ,* 71-72.

in terms of the politically and socially accepted Westminster tradition on both sides of the Atlantic.

Unfortunately, the status of the Massachusetts Commonwealth demanded uniformity under which Baptists would not participate in good conscience. For them, the magisterial church of the reformation had reappeared in Massachusetts, and nothing less than complete toleration would suffice their demands. Conversely, the Standing Church saw open-communion with Baptists as a dangerous idea which would ultimately introduce rebellion, schism, and social anarchy. Any solution to the problem would require the introduction of the Great Awakening doctrine of the new birth which Torbet ultimately said provided "an easy step for Separate Congregationalists to safeguard a regenerate church membership by accepting believer's baptism."[202] As Baptists, they simply adopted a local-church covenant among their membership which replaced the universal Church ideas implicit in covenant theology. However, before looking at the Great Awakening, the historical context for the SBBM first requires a brief look at some earlier historical precedents.

---

202   Torbet, *A History of the Baptists*, 223.

SECTION TWO

Origins and Orthodoxy

Chapter Three

The Development of the SBBM

INTRODUCTION

While Backus would ultimately go back to early "Anabaptist" exemplars to justify his rejection of infant baptism, he employed what earlier Puritan and Puritan/Separatist writers understood as the "continuing" Reformation to rationalize his dissent. The early development of the SBBM was identified later by Backus and other separatists as a movement which demanded a modified ecclesiology not envisioned by the first reformers nor understood by their Puritan successors. The SBBM re-emphasized the same biblical principles in the eighteenth century, and established what their enemies considered to be, ostensibly, a sectarian movement that had snubbed its nose at other contemporary Christian denominations.

FROM THE FIRST TO THE SECOND REFORMATION

Beginning with the early church father Tertullian (c. 160-c. 225), Backus traced infant baptism back to when "heathen philosophy was set up as a rule to interpret Scripture by; when the shadows of the Old Testament were taken to draw a veil over the truth and church order described in the gospel...."[203] Tertullian was the early church's most ardent enemy of Plato. Furthermore, the pastor called antipedobaptism the maxim "which was held by the Waldenses, Petrobusians, Wickliffites, and Hussites, long before Luther's day."[204]

---

203   Backus, *A History of New England with Particular Reference to the Denomination of Christians Called Baptists*, 2: v.
204   Ibid, 2: vi.

This was later modeled in the Anabaptist campaigns of the sixteenth century which Backus interpreted "as the only consistent Protestantism which overcame the perversions of the Church of Rome and brought Protestantism to the goal which Martin Luther, Huldrich Zwingli, and John Calvin did not reach."[205]

In "An Appeal to the Public" (APRL), Backus referred to the entirety of church history—from Constantine (ca. 285- ca. 337) up to the English Reformation—as a long historical episode which claimed one "ecclesiastical head over kingdoms as well as churches...," until in England they "set up the king as their head in ecclesiastical as well as civil concernments."[206] In short, the first reformation leaders, in union with their Constantinian forebears, never became convinced that the union of church and state was the travesty against true religious liberty. Backus, like modern historians, concluded that Luther and Calvin had fallen far short of creating a truly workable Protestant system, Calvin's Geneva notwithstanding. Miller noted:

they ransacked philosophy and science in order to expunge whatever lent support to the pretensions of Rome, they demolished everything in medieval culture that conflicted with reformed doctrine. But they left it still unclear how much of the medieval culture was to remain, or in what fashion the purified body of knowledge was to be reconstituted.[207]

Furthermore, in regard to the English reformation Miller suggested that "the character of Puritanism was determined as much by the questions which Luther and Calvin did not solve as by those

---

205   Walter Klaassen, *Anabaptism: Neither Catholic nor Protestant* (Waterloo: Conrad Press, 1973), 1.
206   McLoughlin, ed., *Isaac Backus on Church, State, and Calvinism: Pamphlets, 1754-1789*, 316.
207   Miller, *The New England Mind: The Seventeenth Century*, 94.

which they did."[208] They did understand that civil government must be restricted from being too dominant in the church, and yet they were not certain how much was enough or too much. However, Backus saw that Luther's shortcoming was partially corrected in the Puritan uprising, their subsequent removal to America, and the establishment of the first Plymouth colony, noting that their founders

> *carried the reformation so far as not to make use of the civil power to force the people to support religious ministers (for which they have had many a lash from the tongues and pens of those who were fond of that way) but the second colony, who had not taken up the cross as to separate from the national church... and so to frame a Christian common-wealth here.*[209]

In the end, Backus concluded that the grand experiment in the colonial wilderness had failed just where the first reformation had failed. The original desires for Christian liberty and freedom of conscience spawned under the duress of their former national church had coalesced afresh in the new world.[210] Instead of fulfilling the dictum of John Robinson's pursuit of new or further light, the early Puritans stopped short of reformation and had become as intolerant to others' pursuit of the pure church ideal just as their Anglican persecutors had been of them.[211] Backus identified their commitment

---

208   Ibid.
209   McLoughlin, ed., *Isaac Backus on Church, State, and Calvinism: Pamphlets, 1754-1789*, 316.
210   Backus distinguishes here between the original Plymouth Colony committed to the Separatist views of John Robinson, and those which came after such as Salem, followed by John Winthrop and nearly fifteen-hundred others who in 1630 planted Charlestown, Boston, Dorchester, and Watertown. These later Puritan communities constituted the Massachusetts Commonwealth which became as intolerant to other views as the Standing Church in England had been to their own.
211   For the Baptists, further light usually referred to their rejection of infant baptism, and the biblical assertion that adult baptism precedes the Lord's Table. For the Puritans, further

to covenant theology as the source of this intolerance, challenged the validity of the New England Commonwealth, and pointed them to their original intention of "making visible that which was formerly invisible." In doing so, however, he looked to historical persons preceding the magisterial reformation who rejected infant baptism on the basis that Separate-Baptists did. Consequently, before examining the magisterial church conceptions, we should look first to those who played a role in what was called the *Radical Reformation.*

THE ANABAPTIST PERCEPTION OF THE CHURCH

Littell calls the study of the Anabaptists' ecclesiology "a study in the origins of 'sectarian Protestantism,'" not in the pejorative sense, but in the context of a sociological perspective of religion.[212] Admittedly, most views, up to the last half century, had been rooted in the polemics of Reformation apologetics. However, recent historians are satisfied to call the Anabaptist church conception a legitimate "third view" within the established radical reformation tradition, because "such a definition can reflect...the verdict of history in favor of those radical groups."[213] Similarly, De Jong follows Troeltsch, who identifies this sect-type influence of the third view among the Anabaptists as something entirely distinguished from the continental reformers in Zurich.[214] This opinion should not be hidden behind the typical Protestant ecclesiology. Why? - Because Anabaptism had courageously distinguished itself from Magisterial Protestantism up

---

light was used to justify their secession from the "Church of England and the tyranny of the king, but they held them in moderation." See McLoughlin, *Soul Liberty: The Baptists' Struggle in New England, 1630-1833*, 49-50.

212   Littell, *The Anabaptist View of the Church*, xxii.

213   Ibid.

214   De Jong, *The Covenant Idea in New England Theology*, 63. De Jong notes that the first Anabaptist to advocate the church covenant idea was Hans Lucher who wrote *Ein Tzeitlang geschwigner Christ licher Bruder* in 1523. It focused on the polity of Anabaptist churches. See De Jong, 63-73.

to and beyond Luther by rejecting infant baptism.[215] Agreeing with this assessment, Williams justified this classification by drawing the distinction between a sect and a church "in terms of the voluntarist and moral criteria of the American scene as distinguished from the religio-political criteria by which the state church was distinguished from the sect in Europe."[216] Williams' definition provides a helpful window into understanding why the SBBM was able to assume the original Puritan mantle of making visible that which was formerly invisible, and it subsequently moves that vision toward its logical end. This perception of the SBBM, along with their use of historical precedents, suggests that they did not recognize the Anabaptists and other Reformation leaders as having acted simultaneously or necessarily out of the same provocations. They believed historical evidence suggested that there were "protestants before Protestantism, reformers before the Reformation-not only individual protestants, as we have already seen, but protestant bodies."[217] The potential problem here lies in some Baptists attempting to claim these disparate groups as direct doctrinal forebears. G.H. Williams said,

An important step in the re-evaluation of the Anabaptists was the work of the Catholic scholar C.A. Cornelius. He assembled and re-worked the surviving documents.... Thereupon the Munster archivist and director of the Comenius Society, Ludwig Keller, sought to give further historical documentation to the claim... that a remnant of faithful Christians had continuously survived down through the Middle Ages.... Keller took from the Mirror the designation "Old Evangelical" and sought to establish a succession

215   William R. Estep, Jr., *The Anabaptist Story*, 3rd ed. (Grand Rapids: William B. Eerdmans Publishing Company, 1996), 201.
216   G.H. Williams and Angel M. Mergal, eds., *Spiritual and Anabaptist Writers* (Philadelphia: The Westminster Press, 1957), 27.
217   Vedder, *A Short History of the Baptists*, 110.

from the Waldensians, the Hussites, and the artisans....[218]

Littell plainly concluded that during the Middle period between
the time of Constantine and the early reformers, the "True Church"
met in the secluded forests and private homes. This conception of
church history should not be viewed as supporting some chain-link
connection back to the apostles or John the Baptizer.[219] It simply
suggests a significant presence of dissent groups under various names
and titles prior to the Anabaptist movement of the sixteenth century.[220]
For instance, Backus pointed out that Peter Bruis and Henry of
Toulouse opposed infant baptism and practiced rebaptism proving,
at least in his own mind, that the Separate-Baptists, including those
dissenters in Munster, were not the first Baptists in the world.[221] But
in doing so, Backus could be accused of making a claim for some sort
of Baptist continuity which could be confused with the later sectarian

---

218   George H. Williams and Angel M. Mergal, eds., *Spiritual and Anabaptist Writers*
(Philadelphia: The Westminster Press, 1957), 26.

219   James Edward McGoldrick, in his repudiation of Landmarkism, goes to
considerable length to expunge the concept of a "True Church" existing in any form in the
time of Constantine or beyond. In doing so, he dispels all claims of organic continuity, but
ignores such fair-minded conclusions as those of those of Baptist historian Thomas Armitage.
His argument from history was that no one group embodied modern Baptist principles
so thoroughly as to be recognizable in the same vein as modern Baptists. However, he
acknowledged that various individuals and groups held certain principles consistent with
modern Baptists, but not in any totality, or in some organic line all the way from the apostolic
period forward. See Thomas Armitage, *A History of the Baptists: Traced by Their Vital
Principles and Practices from the Time of Our Lord and Saviour Jesus Christ to the Year 1886*
(New York: Bryan, Taylor and Co., 1887).

220   Estep, *The Anabaptist Story*, 4. Estep notes various titles given to the Anabaptists
such as Luther's "Schwarmer"; Smith's "Bolsheviki", and Lindboom's "stepchildren of the
Reformation." He then points his readers to Leonard Verduin's work *The Reformers and
Their Stepchildren* as "an incisive theological study of sixteenth century Anabaptism utilizing
the terms of reproach hurled against the Anabaptists as chapter headings" (4). However, this
approbation of Verduin is clearly inconsistent with his own declaration that Anabaptism "must
first be considered as a Reformation phenomena." Leonard Verduin's major thesis in his work
is that of demonstrating the existence of a pre-Reformation vocabulary of invectives used
against dissenters to the State church's policy of infant baptism prior to the Anabaptists of the
sixteenth century.

221   Backus, *A Discourse, Concerning the Materials, the Manner of Building, and Power
of Organizing the Church of Christ*, 32.

doctrine of Landmarkism. As a means of debunking this chain-link
theory, author James McGoldrick used the aforementioned Peter
de Bruys (Bruis) and Henry of Toulouse as illegitimate examples of
Baptist dissent, so claimed by certain Baptists. However, despite the
fact that both came to us through the testimonies of hostile witnesses
and lack credibility as official *Baptists* in their time,[222] Backus' use of
these twelfth-century individuals was not without precedent.[223] He
simply pointed to these men to demonstrate that dissenters rejected
infant baptism prior to the Radical Reformation, not as a means of
justifying Baptist successionism.[224] For Backus, these men served as
historical precedents of what he had experienced in Massachusetts,

---

[222]   The primary record of Peter de Bruys comes through a letter written by
Peter the Venerable who became the abbot of Cluny in 1152, and whose testimony is
"from the perspective of an opponent...of course, heavily prejudiced." In this same
letter McGoldrick affirmed that de Bruys rejected infant baptism, formal worship
sanctuaries, transubstantiation, and prayers for the dead, concluding that "if the
contentions of Peter the Venerable are, however, correct, then the beliefs of Peter de
Bruys do correspond in some measure with those of modern Baptists. But if this is so,
why would the author admit these examples while attempting to debunk a nineteenth
century movement? Similarly, McGoldrick admits that the primary documents we
have concerning Henry of Toulouse are also from hostile sources. One of those
witnesses, Bernard of Clairvaux, accused Henry of adultery, prostitution, financial
deception, and gambling, all of which McGoldrick appears to deny. McGoldrick
chooses not to elaborate on how he rejects Bernard's moral charges on the one hand
but accepts his theological charges on the other. See James Edward McGoldrick,
Baptist Successionism: A Crucial Question in Baptist History, Atla Monograph Series,
no. 32 (Metuchen, N.J., & London: The Scarecrow Press, Inc., 1994), 48-51.
[223]   Crosby was the earliest English Baptist historian. He modeled the view holding
a "continuity of Baptist teachings from New Testament times to the present through earlier
dissenting groups," not any form of visible or chain-link succession akin to the Landmark
position. For a thorough representation of the various positions of Baptist history and their
leading apologists, see McBeth, *The Baptist Heritage*, 48-63.
[224]   This is the name often used to describe the Anabaptist movement in Europe during
the time of the first reformation. The name is descriptive of both the disposition of the
movement, as well as the core values which created their religious and spiritual ethos. For
the best sources of this branch of reformation study see Estep, *The Anabaptist Story*, Guy F.
Hershberger, ed., *A Recovery of the Anabaptist Vision* (Scottsdale, Pennsylvania: Herald Press,
Mennonite Publishing House, 1957), Littell, *The Anabaptist View of the Church*, R.W. Scribner,
The German Reformation (London: Macmillan Press Ltd, 1986), Williams, *The Radical
Reformation*.

and in this sense, he was willing to be identified with pre-Reformation dissenters insofar as it justified his baptismal practice. He rejected such associations when it came to the Munster episode. Littell added,

> *the more historically minded groups elaborated their primitivist historiography in which the small brotherhood groups were the bridge of evangelical faith between the "Fall" and the "Restitution." Among the Anabaptists this was the familiar interpretation: during the middle period the True Church was in dispersion, among those called "heretics".*[225]

The Anabaptist movement did, during the infancy of the Reformation, what Backus did in Colonial New England. They simply determined to drive their principles to their logical conclusions as they believed others had attempted before them. It deserves to be noted that the reformers were not ignorant of their own followers desiring Biblically-based assemblies with the rise of the *ecclesiola in ecclesia* concept.[226] This practice, beginning with Luther's movement, was an effort within the impure churches to establish godly fellowships within the larger inclusive church body without promoting schism or the establishment of another church. This shows that the pure-church ideal was within the grasp of the reformers as clearly as a return to *sola scriptura* had been. In fact, the Anabaptists believed that the latter demanded the former. Luther, Calvin, and Zwingli simply decided that the loss of State-sanction was too dear of a price to pay for a

---

225   Littell, *The Anabaptist View of the Church*, 76.
226   This concept, which originated with Luther's movement, involved believers who wished to separate themselves from the inclusive church to establish godly fellowships among themselves for the purpose of Bible study, prayer, and spiritual fellowship. Although Luther never opposed such practices among his German hearers, he never pursued the idea to its logical conclusion already reached by German Anabaptists. See D.M. Lloyd-Jones, *The Puritans: Their Origins and Successors* (Edinburgh: The Banner of Truth Trust, 1987), 87.

biblical church. Consequently, they turned their backs on true church reformation.

A century later Philip Spener, an orthodox Lutheran, would promote piety and reform within the established church, while at the same time opposing any form of schism (come-outism). Eighteenth-century English reformers George Whitefield, John Wesley, and Howell Harris would promote pietism and godly reform within the Church of England in a similar fashion. As noted later, Whitefield's colonial ministry should not be understood as motivated solely on pietist and reformist principles. The Grand Itinerant's repudiation of unconverted ministers in England and New England, coupled with the admonition of new converts to hear enlightened preachers, does not agree with his self-claim of ecclesiastical neutrality. The Anabaptist movement, on the other hand, operated in the opposite fashion upon a "separated life of holiness."[227] Unfortunately, Luther was double-minded. He admired the practice of church-wide discipline within the Anabaptist churches, but he viciously opposed them as radicals on account of their rejection of the magisterial church.[228]

This "third Church" type is founded upon at least four underlying principles. These would include: *voluntarism, primitivism, exclusivism, and discipline.*[229] Each of these can be identified in principle within the SC and its seven articles. Voluntarism marks all of the seven articles, but notice in the final statement concerning the author's conclusions regarding false brethren: "These are the articles of certain brethren who had heretofore been in error and who had failed to agree in the true understanding...."[230] Clearly, these errant brethren were not failing to operate under the inflexible coercion of a

227   Hershberger, ed., *A Recovery of the Anabaptist Vision*, 148.
228   Avis, *The Church in the Theology of the Reformers*, 21.
229   Ibid, 55-57.
230   Taken from the Schleithheim Confession in Lumpkin, *Baptist Confessions of Faith*, 30.

magisterial church but rather under mutual failure "to agree in the true understanding..." in the context of a local church.[231] Voluntary local-church agreement was necessary for identification of errant believers, not some state-sanctioned Magisterial body. The local-assembly was the only church the Schleithem brethren knew and recognized. Clearly these believers who identified themselves under the SC had rejected the concept of magisterial authority (Corpus Christianum). This concept, which incorporated all Christians under a universal designation, was at the root of what they considered the work of Anti-Christ. They favored the term "body of Christ" (Corpus Christi), a stridently more localized term stressing a gathered body. As a model of the apostolic church, the Swiss Brethren characterized voluntarism by demanding that "the church must be made up of only the regenerate, who voluntarily associate themselves together to live pure lives in keeping with the Scriptures."[232] This reduction and localization of the church concept did not begin with those practicing voluntarism in the Radical Reformation alone, but like other Reformation ideas, was one simply being pursued to its logical end. It was a dissenter idea which had been hated and persecuted since Constantine. Believing it to be a contemporary development, McLoughlin said:

> ...the Baptist movement in New England was not a throwback
> to Munsterism, but instead as the beginning of a new
> concept of individualistic, voluntaristic religion. What they
> denounced as "anti-New England in New England" was
> the inarticulate outreach of seventeenth century pietism
> in the New World environment—a groping toward a new

---

231   Ibid.
232   William R. Estep, Jr., "A Baptist Reappraisal of Sixteenth Century Anabaptists," *The Review and Expositor* 55, no. 1 (1958): 49.

concept of Christian liberty impossible in Europe.[233]

McLoughlin intimates here that New England's Baptist-led pietistic voluntarism originated not with the Baptists but with the individualistic new-birth preaching of the revivalists, particularly Whitefield. However, McLoughlin misses the fact that this individualized ecclesiology was not intrinsic to the Great Awakening phenomena of the new birth, nor should have the Puritans misjudged it as a throwback to Munsterism. Its historical exemplar has to be traced back to the dissent community both before and beyond the Reformation. Earlier Anabaptist conflicts with the reformers over the use of infant baptism forcing infants into the membership of the visible church without conscious regeneration were not new phenomena by any fair assessment of the historical records.[234]

Avis' second principle, recognizable in Anabaptist ecclesiology, was *primitivism.* Concerning their rejection of infant baptism, which they referred to as "the highest and chief abominations of the pope," Sattler, in the S.C considered their position "to have the foundation and testimony of the apostles."[235] Their chief intention was not in parroting a model which was *more* like the New Testament but in *locating the model within* the New Testament and recasting it in their own ecclesiastical milieu. This effort to identify and restore the church to the apostolic model then became the *raison d'etre* of the Anabaptist churches. Incredibly, after some intense debate, along with the Munster debacle, Luther considered this pursuit of radical ecclesiology to be unnecessary and dangerous to their present socio-

---

233   McLoughlin, *New England Dissent 1630-1833*, 1: 32.
234   Both the English and New England Puritans were versed well enough in the anti-pedobaptist literature to know that the new birth, believers' baptism, and voluntaristic ecclesiology possessed historical examples preceding the Munster debacle.
235   Lumpkin, *Baptist Confessions of Faith*, 25.

political situation.[236] Elert argued that Luther's desire for a restoration of the "old church" was "by no means understood to be only the primeval church," but rather "the entire Holy Christian church, which has endured harmoniously in the whole world for more than 1,500 years."[237] Anabaptists had no such monolithic perception concerning the history of the church. Their disagreements with Luther and other reformers were rooted in ancient and longstanding doctrinal battles. Klaassen ties Anabaptist radicalism to the cry for a Biblical church. He noted:

>...in its reform of the church it went consciously and deliberately to primitive models for guidance. Its cry was Back to the Sources: that is, back to the roots of Christianity in the New Testament. The assumption was that what had happened between 325 and 1525 was mostly in error.[238]

The people of the "third church" made no distinction between the reformers and the Western church when referring to the "fallen" church. Their wish was to both identify and restore (*restoration* rather than *reformation*) the "True Church". This pattern of the "True church," as opposed to the fallen church, was always "defined in terms of strict adherence to certain ordinances defined in the New Testament"[239] recognizing that "What Christ said, could be done."[240]

---

236   For instance, Luther argued in 1522 for the right of the churches to elect or dismiss their own pastors. But when he questioned the pastoral call of Karlstadt in Orlamunde, whose call was not only confirmed by the laity but by the town council, Luther argued further that it should have been sanctioned by the greater magistrate which was a complete reversal of his former position. See Scribner, *The German Reformation*, 50.

237   Werner Elert, *The Structure of Lutheranism*, trans. Walter A. Hansen, 2 vols. (St. Louis: Concordia Publishing House, 1962), 286.

238   Klaassen, *Anabaptism: Neither Catholic nor Protestant*, (Waterloo, Ontario: Conrad Press, 1973), 9.

239   Littell, *The Anabaptist View of the Church*, 82.

240   Ibid.

But not only could it be done, it had already been done prior to the official reformation of the sixteenth century. This attitude is evident in Backus' New England approach as he justified his view of baptism from pre-reformation sources.

Avis' third underlying principle of the Anabaptists was *Exclusivism*. The "third church" proponents neither identified themselves nor their churches as parts of an inter-church movement. They refused to be party to the errors of the State-Church. Originally, numbers of the Anabaptists strongly supported the need for a thoroughgoing reformation but became increasingly intolerant waiting for the magistrates to respond to the wishes of mainline reformation leaders.[241] Sattler identifies their exclusive self-image in his opening greeting in the S.C. who says,

to all those who love God, who are the children of light, and who are
scattered everywhere as it has been ordained of God our Father,
where they are with one mind assembled in one God and Father
of us all: Grace and peace of heart be with you all, Amen.[242]

Clearly, they viewed themselves as an identifiable group through mutually exclusive claims of loving God, existing in scattered assemblies (presumably on account of persecution from the territorial church), and being in one accord with their God and Father as opposed to their numerous enemies who basked in doctrinal error. Sattler later defined "that everything," not being in one accord with God and Christ,

cannot be other than an abomination which we shun and flee from.
By this is meant all popish and anti-popish works and church

---

241   Klaassen, *Anabaptism: Neither Catholic nor Protestant*, 4.
242   Broadus, *Baptist Confessions, Covenants, and Catechisms*, 21.

services, meetings and church attendance, drinking houses, civic

affairs..., which are highly regarded by the world and yet are

carried on with all the unrighteousness which is in the world.[243]

Other diverse groups, chafing over notable compromise by reformation deans, demanded the purging of all error which they perceived had satiated the Western Church. This eradication, designed to restore the church to its former apostolic purity, was primarily aimed at the rejection of the pope, sacramental theology, and infant baptism. This purging finds an early example in Zwingli whose early opposition to pedobaptism is well-known, but when the Reformer came to fully comprehend the implications of such reform upon the future of the State church, he rejected his short-lived Biblicism.[244] Along with Luther and Calvin, he consequently became satisfied with the attempt to restore the "purity and integrity of the sacraments," while "distinguishing between the invisible Church of the elect, known only to God, and the visible Church which will always be imperfect."[245] Thereby he stopped short of a full-blown doctrinal reformation on the scale which the Anabaptists desired. Consequently, key reformers abandoned any previous consideration of overthrowing Rome's most deeply entrenched errors. Repudiating such volatile issues as infant baptism consequently resulted in "a bitter and irreducible struggle between two mutually exclusive concepts of the church."[246] Reformation leaders consistently attributed such struggles by the Anabaptists as being an acute form of spiritual pride. Avis said, "More accurately, it was the manifestation of a powerful eschatological vision

---

243   Ibid, 25.
244   Littell points out that Zwingli and Vadian had first rejected infant baptism, but later abandoned their new found conviction because they saw it was totally incompatible with the maintenance of the state church. See Littell, *The Anabaptist View of the Church*, 14.
245   Avis, *The Church in the Theology of the Reformers*, 54.
246   Littell, *The Anabaptist View of the Church*, 14.

and sense of being the persecuted remnant."[247] The controversy of infant baptism assumed infinite importance in the struggle because it represented the critical line of division between the old State system and the "True Church" aspirations of the Anabaptists. The old State system, or the "Church Territorial" was completely rejected by the dissent community. Estep asserted:

The Anabaptists would have no part in such a monstrosity, which was made up of the regenerate and unregenerate alike. This led to the rejection of infant baptism on two counts: First, because it was un-scriptural; and second, because it was the convenient tool of the state church in coercing conformity and membership within its body.[248]

Avis' fourth and final principle of the radical's ecclesiology is *Discipline*. For them, the ban or exclusion of the ungodly from their churches was understood as a compulsory action of voluntary membership not an exclusionary discipline meted out by the State. In a very real sense, the radicals believed that the church could not stand unless its membership would be willing to enforce the breaking of fellowship with the ungodly. The Anabaptist position based its authority on Matt 18 where Jesus gives the church instruction on forgiving and retaining sin, coupled with offended individuals "telling it to the church." Anabaptist leader Dirk Philips said separation was to be preferred over inadvertent forgiveness based on three reasons:

First, that the church may not become a partaker of the sin of outsiders, and that a little leaven may not leaven the whole lump (2 Jn. 1:11; 2 Cor. 5:5; Gal. 5:9); second, that the person who has sinned may be ashamed and his flesh be thus punished, and his spirit saved

---

247   Avis, *The Church in the Theology of the Reformers*, 58.
248   Estep, "A Baptist Reappraisal of Sixteenth Century Anabaptists," 49.

in the day of the Lord Jesus: third, that the church of God be not
blasphemed on account of the evils in it, and be not guilty on their
account before the Lord (Ezek. 36:30 [?]; Rom. 2:24; Josh. 7:20).[249]

The connection between the spiritual prospering of the church
with the ban and excommunication demonstrates that Anabaptists
understood God's certain blessing was the experiential reality of
the ban's practice among Anabaptist churches. Estep asserted that
quite often the churches were hasty in judgment, suggesting that this
oftentimes contributed to the "fragmentation of their fellowship and
left them open for rapid extermination by their enemies."[250] However,
Estep's view is at odds with Anabaptist leader Melchior Hoffman.
He had concluded concerning the practice of the ban, "O how well
it went when such an ordinance was maintained in the true fear of
God," suggesting that contrary to Estep, just the opposite was true.[251]
Furthermore, it may be noted that Hoffman describes the ban as "an
ordinance" demonstrating the importance attached to discipline in
maintaining church purity. Avis observed, "The Anabaptists had made
discipline the *sine que non* of the church: it loomed over every aspect
of the Christian life."[252] While both may be true to some extent, the
Anabaptists themselves acquiesced in the fact that the practice pleased
the godly and fulfilled the demands of the New Testament, regardless
of the internal tensions it sustained in the local assembly.

To this may be added a fifth characteristic of the radical church:
the Anabaptists' intense concept of evangelistic responsibility. For the
Anabaptists, within the milieu of the reformation, Williams observed,
"This new kind of Christian was not a reformer but a converter, not a

---

249   Walter Klaassen, ed., *Anabaptism in Outline* (Kitchener, Ontario: Herald Press, 1981), 225-226.
250   Estep, "A Baptist Reappraisal of Sixteenth Century Anabaptists," 57.
251   Klaassen, ed., *Anabaptism in Outline*, 217.
252   Avis, *The Church in the Theology of the Reformers*, 61.

parishioner but, reviving the original meaning of the New Testament word, a sojourner (*paroikos*) in this world whose true citizenship was in heaven...."[253] Williams adds that these believers simply believed

in the essential unity of all mankind, prospectively redeemed by Christ at Calvary. The Radicals had a gripping conviction as to individual responsibility to witness to Christ in the world and a fresh awareness of covenantal responsibilities accompanying the radical Christianization of ecclesiastically hitherto neglected areas of human relationship....[254]

This conviction to evangelize must be recognized as key to the Great Awakening impetus and the subsequent pursuit by the Separates and Baptists to make this passion the "one thing" from which they could not in good conscience swerve.[255] To the extent, therefore, that the Anabaptists attempted to fulfill what they interpreted in Scripture as their evangelistic mandate, the Separate-Baptists in New England would model New Testament evangelism in the construct of continuous revivalism. Interestingly, in revival practice, the SBBM would eventually identify more with the Anabaptists' view of the unity of all mankind on the basis of their being "prospectively redeemed" rather than arbitrarily elected to salvation. The similarity of these two movements may be understood in their respective dissimilarity to both the Magisterial Protestantism and the Congregational system in the Massachusetts Commonwealth, neither of which embodied a

---

253   Williams, *The Radical Reformation*, 845.

254   Ibid, 863.

255   This characterization by Goen was used in both a positive manner and negative manner. On one side he commends the Separate-Baptists for their commitment to evangelism through the arm of the local church, on the other he condemns their exclusive local-church commitment for neglecting what he termed as the "larger social concerns" of the "total Christian tradition." See Goen, *Revivalism and Separatism in New England, 1740-1800: Strict Congregationalist and Separate-Baptists in the Great Awakening*, 294.

vital missionary principle. The Magisterial Reformers believed that "peripatetic evangelism had been completed in the early centuries; now each Christian has his own parish and each bishop his diocese and no one ought to claim a roving commission"[256] such as the Anabaptists claimed. From a similarly entrenched non-missionary environment, both William Carey and Andrew Fuller bear significant responsibility for modifying extreme Calvinism with a vigorous missionary impulse as well as a new rhetoric which encouraged the practice of calling sinners to respond to gospel preaching. Like the radical Anabaptists, the SBBM distinguished itself from the Magisterial Reformation, namely Massachusetts's Congregationalism, primarily on the basis of believers' baptism and a voluntarist model of the church. In this manner, the Separate-Baptists of New England bore a resemblance and doctrinal lineage to earlier Anabaptist foci and the missionary-minded English Baptists. However, the American Baptists—because of the voluntarist/moral environment in which they operated, as opposed to the religio/political environment of greater Europe—were enabled to extend visible church reformation beyond the Puritan ideal.

THE MAGISTERIAL PERCEPTIONS OF THE CHURCH

Colonial Puritans utilized both the basic Reformed conceptions of the two-church model and a similar application of ideas relating to the fear of schism and the connection of infant baptism to salvation. However, the source of these ideas came hundreds of years earlier.

1. AUGUSTINE

Augustine's theological contributions to Christian thought were both immense and providentially well-timed, basically because they

---

256   Avis, *The Church in the Theology of the Reformers*, 177.

appeared as Rome was in its final years of moral and physical decline. By Augustine's day, the empire and the church had been united under Constantine, before which time the church was perceived by some to be a struggling lower-class sect. By the time of Augustine and the fall of the empire in 410, Christianity became the official religion, with the church becoming the hope for any continued civilization.[257] The Roman Empire would become, in connection with the church, the *ecclesiastical* continuation of the fallen civil state. The Bishop of Hippo desired to preserve the best of the Greco-Roman philosophers and their cultural influence by blending them with contemporary Christian thought in the use of symbol.[258] Consequently, it is significant that it was at the point of Rome's fall that the connection began to be made by Augustine between the church and the kingdom.[259] This made it possible for the future church to be defined by national and geographic perimeters—an *all inclusive*, rather than *sectarian/exclusive*, organization—such as that for which the Donatists argued. This evolving definition would have far-reaching implications for both the church and national-church life forms under reformation ecclesiology.

Augustine's *The City of God*, as the first detailed Christian explanation of the kingdom and church, postulated the existence of two entirely unique ecclesiastical bodies. One was pure, invisible, and consisted of every person living, dead, or yet to be born who had been elected to salvation by God's pre-determination. The other was an earthly church; it was institutional in nature, visible, and consisted of both true Christians and hypocrites. In Augustine's nomenclature "City,"—normally equated with the kingdom—in that final day, would

---

257   Ibid., 64.
258   Norman Perrin, *Jesus and the Language of the Kingdom* (London: SCM Press LTD, 1976), 60. Perrin's extended argument concerning the church and the kingdom is not the subject of any debate here, but only his basic understanding of Platonic thought and Augustine's use thereof in this chapter entitled, "The Use of Kingdom of God by Augustine."
259   Ibid., 64.

be the church in a perfected form. It is not that ideal church now but will be in the final consummation. This merging of terms like church and kingdom did not just occur with Augustine because of sociological and political reasons. Church and Kingdom were also conveniently united on a linguistic basis through the allegorical hermeneutic in Alexandria.[260] The Western school of interpretation was well advanced in the third century under Origen's extreme use of allegory, and Origen's protégé Augustine used allegory as freely as his mentor. In Augustine's comprehension of kingdom reality, there are in effect two stages, one present and one eschatological, but both representing various stages of the church. He explains:

> *We must understand in one sense the kingdom of heaven in which*
> *exist together both he who breaks what he teaches and he who*
> *does it.... Consequently where both classes exist, it is the Church*
> *as it now is, but where only the one shall exist, it is the Church*
> *as it is destined to be when no wicked person shall be in her.*[261]

The church, or the present kingdom—according to this teaching—has both good (those who do the teaching) and evil (those who break the teaching) in it. Augustine identified this as the Church Militant,[262] containing both true and false elements. Because the future kingdom will be represented only by those who have obeyed the teaching he called them the Church Triumphant.[263] Augustine confessed his own affection for Greek philosophy saying, "It is evident

---

260   Shedd observed that the Alexandrian school was "where the Platonic spirit was more intense and extreme than elsewhere...." For the influence of Plato in the Apologetic age, see William G.T. Shedd, *A History of Christian Doctrine*, 2 vols. (New York: Charles Scribner and Sons, 1902; reprint, Solid Ground Classic Reprints, 2006), 1: 67.

261   Saint Augustine, *The City of God*, trans. Marcus Dods, The Modern Library (New York: Random House Inc, 1950), 725.

262   Ibid., 726.

263   Ibid.

that none come nearer to us than the Platonists."[264] Presumably, he meant that theologically, Plato's dualistic view of reality best suited his concept of the church of the New Testament. As a result, Augustine's perception of the visible church was that it was hopelessly impure. He observed,

> *...as long she is a stranger in the world, the city of God has in her communion, and bound to her by the sacraments, some who shall not eternally dwell in the lot of the saints.... These men you may today see thronging the churches with us, tomorrow crowding the theatres with the godless.*[265]

This condition, described by Augustine, only became more profound throughout the medieval period. The Western Church made the safeguarding of the sacraments the singular means of grace to the universal and visible church under the Papacy. Papal Bulls concerning heresy, which came to be considered as any heterodox thinking outside of official church teaching, became the means of creating uniformity, and consequently, deeply ingrained corruption. For Augustine, this perfect, mystical church was understood within Platonism as a perfect church in the eternal state, thus preceding the visible church in both time and thereby, essential importance. In short, the earthly church had no existence outside of its heavenly body. Augustine, in defining this body in Platonic terms believed that

> *The city of the saints is up above, although here below it begets citizens, in whom it sojourns till the time of its reign arrives, when it shall gather together all in the day of the resurrection; and then*

---

264   Ibid., 248.
265   Ibid., 38.

shall the promised kingdom be given to them, in which they shall
reign with their Prince, the King of the ages, time without end.[266]

This differentiation between the heavenly and earthly churches
allowed for both "wheat and tares" in the all-inclusive institutional
church, something which the contemporary Donatists (some would
consider them ancient Anabaptists) could not sanction in their visible,
voluntarist churches. For them, churches comprised of only the
regenerate were not called to capitulate to sustaining a mixed body of
both believers and unbelievers.

Grenz suggested that the inclusive nature of the Constantinian
model was Augustine's method for being able to "exonerate God
and the true Christians from any blame for the fall of the Roman
Empire."[267] Blame, he conjectured, could then be laid solely at the door
of the unregenerate and scandalous members of the visible church,
thereby excusing the invisible counterpart without and the elect within.
Backus affirmed his belief in the universal Church of Augustine as
much as he did in the fact that only the elect belonged to it, but his
Baptist progeny came to accept it under different terms.[268]

---

266   Ibid., 479.
267   Grenz, *Isaac Backus - Puritan and Baptist: His Place in History, His Thought, and Their Implications for Modern Baptist Theology*, 265.
268   Jesse B. Thomas of Newton Theological Seminary illustrated Universal church disuse to a somewhat coming of age of Baptists in the aftermath of Backus and their former dependence upon Reformed-based confessions of faith. He argued that the English Baptists and the early American Baptists used the terminology openly in an effort to maintain religious peace with their Standing Church neighbors, thereby adopting the language of the Westminster Confession in the Baptist Confession of 1689 wherever possible. Thomas made the point that "A hint of disposition to distrust at this point may possibly appear in the circumstance that the later New Hampshire Confession, probably more widely adopted than any other by the Baptist churches of America, excludes all reference whatever to a "Universal church," visible or invisible." See Thomas, *The Church and the Kingdom*, 164.

2. LUTHER

Luther's explanations [269] or treatises established the groundwork for the essential reformation, but his and others' legitimacy as Reformers existed primarily in their ability to defend their official church position from hostile Roman polemicists who asked, "Where was your Church before Luther?"[270] Their answer was simply that they were restoring the original face of the historic church as the one holy, catholic, and apostolic body. The crux of the Reformers' answer lay in developing the doctrine of the true marks of the church (*notae ecclesiae*) by which the true visible church could be identified. Luther's singular contribution focused on the restoration of the gospel. Even at the expense of the unity of the Western church, Werner Elert observed that "For a time it could seem that the reformation in Luther's sense meant the destruction or abolition of the church."[271] Elert justified his summation of Luther on this point for three reasons: Luther's smashing of ecclesiastical authorities, the burning of the book of canon law along with the Papal Bull condemning him, and finally, his proclamation of the priesthood of all believers.[272] His final point is what he essentially uses to tie Luther's restoration of the gospel to his conception of the visible church.[273]

---

269   These treatises were initially Luther's detailed expositions of the theses he nailed to the door at Wittenburg. Luther called these explanations "solutions." They were written with moderation, but at the same time, "he manifested an immovable conviction, and courageously defended every proposition that truth obliged him to maintain." For an excellent, albeit older description of Luther before the Legate between May and December, 1518, see Merle J.H. D' Aubigne, *Scenes from the Life of Martin Luther* (Philadelphia: The Memorial Publishing Company, 1883), 99-127.

270   Avis, *The Church in the Theology of the Reformers*, 2.

271   Werner Elert , *The Structure of Lutheranism*, trans. Walter A. Hansen, 2 vols. (St. Louis: Concordia Publishing House, 1962), 1: 255.

272   Ibid., 1:255-256.

273   Luther did not perceive himself as a founder of a new sect or church, dispelling the idea that his followers considered themselves Lutherans, or Protestants. They wanted to simply be identified as "evangelical Christians." All other titles were normally used in a pejorative manner by their enemies. For a contemporary analysis of the mythology which grew up around the initial movements of reformation see Scribner, *The German Reformation*, 1-5.

Beyond this, Luther's ecclesiastical conceptions were somewhat unique among later reformers in that he excluded any disciplinary function within the visible church as being critically necessary to its development and maintenance. Avis identified in Luther's literary corpus that the church's being and comprehensive development had to be singularly focused within the gospel:

> *Since the Church owes its birth to the word, is nourished, aided and strengthened by it, it is obvious that it cannot be without the word. If it is without the word it ceases to be a Church.... The church is nothing without the word and everything in it exists by virtue of the word alone.*[274]

This was to become Luther's essential departure from Roman Catholicism. Other implications flowed from this tenet but, despite the draconian redefining of its visible make-up, the reformers never entirely abandoned all validity of the Western church prior to the Council of Trent in 1525.[275] It was apostate in their view, but they still felt that it retained semblances of truth sufficient enough to not entirely abandon it to the devil. Logically, however, without this essential and unadulterated gospel, there could be no Christ, and therefore no gospel. In identifying Luther's church, Avis said:

> *The primary and creative impulse of Reformation ecclesiology as we find it in Luther is evangelical and Christological. That is to say that the nature and essence of the Church is understood by Luther solely by reference to the Christian gospel and the reality of the person and work of Jesus Christ.*[276]

---

274   Avis, *The Church in the Theology of the Reformers*, 20.
275   Ibid., 76.
276   Ibid, 2-3.

The gospel is the originating force behind both the invisible church and the individual congregation, but all the spiritual rights and privileges of the individual believer are received through the believer's connection with the universal church. Luther's critics were quick to see this conception as the dissolution of the Roman church, or at least its diminishment to simply a hierarchical structure without sufficiently empowering its priesthood.[277] This, including Luther's priesthood of the believer, "abolishes on principle every organizational element without which, the Church cannot exist as a unit above the individual."[278]

Luther's redefinition invited protests from the enemies of the reformation which suggested that he, as well as the other reformers, in the absence of a visible definition, were simply devising a church in the same fashion that Plato devised his idealistic State:

Meaning not the utopian state for which Plato legislated in
The Laws and had hoped to have seen established in Sicily
(as recounted in his seventh and eighth letters), but an
ideal Church enjoying a disembodied and illusory existence
in the realm of pure abstractions, uncontaminated by the
empirical world of space and time, place and history.[279]

This brought further accusations that Luther's church was not only invisible, but intangible, thus having no actual existence on

---

277   For Luther, the priesthood of the believer was erected upon the three pillars of the word, baptism, and the divine commission given to the entire body of Christian believers. This priesthood included the power to administer the sacraments, baptize babies (for instance, midwives), the absolution of the penitent as a ministry of the word which belongs to all believers. In this way, Luther disarmed the Roman priesthood, and thereby was perceived as directly challenging his former ecclesiastical authority.

278   Elert, *The Structure of Lutheranism*, page number is missing.

279   Avis, *The Church in the Theology of the Reformers*, 4.

earth.[280] This was not the case with Luther, but when his rationale was pressed to its logical conclusion, his view of the visible church was restored only where the gospel and the sacrament were restored. For Luther, this did not mean that his church could not gather or have local perimeters but that the nature of the church could not be described in strictly empirical terms.

Luther thought,

> *the church was created by the living presence of Christ through his word the gospel.... The gospel must shine out at all costs and at whatever sacrifice.... One thing is needful; all else is secondary. To save the gospel, all outward forms of order and structure are expendable.*[281]

The church, with every claimed authority and visible trapping, had to be boiled down to its inviolate essence and recast into a purely biblical form. The second element of change which Luther injected was that of objective authority. With no prelate, pontiff, or visible head to which the church was subjected on earth, the church could then be objectively empowered to preach the gospel and reveal the true Christ. Luther's church conception at this point again plunged deeply below the visible surface to become an invisible reality centered in the mysterious reality of Jesus Christ and His gospel:

> *Because of Luther's commitment to restoring the pure gospel, the church could then be seen clearly in its two aspects as an analogy*

---

280   Millard J. Erickson, *Christian Theology* (Grand Rapids: Baker Book House, 1983), 1033. This Baptist theologian makes mention of this point in his discussion of the church within contemporary theology. Platonic dualism is seldom discussed today as relevant to local-Universal church tensions, but as Erickson suggested, it is argued by some as being an unjustified addition to Christian thought that originated outside of Scripture. However, he believes it to be biblically defensible.

281   Avis, *The Church in the Theology of the Reformers*, 3.

of the incarnation. Like Christ's earthly manifestation, the earthly church was tangible, identifiable, and of course visible. Its universal aspect could be recognized by the visible in the notae ecclesiae which served to connect both aspects of the one True Church.[282]

Because the *notae* were centered solely on the gospel and the sacraments of communion/baptism, Luther considered unnecessary any emphasis on congregational discipline within the visible church. Rather, he maintained that this would promote schism. The civil kingdom, in Luther's ideal, possessed jurisdiction over the external righteousness of the visible church's membership without interfering with purely spiritual matters of the soul. On the other hand, the spiritual authority of the church was only persuasive concerning only the matters of the soul. The church's keys in Luther's eyes were not temporal but spiritual, providing authority to preach the gospel. Both the temporal and spiritual realms relied on one another for the church's ultimate reformation. In fact, there could be no such thing as Christendom until the two acted together as one.[283] Similarly, Congregationalists of New England believed in the magisterial principle, but they thought they had found a perfect balancing point between the invisible and visible churches which set them apart from the first reformation. By the fourth decade after the New England experiment had begun, the fulcrum was already beginning to crumble.

3. CALVIN

---

282   Ibid, 4.
283   Elert, *The Structure of Lutheranism*, 1: 378. This is demonstrated by the Diet of Speyer in 1526, which reiterated the medieval principle of *cuius regio eius religio*, which stated that citizens should follow the religion of their ruler. See Avis, *The Church in the Theology of the Reformers*, 144.

Calvin's view, although consistent with Augustine, made the church's local manifestation more consistent with a national church, which was generally agreeable with most sixteenth century reformers. Calvin, like Luther and other reformation leaders, struggled with what should constitute the outward form of the visible church along with the biblical mandates for its effective administration. Like Luther, Calvin taught that as distinguished from the Church of Rome, God's Word had to be the singular foundation of the church:

Therefore, although they put forward Temple, priesthood, and the rest of the outward shows, this empty glitter which blinds the eyes of the simple ought not to move us a whit to grant that the church exists where God's Word is not found. For this is the abiding mark with which our Lord has sealed his own....[284]

His mind was satisfied as long as the essential criteria of the preaching of the Word and the administration of the sacraments were present while essentially believing the true (invisible) aspect of the church could exist without the aid of any visible form.[285] Theoretically,

The church is called "catholic" or "universal" because there could not be two or three churches unless Christ be torn asunder [cf. I Cor. 1:13]—which cannot happen! But all the elect are so united in Christ [Eph 4:16] that as they are dependent on one Head, they also grow together into one body....[286]

---

284   John T. McNeill, ed., *Calvin: Institutes of the Christian Religion*, 2 vols. Library of Christian Classics (Philadelphia: Westminster Press, 1967), 2: 1046.
285   Ibid, 2: 1015.
286   Ibid, 2: 1014.

The Augustinian concept of election asserted that the invisible body not only consisted of true Christians but also guaranteed absolute unity within the one body, about which no single congregation could boast. As to man's responsibility to the visible church, Calvin said:

Just as we must believe, therefore, that the former church, invisible to us, is visible to the eyes of God alone, so we are commanded to revere and keep communion with the latter, which is called "church" in respect to men...accordingly the Lord by certain marks and tokens has pointed out what we should know about the church.[287]

The visible church was to be understood as one of many assemblies:

Disposed in towns and villages according to human need, so that each rightly has the name and authority of the church... even though they may be strangers to the church, still in a sense belong to it until they have been rejected by public judgment.[288]

Calvin saw no problem with the confluence of regenerate and unregenerate elements in the local church because the unregenerate would ultimately be "rejected" by public condemnation. How could such a significant number of members of the visible church be non-elect? Calvin balanced the problem on Augustine's two-church model: one universal and composed of only the elect, the other visible, and composed of all Christians, national or otherwise, who *claimed* to be Christians, but who were not necessarily elect. The key feature distinguishing the mystical church was its possession of the Word and the sacraments because "it is certain that such things are not without

---

287   Ibid, 2: 1022.
288   Ibid, 2: 1023.

fruit."[289] Therefore, the pure aspect constituting the true elect was eternally certain to bear fruit, even though it was temporarily mixed with a fruitless component. On such a basis he justified the mixed church ideas by using the kingdom parables of the dragnet of fishes (Matt 13:47-58), the wheat and tares (Matt 13:24-30), and the wheat and the chaff (Matt 13:12);[290] and in so doing he condemned all schism and church separations by those wishing to purify the earthly church.[291] This temporary convergence would easily accommodate a church concept with broad connotations because for Calvin a national church by necessity had to be all inclusive.[292]

Calvin also reasserted pedobaptism as traditional church practice. Milner demonstrated that Calvin's meaning of the practice is clear and consistent with itself, but it fails completely in establishing a Scriptural basis for the practice.[293] Milner said Calvin believed children "are born members of the church not because they were born of regenerated parents, but on account of the nature of the covenant itself."[294] Simply put, Calvin believed that it is the covenant's hereditary nature which makes room for the baptism of infants, and, by right of adoption, they enter into communion with Christ, thereby growing into the very reality that baptism represents. Children are incorporated "into the church this way only because they are already

---

289   Ibid, 2: 1024.
290   Ibid, 2: 1027-28.
291   Ibid, 2: 1027. Calvin condemned all such separations by groups such as the Cathari, the Donatists, and the Anabaptists as those "who wish to appear advanced beyond other men." By making the Kingdom parables "church" parables, Calvin, like Augustine, condemned separation within local assemblies as evil and ungodly. This argument has been the basis for ecumenical posturing, and the creation of a monolithic, universal church ever since.
292   Miller, *Orthodoxy in Massachusetts 1630-1650*, 54.
293   Milner's work on Calvin's church doctrine is based on the unifying principle of Calvin's "absolute correlation of the Spirit and the Word" which he affirmed "provides us with the unifying ground for the polarities of Calvin's thought." See Benjamin Charles Milner, Jr., *Calvin's Doctrine of the Church*, ed. Heiko A. Oberman, 5 vols., vol. V, *Studies in the History of Christian Thought* (Leiden: E.J. Brill, 1970), 123-124.
294   Ibid. Milner comments here are taken from Calvin's commentary on 1 Cor. 7:14.

members of it."[295] Historically, the dissent community—all the way
back to the Donatist faction—believed this to be heresy. This is why
the Reformers often referred to the Anabaptists of their day as neo-
Donatists.[296] As with Luther, discipline never officially became a third
mark of the church with Calvin. This is not to say he was not exposed
to more conservative influences concerning its maintenance in the
church. Calvin spent significant time in Strasbourg with Martin Bucer.
Before leaving Geneva in 1538, Calvin had made a church discipline
proposal to the church. In fact Milner suggested: "Failure to get
acceptance of his proposals for Church discipline had been one of the
causes of Calvin's leaving the city of Geneva in 1538, and he insisted on
it as a condition of his return there from Strasbourg in 1541.[297]
Returning from Strasbourg in 1541, Calvin had been exposed to Bucer's
approach to ecclesiological discipline but remained unwilling to make
discipline a third mark of the earthly assembly as certainly as Bucer.[298]
In 1546, Bucer wrote and published a book entitled *The Need and
Failure of the Churches and How To Improve Them*. He focused
on discipline as a singular ecclesiastical responsibility rather than a
mutual concern with the civil powers.[299] Calvin accepted the need
for discipline, but it did not rise in his mind to the level of Word and
sacrament as a true mark of the visible church. For Calvin, discipline
was only to affect the church's *bene esse*, or well-being, not the *esse*
or essential being. To this end, civil ministers effected the well-being
of the reformation church by acting as the nursing fathers of the

---

295   Ibid.
296   See Verduin, 21-62.
297   Avis, *The Church in the Theology of the Reformers*, 30.
298   Martin Bucer departed from the other Reformers in the area of discipline. Although
Bucer believed the foundation of the church was determined solely on its Christological
foundation, its continued existence depended on the church exercising disciplinary control over
its members, and as such, discipline constituted the third mark of the visible church of Christ in
his mind.
299   Jones, *The Puritans: Their Origins and Successors*, 135.

church.[300] In Massachusetts just over a century later, church fathers would echo the same theocratic sentiment as being necessary for civil normalcy in 1630.

However, for most Puritans and even more Separatists, true reformation required a visible church with more than the Word of God and the administration of the sacraments. Local churches would require the ability and right of self-discipline and autonomy without which the infinite distance between the invisible and visible church would remain. As the visible church among New England Puritans developed a greater sense of organization, leadership, membership requirements, and covenantal accountability, the distance between the Augustine/Luther concept of the true church and its visible counterpart was lessened measurably.

Separate-Baptists and their progeny would ultimately drive this principle to its farthest possible perimeters by making the true marks of the local church definitive in arguing that the New England Way had stopped short of a genuine reformation in New England by continuing the age-long error of infant baptism with its introduction of birth-right membership.

4. THE NEW ENGLAND WAY

So what made the Puritans' ideas different from the views of the Reformers? Typically, the New England Way was a philosophy aimed at systematizing not just theology but also a methodology, giving theology a complete and exhaustive physical expression in the visible church. Furthermore, the New England Way was a significant evolution not only of Protestantism per se but of English Puritanism. New Englanders sought to establish church government which vested

---

300   Wilhelm Niesel, *The Theology of Calvin*, trans. Harold Knight (London: Lutterworth Press, 1956; reprint, Baker Book House, 1980), 233.

complete authority in the visible congregation under the sympathetic eye of the civil magistrate. John Robinson had concluded that Luther, Calvin, the Church of England, and the Puritans were all equally wrong in asserting that the true marks of the church were only the preached word and the ministry of the sacraments ministered to churches filled with unbelievers.[301]

Such sentiments by Robinson brought him to conclude that there was "further light" yet to be had regarding baptism and the visible church. Given enough time, Robinson may have ultimately modified his baptismal formula. Unfortunately, he died in Holland in 1625, having never arrived in New England.

In contrast to the national church ideas of old England Anglicanism, the New England fathers envisioned building a society of "visible saints" founded and perpetuated within a quasi church-state theocracy, where the state would insure the unfettered advancement of their churches. True to their pietistic nature, their vision for a community of saints was rooted in their sense of God's perfect, sovereign control. This sense of God's leadership, along with a "preoccupation with the Last Things, seems to have been a selective factor, drawing many *millennial-minded* Puritans to the New World."[302] These "kingdom on earth" expectations, buttressed by the spreading of the gospel in the New World, contributed to their ecclesiological desires of "perfecting and actualizing the pure church and gospel hitherto only partially perceived in England and Holland.

---

301   Miller quotes here from John Robinson who differentiated the Puritan-Separatist church view from all other views. Robinson, who died in 1625 while still in Holland, had left room for "further light" on issues related to the visible church. Had he lived, this may have likely caused him to rethink the entire baptism issue. This may further help to explain why Robinson was hopelessly delayed in Holland while numbers of his congregation waited for him to arrive in the Bay Colony. For historian Perry Miller's explanation, see Miller, *Orthodoxy in Massachusetts 1630-1650*, 55-72.

302   J.F. Maclear, "New England and the Fifth Monarchy: The Quest for the Millennium in Early American Puritanism," *The William and Mary Quarterly* 32, no. 2 (April 1975): 230.

However, the Puritans of Massachusetts Bay, unlike Robinson, were not separatists. Like earlier Reformers,

They shared the original Puritan conviction that the Church of England should be purified, not abandoned. With the vast majority of their English contemporaries, they believed that the church should be protected and supported by the civil government.[303]

The New England Way was in agreement with their English brethren in allowing that just one ecclesiastical orthodoxy had the right to exist at any one time. Consequently, they believed that the civil arm of their system, by necessity, required authority to suppress, punish, and if necessary, banish every example of heresy or dissent. One of their ministers said in 1667, "Separation and Anabaptism are wonted intruders, and seeming Friends, but secret fatall [*sic*] Enemies to Reformation."[304] Augustine believed that schism resulted from one rejecting the principle of *unity* rooted in the universal, invisible body of Christ (The True Church), and for Anglican schismatics this involved the rejection of the bishop.[305] In New England, this simply meant rejecting the authority of the Standing Church.

Just nine years after the Puritan-Separatist landing, King Charles I formally transferred power to the Massachusetts General Court to suppress heresy and deal with dissidents by capital punishment if necessary. It was in this sense that, like Calvin's Geneva, the civil authorities were to become the "nursing fathers" of the church. Schism was, in this context, not only a spiritual breach

---

303   Tull, *Shapers of Baptist Thought*, 36.
304   From an "Election Sermon" by Jonathan Mitchell, 1667; cited in Wood, *The History of the First Baptist Church*, 36.
305   Robert D. Cornwall, *Visible and Apostolic: The Constitution of the Church in High Church Anglican and Non-Juror Thought* (Newark: University of Delaware Press, 1993), 68. Cornwall, echoing Cyprian's sentiment, affirmed that even martyrdom could not atone for the sin of separating from one's bishop.

but a civil-political breakdown of societal and church orderliness. In Massachusetts Bay there would be no distinction between heresy and dissent for nearly a century after their arrival at Plymouth.

John Cotton, the most highly respected proponent of the New England Way and minister of the First Church of Boston, believed that an individual who evidenced doctrinal error should be tolerated "unless his errors be fundamental, or seditiously and turbulently promoted...."[306] If after the subject was properly instructed, he persisted in false teaching, he was to be punished "not for his conscience, but for sinning against his conscience."[307] This demonstrates the balance the original founders thought they had achieved between the civil and spiritual arms of power and the profound arrogance in which they administrated them both! Of course, the failure of the "errand into the wilderness" was, as Simpson observed, "common to Puritans everywhere:"[308]

> *The history of the New England Way is the history of a losing struggle to preserve the intensity of the experience of the saint and his authority over society. On the one hand, a church of visible saints, each of whom could attest the miracle of conversion, is gradually transformed into a church where membership depends on a profession of faith and a standard of Puritan morality.*[309]

One of the key questions involved how the earliest New England Plymouth settlers, along with the non-separating Puritans, tested prospective members for signs of saving grace in their churches.

---

306   Cited in Irwin H. Polishook, *Roger Williams, John Cotton, and Religious Freedom: A Controversy in New and Old England* (Englewood Cliffs, NJ,: Prentice-Hall, 1967), 71.
307   Ibid.
308   Simpson, *Puritanism in Old and New England*, 32.
309   Ibid, 32-33.

Edmond Morgan[310] made a significant contribution to this discussion by demonstrating that until 1640, tests for church membership had not yet been clearly established in actual church practice. Morgan, explaining the origin of the practice stated:

My contention is that the practice came, not from Plymouth to Massachusetts as initially supposed, nor from England or Holland as presently assumed, but that it originated in Massachusetts among the non-separating Puritans there and spread from Massachusetts to Plymouth, Connecticut, New Haven, and back to England. Massachusetts did not imitate Plymouth in this matter, rather the probability is that Plymouth imitated Massachusetts.[311]

Insofar as the struggle for a pure church ideal within the SBBM is represented by the ecclesiological evolution of Isaac Backus and his separate contemporaries, the idea of visible saints in visible churches required no greater precedent than that of the original founders. Even Backus had said, "excepting in the article of sprinkling infants, their faith and practice come the nearest to that of the first planters of New England."[312] Backus, an astute observer of his own history, knew that it would serve the interests of a burgeoning Baptist movement far better to demonstrate their likenesses to the original founders than to a checkered Anabaptist history. In his eyes, the evolution of the position would be best appreciated and most influential when seen in relation to its immediate source.[313] However, as already seen, Backus

---

310   Morgan attests to having depended "heavily" upon the work of Geoffrey Nuttall similarly titled. Nuttall's work is recognized as being a seminal work of the Congregational way, primarily from 1640-1660 in England.

311   Morgan, *Visible Saints: The History of a Puritan Idea,* 66.

312   Backus, *A History of New England with Particular Reference to the Denomination of Christians Called Baptists,* 2: 231-232.

313   William Haller mistakenly assumes the position that Baptists, like other separatists, parties, and sects were all "alike Puritan." He assumes no historical precedent to Backus'

recognized the historical precedents of Henry of Toulouse and Peter de Bruys in calling them Anabaptists who predated the reformation.[314] In doing this, he identified earlier rejections of infant baptism which he saw as more significant than those during the Radical Reformation. This accomplished two things as far as Backus was concerned. First it removed the Munster stigma almost automatically applied by the infant sprinkling clergy. Secondly, it identified conscientious objectors who had preceded the Munster rebellion.

Similarly, Browne and Barrows considered the Lutheran movement to be one that had ignored the ecclesiological implications of those in the radical community. They too had likely been influenced by separatist radicals[315] in Norfolk on the issues of separation of church and state and proposed independence of particular assemblies one from another.[316] De Jong noted that Troeltsch placed the Congregationalist system somewhere between the Calvinistic church-type and the sect-type of the Anabaptists, thereby attributing

---

position on baptism and thereby casts the SBBM under the broader title of Puritan. See William Haller, *The Rise of Puritanism* (Philadelphia: University of Pennsylvania Press, 1938; reprint, First Pennsylvania Paperback Edition 1972), 15-17.

314   In mentioning opponents to infant baptism, Backus makes mention of Dr. Wall's history of infant baptism where Dr. Wall mentions "the names of some in each century" who had opposed the practice. Concerning what to call Peter de Bruys and Henry of Toulouse, Backus then declares, "and I observe that baptist ministers will do as well as any, if people do not know what to call them." See Backus, *A Discourse, Concerning the Materials, the Manner of Building, and Power of Organizing the Church of Christ*, 32.

315   Walker, *The Creeds and Platforms of Congregationalism*, 16.

316   Although, historians like Payne describe the historically organic connections between English Baptists and the continental Anabaptist as "an intricate and thorny problem," he nevertheless contends that such connections clearly existed. Even Lumpkin noted that in the formation of the London Confession of 1644 there were sections remarkably similar to the Aberdeen Confession of 1616. Even anti-Baptist Daniel Featley in his work *The Dipper Dipt*, revealed that there was an unknown Scot who brought this confession before the leaders of the seven churches in London, and that he could be likely identified as one William Gardin of Aberdeenshire who was openly accused of Brownism in 1643 and considered by an associate to be an Anabaptist. Payne makes several of these sorts of connections in his article demonstrating Anabaptistism to have directly and indirectly influenced the Separatist movement within the Church of England. Lumpkin, *Baptist Confessions of Faith*, 145-146 and E.A. Payne, "Contacts between Mennonites and Baptists," *Foundations* 4, no. 1 (1961): 42-43.

Anabaptist influence as the sole contributor to their pure-church ideal.[317] These influences were focused on three primary emphases: "the purity of the church, the necessity of strict discipline and the voluntary character of the covenant...."[318] Unlike the Separatists, the Elizabethan Puritans were not interested in leaving the Church of England, if only she would tolerate their desires for a measure of reform. Underwood noted:

They were as much enamoured of the Church-type of organization as Elizabeth herself and scorned the Sect-type of Christianity. They aimed at capturing for their own party the ecclesiastical machinery and its endowments which has been left over when Roman Catholicism was driven out.[319]

While the Anglicans viewed the Puritan faction as "separatists and would be Anabaptists," the Puritans viewed all who opposed pedobaptism as existing in the "wilderness of anarchy and chaos."[320] However, Puritan Separatists John Robinson and William Brewster both based their Articles on the French Reformed churches which included infant baptism and the aspect of the "church universal."[321] Robinson's own view on baptism[322] had been decidedly drawn from a covenant theological praxis. True to this tradition, he insisted that circumcision as the seal of God's Covenant of Grace was a pledge

---

317   Troeltsch, *The Social Teaching of the Christian Churches*, 664.
318   De Jong, *The Covenant Idea in New England Theology*, 69.
319   Underwood, *A History of the English Baptists*, 31.
320   David S. Lovejoy, *Religious Enthusiasm and the Great Awakening* (Englewood Cliffs, NJ: Prentice-Hall, 1969), McLoughlin, *New England Dissent 1630-1833*, 6.
321   Schaff, *The Creeds of Christendom*, 383-436.
322   The best available work on Robinson has been done by Timothy George. Although somewhat dated, it offers the best overall treatment of his theological views, particularly on election and baptism. Its greatest weakness as a description of the Separatist tradition is the absence of any real discussion on how Separatism as a movement contributed to the development of the visible church covenant.

of His gracious will toward Abraham and his seed. Analogously, he regarded baptism as the "irrevocable seal of election applicable only to the children of the faithful...."[323] Some English Separatists withheld their children from baptism indefinitely rather than submit them to Anglican ministers, while others completely rejected their baptism and submitted to the baptism of the Dutch Mennonites.[324] This repositioning had been anticipated by Separatist John Smyth resulting in his self-baptism (the validity of which he later questioned). Despite this later disavowal of his own baptism, Smith and other Baptists argued against Robinson's baptismal view, offering three fundamental issues which have historically constituted the gist of the Baptist position. Namely, that no express command to baptize infants is found in the New Testament. Secondly, Old Testament circumcision was only for males. Therefore, in a one for one correspondence for New Testament baptism, females would be excluded. And thirdly, infants were unable to manifest true believing faith in the atoning work of Christ. Robinson rebutted each of these positions with the standard arguments from the covenant position. The key to Robinson's view was that "baptism was primarily neither ecclesiologically constitutive nor individually testimonial. It was rather the means by which God communicated to the elect the benefits of His grace."[325]

At this point, rather than repudiate the entire Standing Church on the basis that its practice of infant baptism had truncated Biblical precedent, Backus simply chose to show how the SBBM had pursued many of the same ecclesiological goals. He rejected the baptism of infants in the Robinson tradition, but Backus knew he could reduce any obvious tensions by demonstrating how the Separate-Baptists had adopted the remainder of Robinson's visible church ideology, thereby

---

323   George, *John Robinson and the English Separatist Tradition*, 233.
324   Ibid, 229-230.
325   Ibid, 235.

assuming the mantle of the "first planters."[326] It is clear that the SBBM needed to be associated with the founding fathers insofar that it justified their present claim to biblical orthodoxy. Their self-identity was one of assuming the position of a second reformer whose time had come to restore New England to its first foundation.[327] Essentially the SBBM articulated its *own version* of the reformation as Puritan/ Separatist without the article of infant baptism, thereby validating their movement.[328]

The second statement Backus makes concerning Baptists is in response to the claim which suggested that the Baptists of Backus' day were the distant offspring of the radically errant Anabaptist Munsterites. This was the common retort from those who wished to paint all Baptists with the same broad brush of radicalism. Backus' reply was terse:

As if Christ and his disciples had not been Baptists near fifteen hundred years before the reformation in Germany. And has any man ever been able to produce a mention of infant baptism before the third century? And in the next century, Constantine brought the sword into the church to punish heretics, and to support religious ministers; and blood and slavery, deceit and cruelty, have followed those superstitions ever since, though many good men have been ensnared in their ways.[329]

---

326   Backus, *A History of New England with Particular Reference to the Denomination of Christians Called Baptists*, 2: 231-32.

327   Wood, ed., *Baptists and the American Experience*, 30.

328   This is the dominant thesis of Stanley Grenz's work, Grenz, *Isaac Backus - Puritan and Baptist: His Place in History, His Thought, and Their Implications for Modern Baptist Theology*. Grenz, by placing Backus' thought in Puritan epistemology, puts an undue emphasis on Backus' Puritan roots as a means of projecting Backus' Baptist ideology into contemporary, ecumenical theology.

329   Backus, *A History of New England with Particular Reference to the Denomination of Christians Called Baptists*, 2: 406. Backus very wisely allows Mosheim, the German church historian to establish the historical contradiction to his opponent's faulty assertion.

The author's use of the Lutheran historian offers a good example of how deeply Backus had rejected the entire scope of sacramental theology. His arrival to the Baptist position had evolved one biblical step at a time, but his historical sympathies seemed to develop *en toto*. As a former upstanding Congregationalist, this perspective would have been considered historically biased and deeply tinged with Anabaptist sympathies. By stating that "blood and slavery, deceit and cruelty, have followed those superstitions ever since...," he identifies himself, as well as his movement, with heretics, who since Tertullian in the third century had suffered for the rejection of these "superstitions." In light of Backus' own self-perception of ecclesiastical history, Stanley Grenz's categorization of Backus' ideals existing solely within the Radical Reformation appears to severely short-change Backus' historical views in this area.[330]

For the Congregationalist Puritans, a separation on ecclesiological grounds by purist dissenters seemed to them as unconscionable as their own separation from the Church of England had appeared to church officials more than a century earlier. The Puritan fathers had determined, after James's repudiation of their principles at the Hampton Court Conference in 1604, there was no recourse but to remain in Amsterdam indefinitely.[331] Going back into that hostile environ was not an option. The differences they had with the Standing Church were primarily ecclesiological in nature, and they would have, if possible, removed civil authority from local congregational polity. The King responded with canons making official

---

330   Grenz's argument here is in relation to Backus' identifying himself with movements prior to Luther which rejected infant baptism. Grenz later argues that this issue was not entirely static with Backus and that under the more moderate climate of the prevailing ecumenical culture Backus would have likely rejected his former opinions for a more ecumenical approach. This position will be discussed later under a related heading. For an understanding of Grenz and his treatment of Backus, see Grenz, *Isaac Backus - Puritan and Baptist: His Place in History, His Thought, and Their Implications for Modern Baptist Theology*, 229.
331   Walker, The Creeds and Platforms of Congregationalism , 77.

dissent an unpardonable offense, particularly if that dissent denied the Church of England being of true, apostolic pedigree. In Walker's words, the 161 canons instituted in opposition to the articulated points of difference are

> *...ipso facto to incur the penalty of excommunication, in such severity that naught but a public recantation and the satisfaction of the archbishop as to the genuineness of his repentance can restore the offender to the church. The Separatists might well feel that if Elizabeth had chastised them with whips, James bade fair to chastise them with scorpions.*[332]

The Puritan "Points of Difference" which especially incurred the wrath of James must certainly have been articles five and fourteen. The former affirms the right of each particular congregation to call its own ministers, while at the same time repudiating the claims of "Antichristia Hierarchie or Ministerie, of Popes, Archbishops, Lord-bishop Suffraganes, Deans..."

> *Finally that all churches and people (without exception) are bound in Religion only to receave and submit vnto that constitution, Ministerie, worship, and order, which Christ as Lord and King hath appointed vnto his Church; and not to any other devised by Man whatsoever.*[333] *[sic]*

The inference that these views were Brownist in origin is undeniable, but the civil power which Puritans allowed, that Browne would not tolerate, did eventuate in the Puritan/Separatist divide. But even that would be modified. William Bradford and John

---

332   Ibid.
333   Ibid, 78-80.

Robinson softened their separatism by 1617 when they applied for an English charter to settle in Virginia. The points of difference had to be minimized to accommodate their written declaration to royal supremacy.[334] Article three of the Seven Articles of 1617 discriminates against Royal authority by offering obedience to the King as long as obedience does not contradict "God's Word."[335] While admitting some right of the King to invest civil authority to the bishops and other church officers, they did not give explicit support to the idea that the Anglican prelates carried any divine or spiritual authority over them. This sort of tenuous distinction forced them to appeal at least twice for the assistance of Sir John Wolstonholme of the Virginia Company to persuade the Crown to permit them the right of passage. This tenuous view of the Robinson group was certainly not shared by all the Pilgrim Fathers or the London Merchants who financed them. The Merchants' nebulous support of the Leyden Separatists was evidenced while the colony, without a minister, failed to bring Robinson over in fear they might "injure the plantation in the eyes of the British authorities."[336] Proof of their fear of Anglican reprisal came in the person of John Lyford, a Church of England minister sent to the colony who, while professing Puritan principles, became the Plymouth minister. He was eventually considered a traitor to the Puritan cause and expelled from the colony.[337] This heightened sensitivity to English ecclesiastical authority would guarantee that non-separating Puritanism would eventually guide the colony and set the stage for Puritan settlements at Salem in 1625, Boston in 1630, and shortly thereafter Charlestown,

334   George, *John Robinson and the English Separatist Tradition*, 88. This work by George is the best critical treatment of Robinson and the entire Separatist tradition. Although he does not provide a detailed account of Robinson's requests to the throne for the charter to leave England, he relates how carefully Robinson defined Separatism from the Church of England while remaining firmly committed to the greater Commonwealth.
335   Walker, *The Creeds and Platforms of Congregationalism*, 90.
336   Sweet, *Religion in Colonial America*, 79.
337   Ibid, 78.

Dorchester, and Watertown.[338] The idea of Crown authority,
although distasteful to common sentiment, took another form in
the establishment of the Massachusetts General Court. The Court
was understood as the civil arm of the Congregational system in
Massachusetts. Unlike the other eventual colonies, all who served the
government of the Bay colony were expected by court standards to
belong to the Standing Church.

Sweet credited the intolerance of the Massachusetts system
with the expansion of the majority of New England colonies:

> *The founders of Rhode Island were only the most conspicuous*
> *of the Massachusetts rebels. From the beginning the*
> *Massachusetts leaders had adopted the policy of ridding*
> *themselves of trouble-makers, such as rigid Separatists*
> *and Anabaptists, both of whom they considered especially*
> *dangerous to the welfare and even the safety of the colony.[339]*

Regarding the expatriation mentality of Massachusetts
Puritans, the first permanent settlements which resulted from Bay
Colony intolerance in Maine and New Hampshire were Anglican
communities. These settlements were eventually taken over by
Puritans, and Anglican influence was not revived until the next
century.[340] The Massachusetts religious environ would therefore
serve to provide the primary catalyst for dissention and give impetus
to the Separatist/Baptist churches as they pursued the New England
Way's visible church ideal to its logical conclusions. By justifying the

---

338   These all comprised the Massachusetts Bay Colony which was magistrate-governed
through the General Court in Boston. See Backus, *A History of New England with Particular
Reference to the Denomination of Christians Called Baptists*, 1: 32-38.
339   Sweet, *Religion in Colonial America*, 90.
340   Clifford E. Olmstead, *History of Religion in the United States* (Englewood Cliffs:
Prentice-Hall Inc., 1960), 60.

SBBM as having picked up the mantle of the first planters, Backus sought to make this identification the key to his hope for religious tolerance. Identifying the elect determined the Puritan basis for visible church membership. The hope for extending their influence lay in the continual production of churches and regenerate members living out the covenant expectations in their local churches. Theologically, the constant sticking point was infant baptism. After all, if only regenerate church members were to inhabit the church rolls, how important must infant baptism be in making that determination? Puritan leaders, true to their reformation forebears, thought it critically important. Baptists and other dissenters had serious misgivings about pedobaptism having any Biblical basis whatsoever.

INFANT BAPTISM AND COLONIAL DISSENT

In Colonial New England, particularly in Massachusetts, these social pressures associated with dissenting views were enormous. For many, the cost of dissension was far too high to maintain a consistent resistance. For others, a vocal conscience was the only means of demonstrating truth.

In 1642 three women, Lady Deborah Moody, a Mrs. King, and Mrs. John Tilton were brought before the Salem court for denying infant baptism. The most notable of the three was Lady Moody who had recently purchased a large estate at Lynn, Massachusetts, in 1639, before taking membership in the Salem church. A short time later she became convinced against infant baptism and persuaded two other women in the church to refuse their children baptism. She was censured, along with her two friends Mrs. King and Mrs. Tilton, and brought before the court in Salem and publicly admonished. Refusing to give up her position, she left for Long Island in 1643 and eventually converted to Quakerism.[341] The records of the period reveal no less than forty to fifty legal incidents between 1635 and 1680 which involved those "with anabaptistical tendencies."[342]

Within this period, the Cambridge Platform of 1648 became the social and ecclesiastical structure creating the greatest pressure to conform. One primary objection to this standard was registered by Mr. Obadiah Holmes who had become, after his arrival to the colony, a member of the Salem Congregational Church. In approximately 1645, he was dismissed to the church in what is now Seekonk, Massachusetts, which was newly raised and under the pastorate of Mr. Samuel Newman. Late in 1649 or possibly after the first of the year, Mr. Holmes and several others left the church over an offense evidently not rectified to their satisfaction. They met on their own for some time, and then after adopting Baptist principles were baptized by Baptist preacher John Clarke. Holmes was subsequently arrested and charged with contempt of public worship,[343] commanded to pay a fine of thirty pounds or be thoroughly whipped with a three-pronged cord. He chose the latter. Another less notable example was Thomas Painter of Hingham. Painter was a common laborer who adopted Anabaptist principles in 1644. He remained resolute in his conviction against infant baptism, was convicted, and was publicly whipped in July, 1644.

---

341   McLoughlin, *The Rise of Antipedobaptists in New England, 1630-1655*, 85.
342   Ibid.
343   McLoughlin noted that Holmes was found guilty of holding a private meeting on Sunday, of disrespecting God's ordinances, of not removing their hats in church, of disruption of church services, of discrediting the organizational basis of the church, of offering the ordinance of the Lord's Supper unentitled, of re-baptizing persons, and of denying the validity of infant baptism. McLoughlin, *New England Dissent 1630-1833*, 1: 20.

His judges accused him of reproaching the "Lord's Ordinance," the very charge he had personally made against his own accusers.[344]

Henry Dunster [345] serves as the most illustrious opponent of the mid- seventeenth century. Two points justify his mention here: first, his extraordinary academic reputation among his peers, and, second, the unbiased nature of his testimony. The latter must include the fact that he was called a Baptist for his antipedobaptism, even though he was never removed from the membership of the Puritan Church at Cambridge.[346]

Captain Johnson, confirming Dunster's expertise in the biblical languages, said that he was "fitted from the Lord for the work, and, by those that have skill that way, reported to be an able proficient both in the Hebrew, Greek, and Latin languages, an orthodox preacher of the truths of Christ, and very powerful through his blessings to move the affections."[347] A Mr. Hubbard, while giving testimony of Dunster's call to Harvard's presidency in 1640, said, "Under whom, that which was before, but at best *schola illustra*, grew to the stature and perfection of a College, and flourished in the profession of all liberal sciences for many years."[348] Thomas Prince paid him perhaps the greatest honor by including in his preface to his book on the Psalms, this quote, "For a further improvement it was committed to the Rev. Mr. Henry Dunster, president of Harvard College; one of the greatest masters of the oriental languages, that hath been known in these ends of the earth."[349]

Thomas Armitage, *A History of the Baptists: Traced by Their Vital Principles and Practices from the Time of Our Lord and Saviour Jesus Christ to the Year 1886.* (New York: Bryan, Taylor, and Co., 1887), 2: 637.
345   Historians Thomas Prince, Edward Johnson, and Backus, along with other contemporaries of the period consistently spell the president's name with an "a" on the second syllable. Later writers all spell it "Dunster".
346   McLoughlin, *New England Dissent 1630-1833*, 1: 9.
347   Backus, *A History of New England with Particular Reference to the Denomination of Christians Called Baptists*, 1: 227.
348   Ibid.
349   Ibid.

Dunster's opposition to infant baptism was no doubt connected to his reaction to Messrs. Clarke, Holmes, and Crandall being imprisoned at Boston for not receiving permission to forego services at their respective parishes in Massachusetts. Backus' history confirmed they had been worshipping among themselves.[350]

The Cambridge community was stunned by Henry Dunster holding Baptist principles while the sitting president of a stalwart Congregationalist institution. His own pastor, Jonathan Mitchell, attempted to persuade the college president of his error, but proved entirely unsuccessful. Instead, Dunster proved capable of shaking the young pastor's faith.[351] Dunster was obviously considered dangerous to the Standing Order. In the Harvard community, his message of *soli visibiliter fideles sunt baptizandi*[352] could not be easily ignored. As an academic, he posed a significant threat by virtue of his Harvard office, and his credentials served to provide intellectual gravity to the Baptist position on infant baptism. It is likely the authorities considered the fate of the entire colony could be jeopardized should he become an out and out Baptist. It may very well have been that Dunster understood the tenor of the time period better than his peers and simply decided that a major campaign at this time in his life was not going to benefit anyone, including him. He certainly understood that the Holmes-Clark affair, and several other incidents like it, had not aided toleration of the Baptists.

Secondly, Dunster's reluctance to exploit his influence for the Baptist position also exposes the cohesiveness of the Puritan social fabric. However, his private act of dissent, so owned by such a man of principle, serves to clarify the issue most feared by the Standing Order

---

350   Ibid, 418.
351   Ibid, 1:228-230.
352   (Visible believers only should be baptized) McLoughlin, *The Rise of Antipedobaptists in New England, 1630-1655*, 90.

and most celebrated by those in the dissenting community. There appears in the record no hesitation by the authorities in removing him before the leaven spread. The General Courts' Act of 1644 and the following Cambridge Platform of 1648 was the Bay Colony's effort at codifying religious beliefs and structure to the point that anything outside of it was easily identifiable and punishable. However, this sword cut both ways. On the one hand it strengthened the Standing Order in their pursuit of a cohesive collective community. On the other hand it inadvertently served to give a sense of legitimacy to those organized dissenters who chose to vent their beliefs in the public arena.

Thomas Gould, a close friend of Dunster, was evidently influenced by him in refusing infant baptism in 1655. Wood suggested the tie between Thomas and Dunster to be so strong that he accredits Dunster as being the "immediate forerunner and influential cause of the attitude of Thomas,"[353] and in so doing, the progenitor of the First Baptist Church, Boston. Wood went as far to suggest that if Dunster had lived to 1665, he likely would have become the first pastor of the church instead of Thomas Gould, his friend and disciple, and would have had the joy of seeing his views embodied in a church of baptized believers.[354] In Boston, where tolerance was more noticeable than anywhere in the Bay colony, the First Baptist Church grew from its original nine members in 1665 to over eighty in just twenty-five years. This suggests a considerable dissenting force underlying the thin surface of spiritual uniformity within the Commonwealth.

By 1682, the General Court decided, under direct pressure from the Crown, to allow toleration for the Quakers and the Baptists. Their legal decision appeared to be based purely on expediency rather

---

353   Wood, *The History Of the First Baptist Church*, 29.
354   Ibid, 30.

than a genuine desire to offer Baptists legitimate religious freedom. Congregationalists in Massachusetts had been urged to offer to the dissenting community the same tolerance it had been afforded in England before coming to the New World. The Puritan response was at best a decision to recognize the right to express conscience for dissenting groups. It did not suggest that exercising that right would be fruitful or painless.

Toleration after 1682 offered little change for those committed to open dissension, particularly debates over pedobaptism. Baptists were not able to vote or hold office and were usually forced to build their meetinghouses along the outer perimeters of any given township.[355] Even when the Charlestown Baptists under Gould moved their church to Boston in 1674 and built a meetinghouse, the authorities harassed them, and nailed the church doors shut for two full years before yielding to public pressure to allow public worship.

However, news of the earlier intolerances had already reached certain English Congregationalists who applied some pressure of their own. Gould's incident would prove to mark a clear diminishment of power in the Massachusetts General Court. The debate which occurred over Gould's case actually became an intramural contest between several Puritan laymen and the staunch members of the General Court. Arguing within the context of the New England Way, they asserted that their Baptist brethren were in fact not heretics but simply more excessive reformers than they were on the point of Anabaptism (i.e., denying baptism to infants and re-baptizing believing adults). The Court would not debate the issue of antipedobaptism:

which practice, being also otherwise circumstanced with making infant baptism a nullity, and thereby making us all to be un-

---

355   McLoughlin, *The Rise of Antipedobaptists in New England, 1630-1655*, 84.

baptized persons, and so consequently no regular churches,
ministry or ordinances; as also renouncing all our churches, as
being bad and corrupt that they are not fit to be held communion
with...tending to the destruction of the churches...; all of which
considering, together with the danger of disseminating their
errors, ...this Court do judge it necessary that they be removed
to some other part of this country, or elsewhere....[356]

In October of 1668, the court received a petition signed by sixty-six prominent citizens asking for the release and subsequent pardon of Gould and his friends. In March of 1669, thirteen influential Independent English ministers sent a letter concerning Mr. Gould to the Massachusetts governor with a strong request to end the incarcerations and abuse with a return of liberty to Gould and those of his associates. Both of these reached the Massachusetts' authorities after Gould and his friends had been incarcerated over a year.

Upon their release, Gould moved to Noddle's Island in Boston Harbor, both living there and maintaining the church for over three years. Willing church members rowed out on boats for scheduled services. In the summer of 1674, Gould left the island and began holding services in Boston at the home of Simon Lynd.[357] In October, 1675, Gould died, and John Myles served temporarily as pastor for the next two years. Myles' open-communion sentiments were not at variance with the prevailing opinions of the congregation. John Russell, Gould's permanent replacement, wrote a narrative of the Boston church in 1680, which was, in effect, his response to the Congregational Reforming Synod of 1679. The Synod thoroughly condemned any and all dissension in the Massachusetts Bay Colony

---

356   Backus, *A History of New England with Particular Reference to the Denomination of Christians Called Baptists*, 1:302-03.
357   McLoughlin, *New England Dissent 1630-1833*, 1: 74.

and reaffirmed the Commonwealth's commitment to excoriate and
judge any doctrinal opinion against the Standing Church. Russell's
response was two-fold. First, it demonstrated that the Boston Baptists
felt it necessary to defend their true intentions. Secondly, Russell
wanted to publicly declare that the Baptists did not, as some Baptists
did at the time, consider the Standing Churches to be false churches
because of the practice of infant baptism. He admitted that Baptists
considered infant baptism to be a nullity, but considered this opinion
to be their divine right as interpreters of the Word of God:

> As for not owning their churches to be the churches of Christ,
> we never yet denied them to be Churches of Christ. It is enough
> for everyone to prove his own Work. But we have owned
> them as churches of Christ, and do look at them as such; for
> where there is true matter joined together in the bond of a
> Church, though they may be defective in some things....[358]

These events marked a nearing demise of the old era and the
beginning of a new and tenuous period of imbalanced toleration.[359]
At each turn, dissension—whether introduced by a college president
or by an unlettered laborer—every act appeared to threaten the
entire structure of the Standing Order. The social treatment of the
Baptists by respectable church-goers during the seventeenth century
was similar to that afforded the Adventists and the Mormons in the
nineteenth century and the Pentecostal-Holiness groups at the start of
the twentieth century. Ostensibly, the fear of schism, and the inherent

---

358   Wood, *The History of the First Baptist Church*, 171.
359   McLoughlin, *Soul Liberty: The Baptists' Struggle in New England, 1630-1833*, 44.

challenge to the Standing Order had not been fruitless. Imperceptible change was slowly dissolving away the authority of its vital organs.

By the middle of the eighteenth century, with social pressures somewhat abated by the startling affects of the Great Awakening, Backus and the Separate-Baptists exploited failed Puritan ideas and co-opted them for the purpose of furthering the second reformation.

COVENANT THEOLOGY AND THE PURE CHURCH

There is no record that the Middleboro pastor believed his pursuit of a pure local church to be inconsistent with the old Puritan aim of making "the visible church a spiritual approximation of the invisible church."[360] Backus believed the Congregationalists were in fundamental error in regard to believers' baptism not preceding communion. He thought that once the impediment of pedobaptism had been doctrinally challenged and repudiated by the Separates, they would leave their doctrinal half-way house and pursue the pure-church ideal of the Baptists. In the pamphlet "A Fish Caught in His Own Net" (FCN), Backus boldly attempted to change this image in a reply to nine anti-separatist sermons preached by Rev. Joseph Fish in 1768:

> They allow that the invisible church contains none but the
> first born which are written in Heaven, Heb. xii, 23. but they
> would have the visible church contain abundance more....
> Whereas the proper notion of visible is the making manifest
> what was before invisible.... The only reason why any beside
> regenerate souls get into the visible church is not owing to
> the rule but to man's imperfection in acting upon it.[361]

---

360   Morgan, *Visible Saints: The History of a Puritan Idea*, 65.
361   McLoughlin, ed., *Isaac Backus on Church, State, and Calvinism: Pamphlets, 1754-1789*, 255.

Backus' view of the regenerate church membership required him to reject the idea that God's Covenant of Grace included the children of believing parents. This conception of the visible church had so permeated New England Congregationalism by 1773 that Backus suggested to Rev. Fish, "I know Mr. F. says, 'I have really nothing to do with Mr. B upon this head; tis out of the question, as a particular church is not the church, which my sermons treat of.'"[362] Undoubtedly, Fish spoke for the majority of his contemporary Puritan community in his refusal to see the particular church as a visible representation of the mystical church. His argument, based on the Augustinian interpretation of the parable of the wheat and the tares, involved the inescapable reality of believers and unbelievers comprising the visible church. This became the critical point of difference in his debates with Fish.

In DCM, written in 1773, Backus asserted, "This is the capital point of our dispute."[363] Fish reiterated the Covenant theology of his traditional Puritan roots saying "that children, even infants were always reckoned a part of that body or church, which the Lord gathered in Abraham's family."[364] Backus heartily agreed, but then added, "Is it altogether reasonable to suppose that the Christian church is made up of the same materials, that the Jewish church was?"[365] Answering his own question, he emphatically said no.[366]

For Backus, this pursuit of New Testament church purity demanded a complete separation of the two systems, based on the fact that one was national in scope and the other was particular or

---

362   Backus, *A Discourse, Concerning the Materials, the Manner of Building, and Power of Organizing the Church of Christ*, 17.
363   Ibid, 4.
364   Ibid.
365   Ibid, 4.
366   Ibid.

individual. In his mind, the confounding of the two blurred their separate constitutions and created a false distinction between the invisible and the invisible, notwithstanding the presence of a hypocrite or two. Backus, like others in the dissent community before him, had perceived that the New Testament church could only be entered by regenerate individuals in mutual covenant with each other. This original Puritan ideal of a pure church, in distinction from the Church of England, demonstrated the hope of not being forced to tolerate the corrupting influences of national birthright membership. Morgan's discussion of visible sainthood, mentioned earlier, demonstrated that the Puritan definition was not initially resolute. They had focused on the outward state of the professing believer desiring membership not necessarily on clear evidence of the new birth.[367]

Commonly, individuals believed that if they were elect, God would awaken them in His own time regardless of their own spiritual disposition. Those in church-covenant relation may for years have remained in a state of suspended expectation of God's gracious work in their lives having not experienced the new birth. For some, this gave way to hopeless depression or a cavalier disposition that, if they were elect, God would save them anyway when he was ready. As a consequence, the visible church had become vaguely representative of its so-called universal counterpart prior to the Great Awakening, and Backus was keenly aware of this fact. Consequently, though Backus would use English Puritans as well as some notable New England divines to substantiate the idea of making visible the invisible church, the Middleboro pastor concluded that the

---

367   Ibid, 77. Morgan shows how non-separating Puritans such as William Ames emphasized faith as a mark of the church, but defined believers only as a professors, as long as they remained among the church membership as greater members of the Catholic church. This was no guarantee of genuine conversion.

Massachusetts Standing Churches had skewed the concept through the errors of the Half-way covenant, the preparation doctrine, and infant baptism. They all assisted in institutionalizing birthright baptism, and arbitrarily held in abeyance the new birth of the individual and the person's sense of urgency to own it. The only response to these long-term problems in the collective mind of the SBBM was absolute rejection of the entire system which produced them in the first place. Backus was convinced that the practice of infant baptism was the greatest singular failure of the New England experiment. Unfortunately, as McLoughlin noted of leaders in the Standing Order, "they lived too close to the Munsterite Anabaptists to reject infant baptism"[368] and the covenant system which maintained it.

For them, the images of anarchy and chaos produced by the Munster anarchists made their rigid Biblicism worse than a vacuous religious system. Therefore, the covenant was legitimate if it included, as Robinson conceded, the children of at least one believing parent. By 1662, within forty years of their humble beginnings at Plymouth, New England Congregationalism softened the requirement to also include the children of unbelieving parents through the Half-Way Covenant. By the time of Whitefield and the Great Awakening in 1740, unconverted church members were seen as being led by un-regenerate clergyman! How far they had come! It is at this point that that the SBBM veers into territory previously undiscovered by Robinson and his followers in the previous century and helps to answer the question of why the Backus movement was unique in the Separatist/ Puritan tradition. Ironically, Robinson and Backus defended identical doctrinal perimeters in their respective theological systems with the

---

368   McLoughlin, ed., *Isaac Backus on Church, State, and Calvinism: Pamphlets, 1754-1789*, 131.

exception of infant baptism. Like the later Backus, George conceded that the

concern of Robinson for the visible Church did not attenuate his
interest in the invisible. The tension between a sectarian ecclesiology
on the one hand and a high predestination theology on the other is
the controlling dynamic in Robinson's thought and the resolution
of it, his chief contribution to the English Separatist tradition.[369]

Although, some of Robinson's theology defined Backus, it did not find equal treatment in practical emphasis. There were two clear reasons for this disparity with both his professed theological positions and with the former Separatist/Puritan tradition. First of all, the final rejection of infant baptism appeared to cut infants off from their elect status in the universal Church. Pedobaptists considered infant baptism to have been "neither ecclesiologically constitutive nor individually testimonial" in the visible church[370] but the actual basis on how God manifested his grace to the elect. Children of the Puritan faithful were in fact considered to be elect, though they would have to individually confess and own the covenant in adulthood. Secondly, infant baptism reflected the communal seal to these elect children in the visible church administering their baptism. Thus, this connection between the invisible and the visible churches was made manifest in the act itself and then brought to completion through the "preparation" process between infancy and adulthood. Backus argued in DCM that those in the "Standing Church blamed us because we dare not practically allow that persons may be brought into the Covenant of Grace without their knowledge or choice, many of whom fall away and

---

369   George, *John Robinson and the English Separatist Tradition*, 244-245.
370   Ibid, 235.

perish forever."[371] Thereby, at the point that election became verifiable by adult believers only and evidenced by their baptism in the visible church, the universal and visible aspects of the church became virtually indistinguishable. In reality, the visible church pattern had been laid over its universal model and had, in essence, hidden it, rather than revealed it.

Grenz suggested the Puritans, during the seventeenth and eighteenth centuries, were forced to re-evaluate the pure-church ideal within the universal-invisible context,[372] but Backus, in arguing against them, simply said that the visible church is nothing but "the making manifest what was before invisible."[373] The SBBM freely admitted that while there were many in the Standing Church who had evidenced their election and membership within the universal Church, they rejected the principle of the SBBM "that none should be baptized but visible Christians."[374] Baptists knew that visible churchmanship could not be logically demonstrated by potentially elect infants, since only actual faith and not an infant's inward faith could be considered visible. This is exactly why John Smyth first rejected the practice of infant baptism among English Separatists Richard Clifton and John Robinson.[375] Why had not the radical English Separatists concluded the same thing when it was the pure-church ideal which had motivated them all? Why hadn't the demand for the observation of a genuine faith driven the pure-church ideal of the Brownists to a rejection

---

371   McLoughlin, ed., *Isaac Backus on Church, State, and Calvinism: Pamphlets, 1754-1789*, 466.

372   Grenz, *Isaac Backus - Puritan and Baptist: His Place in History, His Thought, and Their Implications for Modern Baptist Theology*, 266.

373   Backus, *A Discourse, Concerning the Materials, the Manner of Building, and Power of Organizing the Church of Christ*, 6.

374   McLoughlin, ed., *Isaac Backus on Church, State, and Calvinism: Pamphlets, 1754-1789*, 466.

375   Stephen Brachlow, *The Communion of Saints* (Oxford: Oxford University Press, 1988), 151-152.

of sprinkling infants? [376] After all, "Since church membership, for the English radicals in general, belonged only to the visibly elect, Smyth's rejection of infant baptism on this basis was a logically compelling one."[377]

At least part of the answer may be observed in the behavior of Separatist Francis Johnson. This issue motivated John Smyth's first publication as a new professing Baptist, *The Character of the Beast*, wherein he denounced both the practice of pedobaptism and the churches which embraced it. Johnson, responding against Smyth's conclusions, was consequently forced to the unenviable position of having to justify the baptisms of Rome and England, thereby validating the very bodies against which he contended. Brachlow demonstrated that Johnson was able to accept Rome and England as true churches because, despite their apostasy and disobedience, he somehow believed God's grace was "larger than their apostasy."[378]

Backus and his Baptist associates took no such mediating position to preserve the validity of unbiblical churches. In his rebuttal to his former pastor, Backus reported from Dr. Wall's history of pedobaptism the fate of many who

---

376   Although most modern historians downplay any direct influence of Baptists or Anabaptists over the Brownist or Separatist churches in Holland, Backus not only ignored the self-baptism of John Smith, but added, "...his views spread so rapidly that a Baptist church was soon founded of which he became the pastor, and the other English churches in Holland were largely leavened with Baptist sentiments. Churchmen pointed to him as a warning to all separatists and nonconformists, exemplifying the legitimate end of their heresies; and the separatists themselves wrote no less than six distinct treatises against him." For this entire argument by the New England historian see Backus, *A History of New England with Particular Reference to the Denomination of Christians Called Baptists*, 1: 43. For a brief list of historians who reject direct Baptist influence over the Independents, etc., see Winthrop Still Hudson, "Who Were the Baptists?" *The Baptist Quarterly* 16, no. 7 (1956): 305, Nuttall, *Visible Saints: The Congregational Way, 1640-1660*, White, *The English Separatist Tradition*.
377   Brachlow, *The Communion of Saints*, 152.
378   Ibid, 154.

in various parts of Germany and Switzerland, suffered death
for denying infant baptism, sundry years before that affair in
Munster; but also, that at several different times, witnesses
have appeared against that practice, clear back to the third
century; and that is the earliest express mention thereof....[379]

Furthermore, the SBBM's rejection of infant baptism and its
universal Church connection forced them to ultimately reject open-
communion with pedobaptists on the basis that no one was admitted
into the Christian Church "without a personal profession of faith," or
"without water baptism." Therefore opposition to baptizing babies
in seventeenth century New England was equal to rejecting covenant
theology and is vital to understanding the Separate-Baptist movement
a century later. Backus was quite convinced that infant baptism had
been rejected by various religious factions "long before Luther," much
less the English Reformation.[380]

Any attack on this was essentially interpreted as an attack
on the entire Massachusetts Commonwealth. For Backus, this
demonstrated that the identical Standing Church system confronted
both the pre-awakening "Ana-baptistical" brethren and the Separate-
Baptists in consecutive centuries for essentially the same reason.
Identifying the similarities of these movements did not require the

---

379   Backus, *A Letter to the Reverend Mr. Benjamin Lord, of Norwich*, 10, emphasis
added.
380   Backus' quote here is from Lutheran historian Mosheim who connects several pre-
reformation groups together to show their mutual desire for a visible church "inaccessible
to the wicked and un-righteous...." Backus then connects these to the less fortunate German
Anabaptists who saw mixed churches as indicative of confusing civil concerns with the church
but failed in taking the Reformation that far. Then Backus mentions the Munster Anabaptists
in 1525 and 1533 who had hopes "of recovering both civil and religious liberty thereby;
but they perished in the attempt...." Backus then completes the circle by saying, "But the
English Baptists, both in Europe and America have carefully avoided each of these extremes".
See Backus, *A History of New England with Particular Reference to the Denomination of
Christians Called Baptists*.

connecting of historical dots but in recognizing the re-emergence of coinciding principles. The depth of this particular issue is underscored by the fact that no less than four major polemics appeared against sprinkling infants in seventeenth century New England, written by influential Massachusetts divines,[381] demonstrating a significant undercurrent of rejection long before the SBBM made its official appearance.

THE PROBLEM OF SEPARATISM

Reformed theologian Jonathan Edwards had written vehemently against the separatist movement within his denomination. Consequently, the pastor did not see that his defense of infant baptism would only produce the same result from which the deteriorating situation had sprung. Their leaders met this issue in a head-on collision which would prove to be their eventual undoing.[2] In the minds of Separate-Baptists, sprinkling babies represented every evil of a national church, forced religious taxation, birthright membership, and an intolerant magistrate who punished dissent. As Goen, McLoughlin, and others demonstrated, the initial re-entry of converts

---

381   McLoughlin, *New England Dissent 1630-1833*, 1: 27. McLoughlin lists the first of these as having been written by George Phillips, the pastor of the Watertown church. His book was entitled *A Confutation of Some Grounds for Infant Baptism* (1645). This was a reply to the London Baptist minister Thomas Lambe. He lists the second book as being written by John Cotton in 1647 entitled *The Grounds and Ends of Baptisme of Children of the Faithful* (London, 1648). This was based upon a fictitious dialogue between a church member with baptism doubts over his own child and over Cotton himself. A third volume, written by Thomas Cobbet, was entitled *A Just Vindication of the Covenant and Church Estate of Members as Also Their Right to Baptism"* (London, 1648). The fourth was by Thomas Shepherd, Sr, of Cambridge, Massachusetts, and was evidently in the form of a letter written possibly to one of his church members.

into the Standing Churches created a fire-storm of tension and ultimately schism.[382]

Even some, who recognized that bringing their infants to baptism was not rooted in Scripture, struggled themselves with repudiating their own baptism or in being sacrilegious by having taken the name of the Trinity in vain. The importance of this issue cannot be overestimated as McLoughlin suggests.[383] For them this doctrine stood at the threshold of a different theological system. As a point of church entry, the idea of re-baptizing adults challenged the very premise of what constituted actual membership. In reality, it openly challenged the doctrinal core of the Standing Order. In fact, that very thought occurred to Patience Adams who was a member of the Canterbury Separate church before moving to Sutton, Massachusetts, around 1760. In her repudiation of infant baptism in Sutton, she wrote back to her church explaining the discovery that her first baptism was on her parents "account," and that she had opposed it because of her reading of Matt 28:19-20 and Mk 16:16. She concluded that "baptism is anext to beleauours only (for believers only)."[384] Unfortunately, this dilemma was not confined to just church member. The author reported that in 1760, Frothingham, himself a Separate pedobaptist pastor, was aware of eight Separate ministers who had stopped infant baptisms and later reversed themselves under pressure. However, in this first decade after the awakening, most Separate churches based their covenants on a mixed communion standard as a means of dealing with an

---

382   McLoughlin, ed., *Isaac Backus on Church, State, and Calvinism: Pamphlets, 1754-1789.* See Backus' letter, which includes the testimony of a young man who, after conversion, saw the incongruity of the Half-Way covenant, infant baptism, along with other disorders in his family church, and decided the only alternative was to separate. Situations such as this abruptly altered the already tense New England religious scene. The majority of those who came out and separated from their churches during this period never returned.

383   McLoughlin, *New England Dissent 1630-1833*, 1: 428.

384   Ibid. 1: 427.

uncertainty over public sentiment. This battle was much easier fought by the laity than the clergy. Wood asserted:

> *Theologically, "Separates" and Baptists were of one mind,*
> *and the shift to the practice of believer's baptism was*
> *neither difficult to make nor difficult to justify on the basis of*
> *convictions which had been the occasion for the Separates'*
> *break with the churches of the Standing Order.*[385]

However, Wood made no effort to clarify the difficulties experienced by the Separate clergy in dealing with the baptism issue. He seems to overlook the fact that a significant number of converts returned to the Standing Churches within a quarter century, and others of less stalwart disposition never separated in the first place. The two key Separate leaders Solomon Paine and Ebenezer Frothingham had both entertained opposing infant baptism in the early 1740s. Eventually, they both strongly opposed the movement of any Separates into the Baptist fold. This feeling held by Paine and Frothingham must be seen from the perspective of the Standing Church. G.S. Clark reported:

> *Of the forty-five Congregational churches in Massachusetts*
> *that sprang into life during the ten years now under review*
> *(1740-1750), eight or nine had their origin in the spirit of*
> *separatism; while more than twice as many others originating*
> *in the same spirit, grew at length into Baptist churches.*[386]

---

385   Wood, ed., *Baptists and the American Experience*, 28.
386   George Sylvester Clark, *A Historical Sketch of the Congregational Churches in Massachusetts from 1620-1858* (Boston: Cong Pub. Soc,1858), 35.

The loss of people, potential tax revenues, and a shifting status quo provide key elements of understanding how the Separates themselves would respond in the milieu of schism. Pressure from the Standing Order was aimed at driving the fainthearted back to the fold. Backus had little patience for those among his own denomination who had acquiesced in the Bunyan tradition of open-communion and lax baptismal standards. Backus repudiated any mediate position with the Separates saying:

> *Neither could we understandingly act in being buried in baptism, until we were convinced that what was done to us in infancy was not gospel baptism; therefore to commune at the Lord's table with any who were only sprinkled in infancy, is parting with truth, by practically saying they are baptized when we do not believe they are.*[387]

At first, Backus revealed a deep and abiding interest in making toleration work among opposing factions before his own immersion in 1751:

> *...yet many found by degrees that it could not be done in that way; for they saw that if they came to the Lord's Supper with any who were only sprinkled in their infancy, it practically said they were baptized, when they believed in their consciences that they were not. And practical lying is a great sin.*[388]

Unfortunately, Backus' public display of practical honesty regarding his own re-baptism brought the church to council under Solomon Paine in October of 1751. Backus was censured for a denial

---

387   Backus, *A History of New England with Particular Reference to the Denomination of Christians Called Baptists*, 2: 116.
388   Ibid, 2: 178.

of his original covenant with the church based on his original infant baptism. However, Backus and the SBBM continued to baptize those who desired immersion and sent their converts who desired sprinkling to other Separate ministers. This demonstrated that they were initially willing to pastor both parties. Ironically, it was the Congregational-Separates who wanted a closed-communion position for themselves before Backus actually made the decision to separate from them.[389]

For Backus, coexistence eventually became impossible. He reported how that for nearly two years his own church had no peace in order to even celebrate the Lord's Supper bringing him to conclude the truth that immersion of adult believers was the only biblical position. For Backus and his church, this sentiment concluded with their becoming the First Baptist Church of Middleboro on January 16, 1756. Being fully conscious of the irreversible nature of the decision to abandon the baptism of infants, Backus and the five others who signed that first charter did not take this step lightly.[390] The diary inclusions of this entire period demonstrate that in Backus' case no decision about moving ahead on Baptist principles (so-called) were made without mutual prayer, fasting, and continuous dialogue. The cycle of decision began early in July 1755 and culminated on January 16th with six signers; Timothy Briant, John Hayward, Mary Caswell, Esther Forbes, Isaac Backus, and Mrs. Backus. On the January 16th entry

---

389   The close-communion faction was not led by anti-pedobaptists , at least on the level of inter-church efforts to maintain a common cause. The pedobaptists recognized before the Separate-Baptists that separation was essential to preservation. The realization that coexistence was virtually impossible came first to Solomon Paine who, upon seeing the movement of re-baptizers into the Baptist churches, called for the Stonington Convention in 1754 which ultimately was divided over the issue. They knew the life of the movement depended on it. See Ibid, 2: 110-119.

390   William Gerald McLoughlin, ed., *The Diary of Isaac Backus*, 3 vols. (Providence, R.I.: Brown University Press, 1979), 1: 399-401.

Backus transparently offers, "and had not my soul believed that Christ would go before me, I should not have dared to step forward." [391]

No other theological decision more determined the arrival of the Separates to the Baptist destination. The difficulty with which the decision was made, along with the meager number who took that first step, reveals, at least for Backus' church, the motivations were genuine and motivated out of the desire to obey the Scripture as they understood it. Backus almost immediately wrote "A Short Description of the Difference Between the Bond Women and the Free" which set forth the Baptists' fundamental differences with both the Standing Order and the Separates regarding infant baptism. To reject sprinkling was to reject territorial churches and the ecclesiastical authority which constituted the social fabric of the New England Way. By claiming a direct connection to the ideals of the original planters while simultaneously reaching back to Anabaptist exemplars in defending their rejection of infant baptism, Backus marked out a theological position which made it impossible to remain in the half-way house of Congregational Separatism.

SUMMARY

Having discovered that the initial thrust of Luther's campaign was largely soteriological in nature, the Radical Reformation, the English Reformation, and the Second Reformation were predominantly *ecclesiological* or *church-centered* movements. Casting the SBBM as the true progeny of John Robinson and his Separatist tradition (minus infant baptism), Backus not only sought ecclesiastical respect for the beleaguered Baptists but also framed Separate-Baptists as the true heirs of the Puritan ideal by the

---

391   Ibid, 1: 401.

application of their own foresworn principle. This is the light in which the SBBM chose to cast itself, and this ultimately formed the basis from which it spelled out the Baptist position.

Chapter Four

Puritan Orthodoxy and the Development of the SBBM

INTRODUCTION

To further understand the Separate-Baptist movement, it is important to comprehend the merciless resistance the Massachusetts' Standing Order demonstrated to any doctrinal diversity from its original purposes. McLoughlin cited the maintenance of covenant theology as the first of four elements in responding to the direct challenges by the Baptists at "crucial and interlocking points."[392] He noted, "For the church and the state were so intricately interwoven in the corporate system of New England that a breakdown at the local level ultimately compelled a realignment of the whole social and political structure."[393] Backus reminded Dr. Fish during their rancorous debate that even the venerable Puritan Dr. Mather had said by 1700, "If the begun *apostasy* should proceed as fast for thirty years - surely it will come to that in New England, that the *most conscientious* people therein will think themselves concerned to *gather churches out of churches*."[394] Remarkably, his prophecy nearly coincided with the startling implications of Whitefield's new birth message and the separatism which followed it. It also established

---

392   McLoughlin, *New England Dissent 1630-1833*, 1: 28.
393   Handlin, ed., *Isaac Backus and the American Pietistic Tradition*, 24.
394   Backus, *A Discourse, Concerning the Materials, the Manner of Building, and Power of Organizing the Church of Christ*, 114.

the beginning stage for what the Baptists would later exploit in their definition of a regenerate, baptized membership model.

THE CHALLENGES TO PURITAN ORTHODOXY

Maintaining the colonial experience was essentially the same thing as protecting the covenant of its churches. One *was* the essence of the other. Puritan life required a Protestant doctrinaire justifying their "errand in the wilderness" as thoroughly as it did its Geneva counterpart under John Calvin.[395] Separatist John Robinson's use of Calvin's French-Reformed creedal statement served to front-load the Puritan-Separatist tradition as a quasi-Reformed movement consistent with the Protestant national church. By definition, this church consisted of all believers from the beginning of time to its temporal end under the covenant of election, the true church (particular, local church), as distinguished from all other sects. They would adhere to the "pure doctrine" of the gospel, the pristine administration of the sacraments as instituted by Christ, and church discipline exercised by the punishment of sin, etc.[396] Schaff's article thirty-four, entitled "Of Holy Baptism," supplies the critical description of how the covenant community viewed infant baptism as a doctrine. The appropriate section reads:

Neither doth this Baptism only avail us at
the time when the water is poured
upon us, but also through the whole course of our life. Therefore
we detest the error of the Anabaptists, who are not content with

---

395   Miller was correct in his statement that the New England understanding of covenant was entirely different philosophically from its Genevan/Calvinist counterpart. However, the common aim of both of them was a civil-religious union which would produce a true "covenant community". See Miller, *The New England Mind: The Seventeenth Century*, 447.
396   Schaff, *The Creeds of Christendom*, 384-424.

the one only baptism they have once received, and moreover
condemn the baptism of the infants of believers, who, we
believe, ought to be baptized and sealed with the sign of the
covenant, as the children in Israel formerly were circumcised
upon the same promises which are made unto our children.[397]

As a policy for community membership and privilege, infant baptism was to be accepted as the entire foundation for spiritual life. Its broad base connected the Old Testament community with the church of the New Testament and placed them under a continuous covenant begun with Abraham, ratified with the fleshly sign of circumcision to Jesus Christ, who ratified His covenant with the spiritual sign of baptism. The New Testament, in these terms, was merely a continuation of the Old Testament covenant, and to deny the latter was to place it on an uncertain footing, thereby in their minds, making it groundless and disconnected from its originating source. Miller underscored this fact:

That which made New Englanders unique in all seventeenth
century Christendom, which cut them off from all reformed
churches and constituted them in truth a peculiar people, was
their axiom: 'The Covenant of Grace is Cloathed with the Church-
Covenant in a Political visible Church-way'... 'God delights in
us, when we are in his Covenant, his Covenant reacheth to his
church, and wee being members of that Church....[398] *[sic]*

Similarly, Walker uses Browne's definitions as representative of the "usual Calvinistic sense, and nothing peculiar to Browne."[399] He

---

397   Ibid, 427.
398   Perry Miller, *The New England Mind: The Seventeenth Century*, 447.
399   Walker, *The Creeds and Platforms of Congregationalism*, 18.

defines the covenant community in three aspects: first; as a covenant declared by God with certain conditions; second, as a covenant made by man with certain conditions; and third, by using the "sacrament of Baptisme to seale those condicions, and couenantes"[400] [sic]. The covenant community was, in their eyes, under a significant burden to maintain the community standard with no less regard than the Old Testament patriarchs when circumcising their infant males.[401]

THE REFUSAL OF SCHISM

The Puritans' second commitment of repudiating schism was eventually to unravel. Initially, this was observable in Puritan leaders as they refused the Separatist minority their desire for John Robinson's arrival from Holland. Between 1620 and 1625, John Lyford worked with the London Company to make sure Robinson was never allowed passage while he simultaneously manipulated the increase of Puritans and Anglicans in the colony insuring that separatist tendencies did not upset the Puritan desire for *uniformity* of religion.[402] Lyford was responsible for disseminating the falsehood that the Pilgrims were guilty of intolerance because they did not observe the sacraments in the absence of their pastor Robinson. These sorts of tactics, along with the coming in of the Quakers, forced the colonies to adopt a fairly rigid position of uniformity, thus portraying

---

400   Ibid, 19.

401   McLoughlin points to quotes from Thomas Cobbet in *A Just Vindication of the Covenant and Church Estate Children of Members As Also of Their Right to Baptism,* (London: n.p. 1648), 295-296, where he says, "The Baptists sometimes argued that the whole covenant theology was fallacious because a covenant or contract implied and required 'mutuall agreement betwixt the covenanters' which could not be possible between God and a child. They felt they had scored irrefutably when they pointed out that if infant baptism was based on the precedent of circumcision, by what right did the Puritans baptize infant females?"

402   Jacob C. Meyer, *Church and State in Massachusetts from 1740-1833* (New York: Russell and Russell, 1968), 4-9.

schism as something devilish.[403] It is no surprise then that Baptist dissent in the colony was viewed with such suspicion. This Puritan demand for an established religion within the judicatory of the Massachusetts General Court was reminiscent of the Anglicans' order at Hampton Court when they originally sought reform in old England. The similarities are shocking. Bancroft, the Bishop of London, interrupted the Puritan Dr. Reynolds suggesting to King James that schismatics should not be heard and that they should be removed from the conference.[404] Ironically, now they had so treated the separatists siding with Robinson.

John Cotton, who arrived in Boston in 1631, believed church autonomy and individual rhetoric needed to be rigidly controlled. He warned the churches that blasphemers could either join together in any congregation; a Standing Church could apostatize from orthodoxy; or an errant minister could allow hypocrites into the church.[405] Consequently, the fear of dissension was always near the surface in the matrix of Puritan culture. In this environment, Baptist coexistence in the colonies was virtually impossible. This formation of orthodoxy produced an intolerance of any rigid Biblicism. Because all dissension was understood to be a misinterpretation or misunderstanding of Scripture, Cotton taught that although it was wrong to persecute a man against his conscience, no man's conscience could naturally compel him against the truth. Thus, to force the truth upon a dissenter was

403   Ibid, 4.
404   Mountfield, *The Church and the Puritans*, 10.
405   Gaius Glenn Atkins and Frederick L. Fagley, *History of American Congregationalism* (Boston and Chicago: The Pilgrim Press, 1942), 81.

not a violation of his conscience.[406] It was rather a vindication of
biblical truth over the impediment of a faulty thought process.
Cotton's opinions helped in the establishment of both the
Massachusetts' General Court and the Cambridge Platform of 1648
and were voiced in his book *The Way of Congregational Churches
Cleared* published the same year. Consequently, all open dissent
would not be tolerated under the Cambridge system. The "all" in the
1648 measure included "Idolatry, Blasphemy, Heresy, venting corrupt
& pernicious opinions, that destroy the foundation."[407]

THE THREAT OF PIETISM

The third threat to the Puritan communal ideal was the fear
of an encroaching pietism. In real terms it was more actualized
by Baptist doctrine and more personified by individuals like Anne
Hutchinson than anyone else in the colonies.[408] Similar to the fear
of schism, pietism posed a serious risk to a politically structured and
ecclesiastically controlled Commonwealth.

The Antinomian Controversy of 1636-1638 was an occasion
of Puritan control running rampant. For example, the differences
which existed between justification and sanctification were always
under discussion and were most seriously argued by one of John
Cotton's former parishioners in England, Anne Hutchinson. The
Puritans thought her ideas dangerous. One key issue in the Hutchison

---

406   Miller, *The New England Mind: The Seventeenth Century*, 75.
407   Walker, *The Creeds and Platforms of Congregationalism*, 237.
408   Anne Hutchinson stood as the most notorious example of antinomian doctrine in the
Commonwealth. She and her husband William arrived in Boston in 1634, took residence in
Boston and were members of the Boston First Congregational Church under the leadership of
John Wilson. There would be as many eighty people in her home discussing the Sabbath day's
sermon with Mrs. Hutchinson offering obscure and interesting points of Puritan theology. Her
most significant act was in her declaration that the only ministers who preached a covenant
of grace were John Cotton and John Wheelwright: all the other ministers she said preached a
covenant of works.

controversy involved the doctrine of preparation as a stage in the process of conversion. The question of whether or not man needed preparation before receiving God's saving grace was vital to answering the larger question of whether man's response to law was somehow efficacious.[409] Hutchinson's answer to these questions was no, following the view of her beloved pastor John Cotton. Nearly a century later, the Great Awakening preachers would heartily agree by saying that the new birth was an instantaneous event predicated upon nothing but the preaching of the gospel accompanied by the internal urgings of the Holy Spirit to receive the gift of salvation.

Hall rightly observed regarding the ringleaders of the so-called Antinomian Controversy: "Their revolt was the first step toward the 'emancipation' of Massachusetts from the heavy burden of Puritanism."[410] Unfortunately, at the time, Antinomian threats were viewed as insidious doctrinal defects in both the civil and congregational dimensions of the colonies and considered as direct challenges to the well-being of the Commonwealth. The value of Anne Hutchinson to a discussion of pietism lay not in her offensive assertions before the ministerial community in Boston, but in her unqualified love and support of John Cotton, her former cleric in Lincolnshire, England.[411] This friendship begs the question of how John Cotton could be such a respected New England divine, while being held in such high esteem by alleged *pietist* and *antinomian* Anne Hutchinson. The answer lay in determining whether her questions

---

409   David Hall, ed., *The Antinomian Controversy 1636-1638* (Middletown: Wesleyan University Press, 1968), 19.

410   Ibid., 11.

411   Erikson, Wayward Puritans, 85.

and insights reflected similar themes being raised by Cotton, among others, regarding English Puritanism.

Puritans like Cotton had rebelled against the entrenched hierarchy within the Church of England by asserting that salvation was mediated through the authoritative Scriptures and the Holy Spirit to individuals not through an authoritative body of church bishops. Therefore, no spiritual leader had the capacity to determine the validity of an individual's claim of owning salvation. Valid salvation in the Puritan mind was predicated upon observable works in individual professors, or a "reformation of manners" in the same. At the height of the Antinomian Controversy in 1636, Cotton exchanged a series of letters with Thomas Shepherd who questioned Cotton on his views concerning this idea of a believer demonstrating observable works as evidence of their salvation. One man believed that justification was made apparent by external evidences, while Puritan fathers like Shepherd believed the reality of salvation could never be discovered by visible works. Such polar extremes of opinion demonstrated, at least to the Puritan leaders, why "heresy" of this order needed to be dealt with so severely. Simpson explained:

> *They were probably right in thinking that order was possible on no other terms; but so was Anne Hutchinson when she accused them of substituting a covenant of works for a Covenant of Grace. Obedience to an external order, rather than immediate confrontation with God, was becoming, in spite of its formal theology, the criterion of New England Puritanism.*[412]

However, for the sake of a fledgling Commonwealth, such persons could not be tolerated, and the Puritan separation between

---

412   Simpson, *Puritanism in Old and New England*, 34-35.

"the word" and the "inner light" could not be removed. Consequently, in November of 1637, a civil trial was held in Boston in the form of a ministerial synod formed by all Massachusetts ministers including Thomas Hooker and Samuel Stone of Connecticut. The event was considered vital enough to the Commonwealth that all the expenses of the entire proceedings and its delegates were taken from the general treasury.[413] Erikson explained the scene:

> *Governor Winthrop and Mistress Hutchinson faced each other across the bare wooden table which served as a bench, they wore the expressions of an austere magistrate and of a brash, contentious housewife; but the voices in which they spoke carried a tone of far greater significance. Mrs. Hutchinson symbolized the lively enthusiasm of the old Puritanism while Governor Winthrop symbolized the political maturity of the new....[414]*

In the attempt to identify and ultimately excise Antinomianism, no less than eighty-two errors were discovered among the parties of Hutchinson and Wheelwright, along with "nine unwholesome expressions."[415] Both Wheelwright (Hutchinson's brother in-law) and Hutchinson were banished from the colony the same year and settled in what is now New Hampshire and later in New York. As her former pastor, John Cotton recaptured, to some degree, his former image of an austere Puritan father by renouncing all sympathies with Anne Hutchinson and her alleged antinomian opinions. It is doubtful that

---

413   Sweet, *Religion in Colonial America*, 93-94.
414   Erikson, *Wayward Puritans*, 92-93.
415   Ibid., 90.

he ever excised all question from the minds of his peers, but he at least did so publicly.

In retrospect of the first 100 years of the Commonwealth, no event better epitomizes the Puritan effort to rid itself of all forms of piety which exceeded their established criteria or overtly challenged the authority of the clergy class. This resulted in the formation of an ecclesiastical code, a standard of orthodoxy which became the means of censoring all dissension by the ruling Puritan party. As an addend to the 1638 decision came the more formal decision of November 13, 1644,[416] which sanctioned the State banishment of "Anabaptists." Backus reported the ominous decision of the General Court:

They have been incendiaries of the commonwealths, and
the infectors of persons in main matters of religion, and the
troublers of churches in all places where they have been, and
that they who have held the baptizing of infants unlawful, have
usually held other errors or heresies together therewith....[417]

Cotton admitted that for many of these Anabaptists, heresy did not involve the denial of civil authority, predestination, apostasy, or original sin but only their refusal of infant baptism.[418] Therefore the 1638 decision became the benchmark to which all expansions of the original decision would be justified. Heterodoxy would be easily defined as anything outside of the established orthodox standard, and

---

416   In essence, this legal decision was just an extension of the Commonwealth's authority against the threat of piety outside the perimeters of the Standing Order Churches. This act of the General Court was aimed at dealing with the fact that "Anabaptists increased and spread in the country." Backus noted that the specific intent of the law was to guard against such as refused to countenance infant baptism and the use of secular force in religious affairs, which the Baptists have ever done from that day to this. See Backus, 1: 126-127.
417   Backus, *A History of New England, with Particular Reference to the Denomination of Christians Called Baptists*, 1: 126.
418   Ibid, 1: 53.

the refusal of infant baptism was considered central to heterodoxy and dissent.

THE DOCTRINE OF PREPARATION

The Puritan view of election was a modification of classical Calvinism found in the Westminster Confession. With its inherent suggestion that the hopeful election of an infant child begins with sprinkling, Puritan salvation became a multi-layered morphology of steps culminating in the soul that eventually closes with Christ. When Backus and the Separate-Baptists called infant baptism a biblical travesty, they were not just rejecting it, but an entire ideology which they saw as stretching all the way back to the early third century.[419] This is precisely where the SBBM broke ranks with the first reformation as the progenitors of its second wave in the New World.

Preparation involved two separate ideas in the Puritan mind. First was the concept of bringing up of covenant children under the care, teaching, and necessary discipline of the church. These children, *presumably* in adulthood, would be qualified to personally believe the gospel. The second element of the preparation process was that children must enter adulthood before reaching a salvation experience finally identifying them as part of God's elect. Miller explains that process:

A phenomena of Calvinism everywhere in the century was a tendency
to analyze the process of regeneration into a series of moments,
but that strain which invented the federal theology was impelled,

---

419   Backus recognized that infant baptism, state control of the church, and the enforcement of temporal penalties for dissent groups as capitulation to "heathen philosophy" which could all be traced to the early third century and continuing on through the first Reformation up to the Puritans in New England. See Backus, *A History of New England with Particular Reference to the Denomination of Christians Called Baptists*, 2: iii-vi.

by the nature of the metaphor, to set off an initial period wherein
he who is about to believe begins to learn what to expect.[420]

Under the Puritan system, men could make themselves ready
for salvation by studying the requirements of the covenant and how
they fell short of its demands. This mindset often produced a sense
of intense personal introspection. Puritan sources of the period tell
us that the colonists often felt disheartened by it. They pleaded their
unworthiness; they spoke of themselves as sinners lacking any hope
that God would spare them from his anger, yet they voiced their
dependence on the risen Christ. Puritan fathers like John Cotton
systematized the doctrine of salvation into a series of preparatory steps
which articulated Calvinism in a manner previously not known. This,
of course, differed from Calvin's idea of salvation which to him was a
forcible event and allowed no time for preparation. The idea of some
form of preparation would have smacked of a meritorious work, an
affront to the sovereignty of God. Recognizing this, Miller asserted
that "regeneration through covenant meant that men could make
themselves ready, at least by studying the nature of covenants."[421]
Consequently, the preparation idea suggested that every man was able
to *predispose* himself for grace even though grace was arbitrarily and
efficaciously offered by God.[422]

This kind of thinking has often gone unnoticed by observers
of Puritan theology. By ignoring the implications of the preparation
doctrine upon the typical New England minister, much less his

---

420   Miller, *The New England Mind: From Colony to Province*, 55.
421   Miller, *The New England Mind: The Seventeenth Century*, 56.
422   This breach in classical Calvinist doctrine may be seen as one of the precursors or
catalysts of the future "evangelical Calvinism" and its continued development into the broad
understanding of the general atonement doctrine which was exacerbated by the individual
"new birth" experience and its attendant voluntaristic churches. This shift of the election
doctrine directly affected the Separate-Baptist's view of the church-universal eventuating in its
near abandonment by the close of the nineteenth century.

parishioner, historians are forced to assume that nothing within the pre-existing Puritan theological system contributed to either the need for or the justification for the Great Awakening. If that were true, one may ask of the Whitefield revival, awakened from what? Wright recommended New England had actually been moving in that direction for over a century, and in fact, whose roots, were deeply rooted in Puritanism *itself*.[423] Heimert called this the essential working out of Puritanism's "own modifications" of classical Calvinism which he identified to be in the preparation doctrine.[424]

The preparation doctrine further demonstrates that many of the clergy observed the instantaneous nature of the new birth in their own churches during the Awakening and considered it to be "enthusiasm" or emotion-based because there was no logical or *observable* pattern to the phenomena of conversion. Early Puritan concerns about uncontrolled enthusiasm and subsequent civil disorder with Anne Hutchinson differed little from the Awakening concerns regarding instantaneous salvation.

By 1740, with the advent of Whitefield's new birth sermon, the idea of preparation for salvation was essentially dealt a death blow by the new-birth experience. The multi-layered conditioning and morphology of the election process would nearly vanish in religious discourse as a result.[425] Technically, election would remain, but its role

---

423   Conrad Wright, *The Beginnings of Unitarianism in America* (Boston: Starr King Press, 1955), 10.
424   As a co-editor, Heimert makes this observation in an opening discussion which included the preparation doctrine in New England theology. See Heimert, ed., *Religion and the American Mind: From the Great Awakening to the Revolution*, 4.
425   For the latest and best appraisal of New England Theology and how Edwards' theology evolved, see Sweeney, ed., *The New England Theology: From Jonathan Edwards to Edwards Amassa Park*, 26. The editors, by careful documentation, demonstrate the logical progression of theological thought which came to be identified as the "New Divinity," and concluded that Edwards's distinction between a sinner's "natural ability" and "moral inability" to repent was theological grist for the mills of countless New England churchmen up to the time of the Civil War.

in a visible congregation now controlled by voluntaristic acts would remain under constant pressure in the SBBM and its subsequent commitment to revivalism.

THE TRANSFORMING DYNAMIC: THE NEW BIRTH

The doctrinal controversies of the New-Light Separates all were fundamentally connected to the reformation doctrine of the new birth. The biblical injunction "ye must be born again" was the primary, even the exclusive message of the Awakeners. Whitefield's sermon on "The Necessity of the New Birth" was given credit by the evangelist himself for the initial English awakening in London, Bristol, Gloucester, and Gloucestershire. He reported that the sermon sold well to persons of all denominations and was "dispersed very much both at home and abroad."[426] Lambert demonstrated that Colonial printer Ben Franklin made "large sales" of Whitefield's journals and printed sermons heavily weighted by conversion themes.[427]

The revival model actually had its immediate roots in the "Justification by Faith" doctrine of Edwards, who in 1735 initiated the Northampton revival with a series on the subject of salvation through faith in Christ. The new birth and its associated biblical assurances of God's vital presence in the believer's life stood in stark contrast to the Standing Orders on both sides of the Atlantic. In Colonial New England, the Calvinist doctrines of the reformation fathered by John Cotton, William Ames, and Thomas Hooker, had drifted into a theological fog of irrelevance by a shifting Puritan ideal of gaining membership at the expense of doctrinal purity, particularly since 1662. Some Congregational leaders discovered, to their chagrin, that

---

426   George Whitefield, ed., *Whitefield's Journals*, new ed. (London: Banner of Truth Trust, 1960), 86.
427   Frank Lambert, "Subscribing for Profits and Piety: The Friendship of Benjamin Franklin and George Whitefield," *The William and Mary Quarterly* 50, no. 3 (1993): 540.

they could not maintain doctrinal purity and societal control in an increasingly market-driven culture,[428] especially when conversion in its biblical form was presented in the marketplace by those who, unlike themselves, had personally experienced it.

In light of the Puritans' earlier commitment to the visible church identifying the elect, Goen suggested that the "golden age for the Separates lay no farther back in history than the early Puritan era, when a testimony of 'personal' religious experience was expected from everyone who applied for membership in a visible church."[429] However, Goen appears to underestimate the entrenched, almost subconscious sentiments held by the Puritan fathers concerning infant sprinkling, making this assertion even more doubtful. It also seems to equate the phenomenon of new birth theology with an already- existing mindset within the Puritan order, thereby gravely underestimating the shocking response most Great Awakening converts had to the *immediacy* of their own conversions. Whitefield stressed this as the touchstone of the new birth. Marini explained:

Whitefield shortened the morphology of conversion, swept away the casuistry of covenantalism, and focused the issue of salvation on the moment of conversion itself. His God, though still demanding just punishment for sin, actively sought the sinner's salvation, requiring them only to reach out for the "free grace" available through faith in Christ. For Whitefield did not operate through slow-moving "legal" stages of growth.[430]

---

428   Gaustad, *The Great Awakening in New England*, 15.
429   Goen, *Revivalism and Separatism in New England, 1740-1800: Strict Congregationalist and Separate-Baptists in the Great Awakening*, 159-160.
430   Marini, *Radical Sects of Revolutionary New England*, 13.

But once again, by placing regeneration within the grasp of the individual hearer, the election doctrine tended toward a theological arbitrariness. The language of the revival sermons blasted away at the entrenched morphology of Puritan salvation and asserted the need of immediate repentance without life-long preparation. In his "Solemn Warning" sermon of 1735, Gilbert Tennant commanded his listeners:

Arise, call upon thy God, if so be he will think upon us that we perish not.... And especially knowing the Time, that now it is high Time to awake out of Sleep.... Awake unclean ye Adulterers, and Whoremongers, and remember that without a speedy Repentance.... Awake ye Sabbath-Breakers and reform....[431]

Secondly, if immediacy was shocking to the Standing Order, so were the implications of the Whitefield's brand of evangelicalism. Although the evangelist flatly subscribed to the rigidly Calvinist thirty-nine articles of the Anglican Church, his invitation to sinners in the course of his sermons implied, even demanded an arbitrary, highly individualistic response to the gospel. In these terms, the concept of salvation could no longer be understood as belonging solely to an act of God's sovereignty but man's willing response to the gospel. Gillies reported Whitefield wept on one occasion:

You blame me for weeping...but how can I help it, when you will not weep for yourselves, though your immortal souls are upon the verge of destruction, and, for aught I know, you are hearing your last sermon, and may never more have an opportunity to have Christ offered to you.[432]

---

431   Richard L. Bushman, *The Great Awakening, Documents on the Revival of Religion, 1740-1745* (Chapel Hill and London: University of North Carolina Press, 1969), 16-17.
432   Rev. John Gillies, *Memoirs of the Life of the Reverend George Whitefield, A.M.*

But what would a second, third, fourth, or one hundredth offer of Christ do if one was not one of the elect? Furthermore, the proximity of one's soul to hell and "destruction" would have no significance for one of the chosen if, after all, God arbitrarily saves only those whom he foreordained to salvation. If in fact, as Edwards had asserted, that man would only exercise affections because God had placed them there, why would such subjects need any human coaching such as that suggested by Whitefield? For him, Calvinism was defined more from the perspective of the individual gospel-hearer who needed to respond to God's irresistible grace because that individual "may never more have an opportunity to have Christ offered to you." This tacit approval of the power of the individual to decide for Christ brought criticism by those who accused Whitefield of Arminianism equal to that of Wesley. Such criticisms were not entirely unfounded. On another occasion aboard ship he disciplined a boy for disobeying his command to say his bed-time prayer. After the boy recanted, Whitefield remarked that if more parents would be faithful in breaking the wills of their children, conversion would come much easier and oftener.[433] This is similar to both the sermons and songs among Second Great Awakening evangelists who, despite their professed Calvinism, preached the Bible and encouraged hymns which taught free-will principles,[434] particularly about reaching children before they became hardened in sin. On yet another occasion, the evangelist's reply to a group of questioning Presbyterians suggests that he was forced to defend his own understanding of contemporary Calvinism.[435]

(Hartford: Andrus and Starr, 1812), 25.

433   Whitefield, ed., *Whitefield's Journals*, 146.

434   This phenomenon, which began in the first Great Awakening, was much more fully developed by the turn of the nineteenth century and will be discussed later in some detail.

435   George Whitefield, *George Whitefield's Letters* (Edinburgh: Banner of Truth Trust, 1976; reprint, This edition, with additional letters, first published by the Banner of Truth Trust 1976), 256.

In reality, it was this—not the later revivalism, nor Finney and the New Divinity—which marked the beginning of what came to be called evangelical or moderate Calvinism and its evolution within the revivalist tradition.[436] By preaching the new birth as if all needed to respond to the gospel message, which essentially meant (to the common man) that all could respond, Whitefield set forth a whole new methodology of gospel preaching and, as a professed Calvinist, appeared to place his tacit approval upon it.

Churches which fully participated in the Awakening were now confronted with the explicit problems brought on by new-birth preaching, requests for believers' baptism, and their relations with those who testified of membership but had not yet been converted. Additionally, these new Awakening Congregationalists (Separates) were unwilling to compromise the principle that "visible saints are the only fit matter for a gospel church,"[437] and the context of such unwillingness was inextricably tied to an instantaneous new birth preachment.[438] Later, Backus would unwittingly qualify the extension of Baptist principles as first being "that saving faith is necessary

---

436   Boardman, one of the seminal authors who traced the developments within New England Theology from its inception to the middle of the nineteenth century almost ignores the unique changes which Great Awakening revivalism placed upon the election doctrine, particularly by Whitefield. This modifying of the election doctrine—in the preaching (not Calvinistic creed) of Whitefield and those in the frontier revivals—did not result in the same theological heresies associated with Finney and the "New Divinity."

437   Goen, *Revivalism and Separatism in New England, 1740-1800: Strict Congregationalist and Separate-Baptists in the Great Awakening*, 38.

438   The new birth, usually connected with revival was, in effect, the beginning of the long evangelical tradition of holding gospel preaching as a fundamental tenet of their movement. The implications of this early tradition proved to be important for church growth, particularly among the Baptists during the Second Awakening. Participating Presbyterians often jettisoned creedal Calvinism in favor of preaching the new-birth to teeming crowds attending camp-meetings in Virginia, North Carolina, Kentucky, and Tennessee. Many of these converts submitted to believers' baptism and entered directly into Baptist churches throughout the developing westward frontier. For an excellent treatment of the Second Awakening and its contribution to denominational development, particularly the Baptists, see John B. Boles, *The Great Revival* (Lexington: The University Press of Kentucky, 1972).

to give any soul a true right to communion in the church of Christ."[439]
When converts began to pour into existing Congregational churches
in Boston in 1742, immediately, battle lines began to be drawn on
spiritual issues perceived by new converts as being directly related to
their new life in Christ.

As Whitefield, Tennent, and others had demonstrated earlier,
separation in some form was to become an axiom of new birth
theology, which the Separates, and finally the Baptists, fully exploited
to their own advantage.

SEPARATISM: THE GREAT AWAKENING REALITY

The Great Awakening left its most enduring legacy not
necessarily with the populace who heard its famed evangelists but with
the churches left to absorb the newly converted after the preachers
were gone. Guelzo and Sweeney argued that the need for revival itself
was a judgment upon the Standing Order's failure and that "its logical
end was to turn people into come-outers...and to inflate a radical
individualism."[440] The Great Awakening insured that any revival,
and any subsequent separations, would not rest on the Baptists. It
would in fact come strangely through Anglican George Whitefield
who *publicly* rejected sectarianism and denominational disputing.
Despite Whitefield's attempt to walk a non-partisan line of advancing
the doctrine of new birth, schism became an inevitable product of a
revitalized soteriology. Hard-line separatism disseminated by James
Davenport is often noted as the progenitor of the cleavage in churches
in the post-awakening period, but its perennial seeds were likely

---

439   Backus, *Church History of New England from 1620 to 1804: Containing a View
of the Principles and Practice, Declensions and Revivals, Oppression and Liberty of the
Churches, and a Chronological Table With a Memoir of the Author*, 176.
440   Sweeney, ed., *The New England Theology: From Jonathan Edwards to Edwards
Amassa Park*, 17.

planted by Whitefield in New England during the course of his initial preaching tour in 1740-1741.[441] This same upheaval, precipitated by the preaching of the new-birth, bringing schism to the Standing Churches, also demanded a refocusing on requirements for church membership.

For the most part, conscientious historians, determined to demonstrate a fair-mindedness on the subject, are reticent to ascribe separatist principles to the Grand Itinerant, not only out of a respect for his extraordinary piety but also because he himself denied such charges.[442] Whitefield's professed position on the matter of denominationalism was clearly non-committal.[443] He wished to remain neutral in relationship to sectarian views, but with his undying commitment to the doctrines of new birth, regenerate church members, and ministers, such a position was little more than idealism born of virtue rather than genuine experience. This trans-denominational attitude was made clear in one instance by his refusal to acknowledge the exclusive claims of the Erskine brothers over a church government skirmish in Dunfermline, Scotland. Upon his initial visit there during the summer of 1741, Whitefield rejected the claim that it was necessary for him to leave the Church of England in order to prove himself an "Instrument of the Reformation."[444] He clearly saw himself as a Church of England priest wholly committed to the orthodoxy of the thirty-nine articles.[445] Filial biographer Arnold Dallimore was even forced to admit that, Whitefield's Anglican

---

441   Maurice Whitman Armstrong, "Religious Enthusiasm and Separatism in Colonial New England," *Harvard Theological Review* 38 (1945): 127.
442   Whitefield, ed., *Whitefield's Journals*, 529.
443   Ibid, 458.
444   Gillies, *Memoirs of the Life of the Reverend George Whitefield, A.M.*, 51.
445   Ibid, 185.

orthodoxy aside, his preaching opposed unregenerate men of his own communion. Dallimore noted that his ministry:

...brought him into this close fellowship with Presbyterians,
Dutch Reformed and Baptists. Thus he had come to a
position in which not denominational adherence but
evangelical soundness was the criterion, and his work
had become non-denominational in character.[446]

The evangelist's desire to remain above the denominational fray became intensely apparent after his return to America in 1744 to find the revival to be in serious disrepair. By his own design, having left it in the hands of Gilbert Tennent and James Davenport to forward the revival's progress, the lesser itinerants began a scorching campaign against unconverted ministers and the need of people to separate from their parish churches to establish separate congregations led by regenerate clergymen. Tennent's message went beyond Whitefield's mere identification of unconverted clergy to a near savage denunciation of them.[447] Davenport then went from denunciation to disassociation by urging new converts to seek out converted ministers and spiritually awakened groups of Christians.[448] Now, with separation principles severely dividing his earlier alliances, Whitefield was forced to make apologies to several key Boston clergymen on account of the possible misunderstanding of his words:

I would promote or encourage separations and that some would
have been encouraged to separate by my saying in my journal

---

446   Arnold A. Dallimore, *George Whitefield: The Life and Times of the Great Evangelist of the 18th Century Revival*, 2 vols. (Oxford: University Printing House, 1970), 1: 438.
447   Leonard J. Trinterud, *The Forming of an American Tradition: A Re-Examination of Colonial Presbyterianism* (Philadelphia: Westminster Press, 1949), 56-58.
448   McLoughlin, *New England Dissent 1630-1833*, 1:341.

that I found the generality of preachers preached an unknown
Christ, that the Colleges had darkness in them, even darkness that
might be felt, and that speaking of the danger of an unconverted
ministry, I said, How can a dead man beget a living Child? But I
told them these words were not wrote to imply that it was absolutely
impossible but that it was highly improbable that an unconverted
man should be made instrumental to beget souls to Christ.[449]

The distinction Whitefield needed to make here between
impossible and *improbable* to avoid open disruption reveals a kind of
reductionist methodology aimed at smoothing injured relationships
and ending discord. Similar apologies to Harvard College
demonstrated a novel willingness to coexist in the same religious
environment with unconverted clergy previously not seen in the
evangelist.[450]

In his spring tour of 1745, he preached outside Boston for
Benjamin Adams, pastor in New London. Just two years prior,
Davenport had personally declared Adams to be unconverted
and encouraged his flock to found a separate house of worship.[451]
Although, Whitefield, as leader, clearly understood the implications
of the new birth theology and its effect upon existing congregational
norms, he sought to remain outside the ecclesiastical paroxysms his
ministry created and simply preach the gospel. By maintaining this
stance, the itinerant established the greatest possibility for future
evangelistic opportunity.

Historians at this point are often guilty of a lack of real
objectivity regarding the evangelist's professed neutrality regarding

---

449   Whitefield, ed., *Whitefield's Journals*, 529.
450   Harry S. Stout, *The Divine Dramatist* (Grand Rapids: William B. Eerdmans
Publishing Company, 1991), 194.
451   Ibid, 91.

issues of separation.[452] It is clear that separation was not the solution he personally promoted, but since it was not openly repudiated at the first, division was viewed as a viable option by his ministry associates and new converts. In this case, an evangelical call to salvation clearly meant the probability of dissension leading to schism within existing churches. Marini goes even further:

> *Whitefield rejected the century-old New England principle of theological diversity within ecclesiastical unity, demanding the indwelling Spirit rather than the all-too human workings of Puritan tradition...he also outlined a social and cultural structure for the saints to adopt and urged them to do so regardless of the consequences to themselves or to worldly institutions.[453]*

By the time of Whitefield's second tour, this pattern of separatist preaching had been recognized and publicly criticized by several leading ministers in Boston, including prestigious Harvard College. Harvard's leaders made their vitriol public in their "Testimony" pamphlet war against him.[454] He answered it with

---

452   Arnold Dallimore, author of the splendid two-volume work on Whitefield was reticent to attach any separatist tendencies to the evangelist personally. Likely, speaking of the new birth message, he said that "sometimes the separations were based on doctrinal necessity, there were also those that arose merely from personal strife and a desire for notoriety" which entered the Awakening during 1742 and 1743, and "did great harm to the work." Here Dallimore is obviously referring to James Davenport and Gilbert Tennent who took over the reins of the revival directly from Whitefield. See Dallimore, *George Whitefield: The Life and Times of the Great Evangelist of the 18th Century Revival*, 2: 187. Gaustad, wanting to exonerate Whitefield from any substantive blame for separatism and schism, said that with the entrance of Davenport and Tennent "the Awakening had been brought to a sad pass." Gaustad, *The Great Awakening in New England*, 39. Diminishing the utter impact of Biblical revelation upon the Standing Order in New England and the Middle Colonies, editors Alan Heimert and Perry Miller said, "The central conflict of the Awakening was thus not theological but one of opposing theories of the human psychology."

453   Marini, *Radical Sects of Revolutionary New England*, 14.

454   Perry Miller and Alan Heimert, eds., *The Great Awakening, Documents Illustrating the Crisis and Its Consequences*, The American Heritage Series (New York: Bobbs-Merrill, 1967), 340-353.

profuse apologies and humble admissions of immature judgments, but the die had effectively been cast, whether or not Whitefield perceived himself to be an apologist for separatism.

Elsewhere, it was plain that the scatter gun which shot broadside at unconverted clergyman had been aimed like a rifle at the Church of England. Whitefield had become "an Anglican Jeremiah"[455] against the perceived apostasy of his native church. Similarly, in South Carolina, with tensions running high between the dissenters and the Society for the Propagation of the Gospel (hereafter the S.P.G.) missionaries, Whitefield had earlier taken up their cause against Alexander Garden, the Bishop of London's Commissary in Charleston in several well-publicized skirmishes. Like Commissaries William Vessey of New York and Archibald Cummings of Philadelphia in November of 1739, Garden refused Whitefield the use of his church pulpit at St. Philip's in January of 1740.[456] Whitefield instead preached that afternoon in the meeting house of a local congregational dissenter Josiah Smith. In that same month the evangelist wrote and printed his letter stating that the seventeenth century Anglican Archbishop Tillotson..."knew no more of Christianity than Mohamet."[457] The

---

455   Kenney 3d, "George Whitefield, Dissenter Priest of the Great Awakening, 1739-1741," 88.

456   Whitefield, in keeping with the practice in the Church of England, would request the use the church in a community he was visiting. If accepted, the evangelist would preach there, if not, he would go to a common meeting area or to a private home. In both Philadelphia and New York, the Church of England Commissaries refused him use of their church pulpits, and he was forced to preach outdoors to far greater crowds than either of the churches could have accommodated. See Dallimore, *George Whitefield: The Life and Times of the Great Evangelist of the 18th Century Revival*, 1: 434, William Howland Kenney 3d, "Alexander Garden and George Whitefield: The Significance of Revivalism in South Carolina, 1738-1741," *South Carolina Historical Society* 71 (1970): 3.

457   Whitefield, *George Whitefield's Letters*, 505.

evangelist appeared to desire that nothing be left to imagination in his spiritual description of the Anglican leader.

Garden decided against the open dissension going any further and cited the itinerant to appear before his own ecclesiastical court to answer charges concerning his preaching in dissenting meeting houses and failing to use the Book of Common Prayer. The four-day trial accomplished little more than deepening the schism between the dissenting community and the Standing Order and served to further widen their perception of the commissary's imposition of authority over colonial religious interests. Garden had inadvertently reminded New Englanders, "whose religious traditions stemmed from seventeenth century English dissent,"[458] of their own efforts to live free from autocratic religious conformity. It was only weeks after the Garden trial was over that the evangelist entirely gave up his Sunday morning attendance at his own church and instead began to attend the Baptist, Presbyterian, and other dissenting meetinghouses.[459] Whitefield would later comment on his pronounced influence upon the growth of Baptists, particularly in New England through itinerant evangelism, having been reported to have "pleasantly said, many of his chickens had turned to ducks, and gone into the water."[460] Speaking of those who had received the new birth as chicks he appeared dispassionate about them turning into Baptists. This evolutionary step would have been unconscionable without countenancing a separatist mentality. He offered no apology about them having "gone into the water," as if they had gone too far. The non-rancorous metaphor seems to say that the "duck" status effectually culminated their "chick"

---

458   Kenney 3d, "Alexander Garden and George Whitefield: The Significance of Revivalism in South Carolina, 1738-1741," 12.
459   Whitefield, ed., *Whitefield's Journals*, 400-402.
460   David Benedict, *A General History of the Baptist Denomination in America* (New York: Colby, 1848), 1: 141.

beginnings, suggesting that they had pursued their ecclesiological principles all the way to the most notorious in the dissent community. This summation serves to identify Whitefield with the separatism which characterized the schismatic Congregational New Light Separates, many of which would go all the way to the Baptists by the end of the century.

He further commented that "two or three dissenting ministers, by my advice, agreed to set up a weekly lecture. I advised the people, since the gospel was not preached in the church, to go and hear it in the meetinghouses."[461] Any claims to the contrary in regard to the newly converted being influenced toward some form of separatism by Whitefield should likely be abandoned. Bruce Hindmarsh suggested here that separatism in relation to Whitefield and the Awakening was less intentional than Whitefield's stated ambivalence to visible church forms. However unintentional though, he admitted that "Whitefield could not prevent divisions within the evangelical movement. In some cases he even precipitated them."[462] The separatist demands of the new birth doctrine were probably understood by the evangelist far more than he verbalized them openly. His inability to encourage fresh converts to maintain their allegiance to the Church of England only underscored his own unwillingness to continue outward support.[463] The openly hostile opposition of Garden in Charleston, and those like him in New England, had convinced him of this course of action.

Whitefield's dissenting persona was further substantiated by Dr. Benjamin Colman, a dissenting Boston minister who wrote the Bishop of London and suggested that New England could get along

---

461   Whitefield, ed., *Whitefield's Journals*, 444.
462   Mark Husbands and Daniel J. Treier, ed., *The Community of the Word: Toward an Evangelical Ecclesiology* (Downers Grove: Inter-Varsity Press, 2005), 27-28.
463   Peter Naylor, in his study of English Particular Baptists, thought that the nub of Anglican dissent rested with Whitefield and that the Baptist sympathy with him was vested in the evangelist's dissenting persona. See Naylor, *Calvinism, Communion, and the Baptists*, 64.

quite nicely without the S.P.G. (Anglican) missionaries.[464] What
Colman was cynically suggesting to the Bishop was commonly felt
in the breast of many a colonial citizen who understood their brief
American history. This not only identified Whitefield with the latent
dissent within the early Colonial Puritan establishment but also served
to justify the continued existence of dissenting clergyman like Colman,
Foxcroft, and Prince, along with their respective meetinghouses. The
fine line of demarcation between Whitefield's dissenting and the
excesses of Tennent and Davenport is revealed in the complaint letter
of fourteen revival-supporting ministers printed in the Boston Evening
Post of July 5, 1742, wherein they condemned the latter's methods
and confirmed their intentions of refusing Davenport their pulpits.[465]
The presence of Colman's signature, along with the thirteen other
dissenters, serves to demonstrate that a respectable dissension existed
which opposed the uncontrolled schismatic tendencies of Davenport
and others.[466] White, prejudiced in his treatment of Whitefield and
his association with Tennent and particularly Davenport, stated that
on December 13, 1740, Gilbert Tennent, after Whitefield's departure
for England, "according to agreement with revivalists in New England
and in the Middle colonies, arrived in Boston to help maintain the
emotionalism of the Awakening."[467] However, emotionalism was never
clearly attached to Whitefield as it had been to Davenport at this point
except by his most virulent enemies.[468] Clearly, the pro-revivalists

---

464   *Papers Relating to the History of the Church in Massachusetts, 1676-1785*, ed.
William Stevens Perry (Hartford: 1873), 302-303.
465   As quoted from Eugene E. White, "Decline of the Great Awakening in New
England: 1741-1746," *The New England Quarterly* 24, no. 1 (1951): 42.
466   Ibid.
467   Ibid, 36.
468   One of Whitefield's most implacable foes at this point was Charles Chauncy,
pastor the First Church of Boston. Chauncy believed that the presence of any emotionalism
or fanaticism in the revival made null and void the revival being a work of the Spirit of God.
Several Boston ministers and Harvard University were influenced by Chauncy's virulent
rejection of the Awakening. For an excellent treatment of Chauncy's view of the Awakening

wished to maintain the thesis that dissent and desire for church clarity were not rooted in emotionalism and schism but in pre-established Puritan principles. Backus would later do the same but also would demonstrate a commitment toward ecclesiastical purity shared, in his view, by Anabaptist forebears three centuries earlier.[469] The revivalists understood that Whitefield was irreplaceable in his ability and power to strengthen this present cause. Kenney commented on this issue:

George Whitefield's unique position as an anti-establishmentarian Anglican defined much of his revivalistic power in the American colonies. Widespread colonial resentment of Anglican influence in America provided a recurring source of tension which he, like no other preacher, could exploit.[470]

The Colonial resentment forged within the Puritan heritage of New England Whitefield found deeply attractive.[471] To him it was his native land without the exclusivity of his native church. The freedom to preach the gospel under so many different worship expressions appeared to him to be the essence of an unfettered Christianity. This would eventually manifest itself in demonstrable growth among the Presbyterians, Congregationalists, and the Baptists (particularly those Baptists in the southern colonies).[472] Gaustad counted

---

as opposed to Jonathan Edward's view see *Rationalism and Enthusiasm* in Conrad Cherry, *The Theology of Jonathan Edwards: A Reappraisal* (Garden City, New York: Doubleday & Company, Inc., 1966), 164-185.

469   Backus, *A Discourse, Concerning the Materials, the Manner of Building, and Power of Organizing the Church of Christ*, 32.

470   Kenney 3d, "George Whitefield, Dissenter Priest of the Great Awakening, 1739-1741.", 92.

471   Dallimore, *George Whitefield: The Life and Times of the Great Evangelist of the 18th Century Revival*, 543.

472   Ibid., 522

...nine pro-revivalist, three anti-revivalist, and three neutral.
Five churches fully supported the Awakening (Brattle St,
Old South, Second, New North, and New South), while one,
Hollis Street, was opposed to it. New Brick and West were
neutral, first was divided. The City's one Presbyterian
church, pastored by John Moorhead, was as determined in its
support as the one Baptist church was in its opposition.[473]

The greatest effects of the revival were felt in its aftermath. Gaustad comments, "Flood waters normally display all their vengeful fury as they advance, while their retreat is chastened and still. But in New England, the religious 'Broyls' were far more in evidence as the Great Awakening departed than as it entered."[474] Therefore, the questions washed up by biblical conversion, namely, separatism, did not really involve its legitimacy but rather the degree of its manifestation. The strict Separate-Congregationalists, especially the Baptists, were willing to follow these doctrines to their logical conclusions. Those separates not willing, eventually re-assimilated into existing Congregational churches or simply ceased to exist.[475]

In the receding waters of the Awakening flood, one can identify how these doctrinal issues divided the Old Lights, New Lights, and Separates,[476] and specifically, how those issues evolved into the strict Biblicism among the Separates into an emerging Baptist movement.

---

473   Gaustad, *The Great Awakening in New England.*, 59.
474   Ibid, 62.
475   Marini, *Radical Sects of Revolutionary New England*, 4.
476   Goen, *Revivalism and Separatism in New England, 1740-1800: Strict Congregationalist and Separate-Baptists in the Great Awakening*, 33-35.

THE SBBM: IN PURSUIT OF THE PURE CHURCH

The Puritans had concluded that the earlier notion of a gathered church, consisting only of visible saints, was not workable in the New England experiment. McLoughlin explained:

> *Puritans feared the depravity of man too much to trust that*
> *God would be willing to save souls with sufficient regularity*
> *to preserve Christian civilization without considerable*
> *support and assistance from the institutions of Church*
> *and State. That was why he had ordained them.*[477]

By "Christian Civilization" McLoughlin was referring to the Massachusetts theocracy. The idea of any particular church having absolute autonomy to self-government, which included the right to pursue a pure-church comprised only of regenerate souls while rejecting infant baptism, was an unthinkable possibility in the Massachusetts Commonwealth. The authority of the Massachusetts civil officials vested in the Commonwealth is revealed in the nature by which they described those who dissented from the General Court and the parish system not the individual church. Their conjecture was that the Separates and the Baptists had broken the covenant of the covenantal system and therefore were "going fast into a dreadful apostasy,"[478] maintaining that they were as guilty of rejecting the General Court as Korah was in rejecting the authority of Moses![479] This

---

477   McLoughlin, *Isaac Backus and the American Pietistic Tradition*, 63-64.
478   Backus, *A Discourse, Concerning the Materials, the Manner of Building, and Power of Organizing the Church of Christ*, 81-82.
479   This assertion from Numbers 16 is based on the narrative of Korah and his associates who believed that Moses had circumvented God's authority and was not actually the leader that God had placed over them. God's judgment upon these "dissenters" was both swift and severe, and such a judgment was suggested to Backus and his associates as a potential consequence of their separation from the Standing Church, and consequently from the Massachusetts Commonwealth.

perception underscores the civil paranoia felt within the Standing Order against Baptist antipedobaptists. It also highlights the divide which separated Puritan and Baptist views of the visible church. By perceiving the church through a *vertically* directed covenant (from man to God), infant baptism became the key to eventual salvation. Conversely, the Baptists saw the individualistic, new birth as requisite to adult membership, baptism by immersion, and the joining/ support of a church left to one's voluntary choice. This is the same type of voluntaristic membership which Briggs said characterized many English Baptists who rejected Puritan approaches for John Locke's voluntaristic church concept.[480] Briggs is accurate as he describes English voluntarism in its connection to the enlightenment views of John Locke, but colonial Baptists saw Locke's voluntarism more through the prism of believers' baptism and the free exercise of conscience in supporting the church of choice in the absence of a national church. This is why Backus saw the Baptists as having become the rightful heirs to the Second Reformation, because he perceived Puritans as having left England in search of the very ecclesiological liberty they subsequently denied Baptists. For Backus, the Congregationalists had lost both their vision and right to be called true *Puritans*. In the pursuit of true church reform, they had veered into building the same sort of intolerant national church from which they had fled.[481]

At this point in the Separate-Baptist view, the church as an institution became secondary to the individual who stood apart from

---

480   Briggs, *The English Baptists of the Nineteenth Century*, 142.
481   Backus went to some length to explain the Baptist prerogative his chapter subtitled "The Sentiments and Character of the First Planters of This Country, With Their Proceedings Down to the Year 1634." Using John Robinson and the first Plymouth Colony, Backus allows their testimony to justify the Baptist's demand for equal liberty for all people, and the right to pursue a complete reformation of the church according to their own consciences. See Backus, *A History of New England with Particular Reference to the Denomination of Christians Called Baptists*, 1: 1-38.

the visible church and alone before God. By insistence on personal conversion, consistent with Great Awakening revivalism, the SBBM "heightened the mood of Evangelicalism to its highest degree, making conversion everything, and finally stereotyping and institutionalizing this conception of Christian experience."[482] By definition then, the pure-church became a sect-style church which admitted members "only by personal choice, that is, on the basis of conscious conversion."[483]

This native individual ability to decide for salvation argued against nearly everything the State-Church professed. McNutt asserted:

> It consistently throws the whole weight of a creative idea against every form of legalism in religion, it will have no intercourse with sacramentalism of any sort, it eschews creedalism in every form, and lifts a hue and cry at every indication that civil government intends to make into religious territory.[484]

Consequently, an individual's pre-temporal election began to be seen only in the individualistic terms of the new birth. It was precipitated through the individual by the agency of the Holy Spirit and resulted in an equally individualistic priesthood of the believer before God as believed by earlier Anabaptists. McNutt further argued, "It is the doctrine of soul competency that produced the Baptist doctrine of the church."[485] Election was actually beginning to be understood through the prism of personal experience and the new

---

482   Samuel S. Hill, *Southern Churches in Crisis* (New York: Holt, Rinehart & Winston, Inc., 1967), 58.
483   Underwood, *A History of the English Baptists*, 17.
484   William Roy McNutt, *Polity and Practice in Baptist Churches* (Philadelphia: The Judson Press, 1935), 25.
485   Ibid, 22.

birth and made available through the leading of the Holy Spirit. For Backus, profession had to be connected to an actual life-change or produce an alteration in one's previous behavior, hence hearing and doing. While speaking of saving faith, Backus likened regeneration to a radical work of the Spirit whereby "the roots naturally in it are broken up and the wheat sown therein; so the new birth cannot be wrought in any but by divine revelation. It is not a creation of new faculties but the giving of new ideas and dispositions...."[486]

As Backus discussed the order of the new Separate-Baptist churches in his New England history, he set forth the soteriological standard of the movement. He affirmed his affinity for Calvin's view of election explaining:

> *That by the influence of the Holy Spirit, these persons individually, as they come into existence, are effectually called in time, That, according to God's institution, regenerate souls are the only materials for particular churches. That the right way of building such churches is by giving a personal, verbal account to the church of what God has done for their souls....*[487]

This pattern of Holy Spirit influence leading to the individual reception of Jesus Christ by faith in Christ's atonement was continually alluded to in Backus' diary insertions as a part of the standard salvation format. As a Reformed thinker, he rejected any notion that the sinner could do anything to assist God in his own salvation prior to regeneration. However, it is important to recognize

---

486   Backus, *A History of New England with Particular Reference to the Denomination of Christians Called Baptists*, 2: 264.

487   Ibid, 2: 232.

that with Backus' own conversion experience, he, like Whitefield, had begun to diminish rigid sovereignty and elevate personal choice:

My soul yielded all into his hands, fell at His feet, and was silent and calm before Him. And while I sat there, I was enabled by divine light to see the perfect righteousness of Christ and the freeness and riches of His grace, with such clearness, that my soul was drawn forth to trust Him for salvation. And I wondered that others did not also come to Him who had enough for all.[488]

Interestingly, he admitted two things here that would appear to contradict his own strict Calvinist creed. First, he suggested that God comes *not* to the elect sinner with irresistible grace but that "my soul was drawn forth to trust him," establishing salvation in the realm of the human will by *actively trusting.* In contrast, Baptist historian Francis Wayland illustrates how personal salvation had been formerly comprehended by such Baptists as John Gill. Wayland, a Massachusetts pastor, told of a conversation he had with one of the members of his church who had a very worldly family. He told the father that he wanted to discuss religion with him and his family. Wayland offered the testimony of the father who admittedly followed Gill.

He plainly told me that he did not wish any one to converse with his children on that subject. If they were elected, God would convert them in his own time: but if not, talking would do them no good, it would only make them hypocrites. He was, I believe, the last pillar of Gillism then remaining in the church.[489]

---

488   McLoughlin, *Isaac Backus and the American Pietistic Tradition*, 14, emphasis added.

489   Francis Wayland, *Notes on the Principles and Practices of Baptist Churches* (New

Secondly, the Middleboro pastor *wondered that others did not come to Him*, appearing to suggest (at least inwardly) that others could come if they so chose but ultimately chose not to come. This is clearly a gospel liberty which Backus did not technically support but one that Separate-Baptists had begun to accept as a credible position well before Backus died.[490] Secondly, in his closing phrase about God's grace *who had enough for all*, he appears to have thought that the grace he experienced was somehow *inexhaustible* and *universal* rather than restricted to the elect by a limited atonement.

However, the critical difference between the Separate-Baptists and the universal church idea found within typical Protestant/Puritan ecclesiology lay in how Backus perceived the believer's salvation/election as *requisite* for local/particular church membership. Backus' re-orientation of election into the new birth vernacular, as necessary for membership into the local/particular church, began a perceptual change, not only of election but also its vital connection to *anything* beyond the visible church. Baptist historian Francis Wayland, writing just half a century after Backus' death, confirmed this change in strict Calvinism which had begun to take place in the late eighteenth and early nineteenth centuries saying,

> *Within the last fifty years a change has gradually taken*
> *place in the views of a large portion of our brethren. At*
> *the commencement of that period Gill's Divinity was a*
> *sort of standard, and Baptists imbibing his opinions were*

York: Sheldon, Blakeman, and Co., 1857), 19.

490   Backus had lived to hear about the tremendous results of the frontier revivals taking place in North Carolina, Tennessee, and Kentucky. The methods utilized in the great camp-meetings by the Presbyterian evangelists contradicted creedal Calvinism and therefore attracted the Methodists and the moderately Calvinistic Separate-Baptists to participate. Backus' support of these events demonstrates the Middleboro pastor's commitment to revival as the principal means of Baptist expansionism beyond his lifetime. For how Backus saw these results as "good news," see McLoughlin, ed., *The Diary of Isaac Backus*, 3: 1473.

what may be called almost hyper-Calvinistic.[491]

Despite this theological shift which had slowly crept into the evangelical position, ironically, Backus publically defended Gill's position until his death in 1806. The individual event of the new birth became the singular issue for the Separate-Baptists in being eligible for coming into the household of God giving individuals the right to both baptism and the Lord's Supper. For the SBBM, the principles of individual conscience and personal volition would form the basis for voluntarism. Upon this the Baptists in the Commonwealth would stand and fight for the right to support their own local churches over the State-backed Standing Churches and their ministers. Concerning their singular, consuming passion for evangelism and voluntarism in the local church, Goen commented:

> *Their chief task was to prepare individuals for eternity, and they pursued it with vigor. Every other concern, at least in the realm of religion, was subordinated to the primacy of the evangelistic imperative. This wrought significant changes in their doctrinal stance, as well as bound them to an emasculated doctrine of the church.*[492]

Goen does not suggest that Separate-Baptists were the only bodies of believers who were committed to evangelism, but he did blame the Baptists for an "emasculated doctrine of the church." For this indictment, he cites their "evangelistic imperative" which had altered their doctrinal stance or, in other words, changed their views on election. This is the closest Goen ever came to admitting a direct

---

491   Wayland, *Notes on the Principles and Practices of Baptist Churches*, 18.
492   Goen, *Revivalism and Separatism in New England, 1740-1800: Strict Congregationalist and Separate-Baptists in the Great Awakening*, 294.

connection between a declining Calvinism and the absence of a universal church concept among the Baptists. For the Baptists, this insistence on the new birth was followed by an insistence for believers' baptism for admission into a local body of believers. Goen again comments:

> *Their concentration on "this one thing" was at once the secret of their greatest strength—the harvesting of converts and the planting of churches—and of their greatest weakness—the refusal to work out the full implications of personal religious experience in the context of the total Christian tradition and its larger social concerns.*[493]

However, Backus and the Separate-Baptists did not see themselves as stopping short of reformation, they thought they had simply brought the first principles of the original founders to their logical conclusions. Visible saints, who had clearly experienced the grace of God in regeneration, were the only fit material for Christ's visible churches who concentrated primarily on evangelism and the planting of new churches. The question of why they did not work out the implications of such personal religious experience in the context of the "worldwide fellowship of faith"[494] and the bounds of "the whole church"[495] is an expectation which assumes such matters concerned Baptists at all. Why would it be so incumbent upon the Baptists to assume such broad concerns when their State-Church persecutors had never given thought to working out similar implications? Why had the Church of England never considered those same implications? The fact is, even ecumenical efforts are driven by doctrinal guideposts. For Backus, this hindrance to the "full implications of personal religious

---

493   Ibid.
494   Tull, *Shapers of Baptist Thought*, 76.
495   Ibid.

experience" was not caused by the Baptists but by those in tax-supported, State-sanctioned churches who advocated admission to the Lord's Table *before* adult baptism. Intercommunion, upon any other basis, would be to question, in Backus' mind, "that we can duly regard the law of Christ."[496]

No other area of Backus' theological thought has engendered as much controversy and intramural debate among scholars as this Baptist's ideas about the church, particularly as it relates to his diminishment of the universal Church in favor of visible church interpretation.[497] The debate does not concern his belief in the Augustine's universal idea, but rather how it eventually worked itself out in practical theology. Goen blames Backus and the Separate-Baptists for atomizing the doctrine of the church to the point where the Universal Church became almost non-existent.[498] This charge would appear to better fit the architects of the Landmark Baptists, such as J.R. Graves, who completely repudiated the coexistence of

---

496   Backus, *A Discourse, Concerning the Materials, the Manner of Building, and Power of Organizing the Church of Christ*, 143.

497   This debate centers largely on the ecumenical implications of Universal church theology. Usually the universal concept of the church becomes the link providing the theological foundation for inter-church cooperation, denominational unionism, and the various expressions of Bible-centered Christianity working together as a universal, worldwide body of Christ. For the best treatment of how this operates among the Baptists, see Stanley Grenz, *The Baptist Congregation* (Valley Forge: Judson Press, 1985), Hudson, ed., *Baptist Concepts of the Church*. For the various views and opinions among English and American churchmen, see Ernest Best, *One Body in Christ* (London: S.P.C.K., 1955), Edwin S. Gaustad, *Baptists, the Bible, Church Order and the Churches: Essays from Foundations, a Baptist Journal of History and Theology* (New York: Arno Press, 1980), Goen, *Revivalism and Separatism in New England, 1740-1800: Strict Congregationalist and Separate-Baptists in the Great Awakening,* Paul S. Minear, *Images of the Church in the New Testament* (Philadelphia: The Westminster Press, 1960), Wolfhart Pannenberg, *The Church* (Philadelphia: Westminster Press, 1983), Thomas Riplinger, *An American Vision of the Church* (Frankfurt: Herbert Lang Bern, 1976), Malcomb G. Shotwell, "Renewing the Baptist Principle of Associations" (Eastern Baptist Theological Seminary, 1990). For Post-modern conceptions of Evangelical ecumenism and the church, see Stanley Grenz, *Renewing the Center: Evangelical Theology in a Post-Theological Era* (Grand Rapids: Baker Academic, 2000).

498   Goen, *Revivalism and Separatism in New England, 1740-1800: Strict Congregationalist and Separate-Baptists in the Great Awakening,* 293.

both church conceptions.[499] Gaustad, in his appraisal of the so-called "Backus-Leland Tradition," asks of their position, "Can the churches ever become the church?"[500] However, the shift which Backus started, and others developed yet further, was driven by his own theological evolution as a Separate-Baptist, not by a total repudiation of his Puritan roots or reformation ecclesiology. The Middleboro minister did not likely foresee the ecclesiological implications of his own spiritual and theological development, such as some of his progenies' forays into the Landmark error.[501] The opinions of Goen and Gaustad in regard to the Backus movement, intimate only the succession aspect of the Landmark error.[502] Cathart asserted that the primary issue of Old Landmarkism was that which opposed the recognition of

---

499   This movement had its beginnings in the *Cotton Grove Resolutions* held in Cotton Grove, Tennessee, in June of 1851 with J.R. Graves being the leading proponent. Its tenets were built on Baptist church succession sustained by a chain-link baptismal authority beginning with John the Baptist or Christ's calling of the apostles in Luke 6. For a generally fair treatment of this movement and its relation to other Baptists see McGoldrick, *Baptist Successionism: A Crucial Question in Baptist History*, Ross, *Old Landmarkism and the Baptists: An Examination of the Theories of Church Authority and Church Succession.* McGoldrick's work is somewhat contentious, and he uses some historical cases uncritically in attempting to prove his case. However, Backus never intimated such a view of Baptist history in any of his own writings, having depended on English Baptist historian Thomas Crosby who held to what Morgan W. Patterson called a "spiritual succession." Moreover, Backus' acceptance of the Protestant view of the universal-invisible church precludes him from any direct connection to the later Landmark movement. The Middleboro pastor's emphasis on local-church theology was predicated on his perception of the ordinances, particularly immersionist baptism as a prerequisite for the Lord's Table, coupled with strict local-church autonomy. For Patterson's quote, see McBeth, *The Baptist Heritage*, 57.

500   Hudson, ed., *Baptist Concepts of the Church*, 262.

501   This is not a suggestion that Backus had a blind side in his ecclesiological opinion but that he did not anticipate future developments contingent upon his own theological ideas. McLoughlin conceded this same point when referring to the demise of Calvinism in the latter part of the eighteenth century. Despite Backus' defense of strict Calvinism, as "a child of his times, he was led to make concessions without realizing that he was doing so." McLoughlin reveals this pattern of concession in several key areas. See McLoughlin, ed., *Isaac Backus on Church, State, and Calvinism: Pamphlets, 1754-1789*, 56-57.

502   Neither author appears to see as critical the connecting of the visible and Universal church concepts. Their reaction to the emphasis of the Separate-Baptist ecclesiology was focused more on the Baptists' practical unwillingness to entertain any ecclesiological obligations beyond the local-church.

pedobaptist ministers as legitimate gospel ministers.[503] On this basis Graves felt that William Kiffin was a consistent Landmarker by his refusing pedobaptist ministers in his church pulpit.[504] Backus may have likely been guilty of this charge, but he could never have been accused of being a successionist. More importantly, Backus would not have had a Congregational pastor in his Middleboro church to preach, if at the same time the communion table was closed to unbaptized Christians. He flatly denied the possibility of meeting those at the communion table who had not been immersed.[505] However, neither Kiffin nor Backus would have denied that the pedobaptist minister would be joined with them in the Universal-invisible church on the basis of their mutual election/salvation. The key to the problem lay in Backus' incontrovertible opinion that the communion table was closed to all except regenerate, immersed members, but by not attaching an *a priori* position to the universal concept, he appeared to be doing so for the visible church. It is precisely here that the distinction between the universal and the visible enters the argument, because in his mind the visible can only reflect its invisible counterpart in terms of election, therefore the baptism of believers by immersion became the divider of the two ecclesiological concepts. What apparently frustrates Goen and Gaustad was Backus' willingness to make visible church order the basis for denominational separatism. Backus would make no additional allowances for intercommunion among denominations

---

503   William Cathart, a contemporary historian of the Landmark movement, does not even mention successionism in his article on "Old Landmarkism" as one of its fundamental ideas. Rather, Cathart suggests that this non-intercourse position of the Baptists in regard to pedobaptist ministers and churches can be traced to English Particular Baptist William Kiffin in 1640. Cathart bases this on Cramp's Baptist History, and Ivimey's "Life of Kiffin." See Cathart, ed., *The Baptist Encyclopedia*, 867-868.

504   J.R. Graves, *Old Landmarkism: What Is It?* (Texarkana: Baptist Sunday School Committee, 1928), 264.

505   Backus, *A Discourse, Concerning the Materials, the Manner of Building, and Power of Organizing the Church of Christ*, 143.

beyond what he allowed for any visible church. In this sense, Backus answers Gaustad's question in the negative. Perhaps Backus would have responded with yet another question, such as, "Why should we overlook baptism as a basis of communion in the universal church when we are unwilling to do the same in the particular church, supposing that one reflects the other?"[506]

SEPARATISM: PEDOBAPTIST SCHISM

The non-separating Puritans, like their Reformer exemplars, thought separation from the Standing Church to be mere presumption, devilish, and potentially destructive to the Commonwealth, even to the point of calling some of the first Salem immigrants Anabaptists for their failing to use the Common Book of Prayer and their denial of *scandalous offenders* into the communion of the church.[507] Similarly, English Separatists like Johnson and Ainsworth had attempted to mitigate separation solely on the basis of perceived apostasy in Rome and England rather than any explicit practice like infant baptism. As a consequence, the visible church continued to be filled with pretenders and hypocrites right up to the Great Awakening.

By the time of the post-Great Awakening period, Goen referred to the Separate-Congregational churches as the "nurseries of Baptists."[508] By demanding equal fidelity to the baptism of believers as vigorously as they emphasized the biblical doctrine of the new

506   This is the essence of his argument with Mr. Fish in DCM when Backus asked him, "Is any other visible church-state instituted in the gospel, but a particular one?" Then he answers his question by saying that the seven churches of Asia are "not as one national or provincial church, but as so many distinct churches...in each particular community." See Ibid, 17.

507   Kenneth B. Murdock, ed., *Cotton Mather: Magnalia Christi Americana* (Cambridge, Massachusetts, and London, England: The Belknap Press of Harvard University Press, 1702; reprint, 1977), 155.

508   Goen, *Revivalism and Separatism in New England, 1740-1800: Strict Congregationalist and Separate-Baptists in the Great Awakening*, 208.

birth, the SBBM was able to doctrinally justify the historical baptismal practices of earlier dissenters and issue a challenge to the Separates to come all the way out of their pedobaptist heritage.

Conversely, Backus, and other Baptists in New England, saw, experienced, and finally came to repudiate what such ecclesiastical sentiments had produced in Massachusetts. Unlike their predecessors who considered election to be the hopeful end of infant baptism, the Separate-Baptists viewed baptism to be the testimonial of a salvation "already secured."[509]

In speaking for Baptists, Backus would ask his readers to be his judge as to "what cause we had for a new separation...."[510] Backus argued this point in his response to John Cotton's claim that church members were all to be baptized. Actually, Cotton's point was that infants were members upon their baptism. Backus argued that infants were brought into the covenant while in their natural state, and on that basis, were entirely out of order with the Covenant of Grace they claimed to possess.[511] Therefore, the only means to the pure church ideal for the SBBM was in repudiating the practice which they determined had corrupted all reformers in the first place and then separate from those who embraced it. Speaking of the unkind reception this position invited, the Middleboro pastor and like churches were accused of schism. Backus rejected such a notion:

...and only because we will not meet such persons there, as we cannot believe in our conscience to be baptized according to our Lord's direction...but if the truth breaks up churches, it highly concerns all that belong to them, to awake and consider what churches they are.[512]

---

509   William Latane Lumpkin, *Colonial Baptists and Southern Revivals* (New York: Arno Press, 1980), 17.
510   Ibid.
511   Ibid, 134.
512   Ibid, 142-143.

For Backus, all middle ground formerly inviting conciliation had vanished. In a letter, Backus reminded Mr. Valentine W. Rathbun that separation from the Titicut church was made necessary by pedobaptist brethren who would not accompany Backus and other church members to the river for baptismal ceremonies. In light of such activities, the Middleboro pastor told Mr. Rathbun that they had not been able to celebrate the Lord's Supper under such conditions and, therefore, "could not commune anymore with unbaptized persons."[513] A few lines later Backus tells his friend that many practices such as prayer, preaching, and singing could be done without the aid of church authority, but it was not lawful for any unbaptized person to come to the Lord's Table, and for anyone to do so violated the practice of early Puritans.[514] These appear to be little more than detailed expressions of latent Great Awakening tendencies noticed among Whitefield and his associates with separation being the great underlying tension. Separates had simply brought to a logical end what Whitefield had begun.

Here, the SBBM became the latest part of the broader dissenting stream of non-conformists. George suggested that the English Separatists' demand to separate from Rome actually identified them with the Donatists who had done the same thing. Interestingly, George makes this connection of ancient Donatism and English Separatism because both systems rejected Christian sacramentalism. George does not mention the apparent connection to infant baptism by these ancient dissenters! Backus, in his use of Lutheran historian Mosheim, would point out that prior to Constantine infant baptism had appeared and had been repudiated by Tertullian, along with many

---

513   Isaac to Valentine W. Rathbun Backus, in *American Baptist Historical Society* (Middleborough: 1805), 1.
514   Ibid.

in the Donatist group.[515] Also missing is how the English Separatists disagreed with their Baptist brethren on the latter's separation from Rome because of the Baptists' fidelity to believers' baptism not simply their rejection of sacramentalism.[516] However, George does mention that:

> *We should recognize that many of the motifs first articulated by the Anabaptists were indeed later picked up and owned afresh by the Baptists. These include the principles of religious liberty, believers' baptism, congregational autonomy, and a zeal for missions and evangelism.*[517]

This continuity of principle demonstrated by George affirms that truth appearing throughout the course of human history is not handed down from one human hand to the other but asserts itself spontaneously through the application of first principles previously ignored or repressed. Backus never attempted to argue for any organic connection but utilized early Anabaptist models to justify his contemporary movement.[518] Certainly, by 1756, Backus no longer considered the Separate movement to be consistent on this matter of biblical separation. Elisha Paine, an apologist for sprinkling, admitted

---

515   George, *John Robinson and the English Separatist Tradition*, 101.
516   For the Backus argument concerning this problem, see "Truth is Great" in McLoughlin, ed., *Isaac Backus on Church, State, and Calvinism: Pamphlets, 1754-1789*, 415-416.
517   Ibid, 6.
518   The New England historian utilized the testimony of Lutheran historian Mosheim to point to pre-Reformation groups such as the Waldenses, Petrobusians, Wickliffites, and Hussites, long before Luther's day... "who rejected, as did the English and American Baptists of his day, the practice of infant baptism, and State-Church alliances." See Backus, *A History of New England with Particular Reference to the Denomination of Christians Called Baptists*, 2: v-vi.

the possibility of inconsistency in his remarks at the Stonington
conference in May of 1754 saying,

*...if you can reconcile the above principles in the essential parts
thereof, you will remove all the grounds of bars and disputes; but if
there be an essential difference in the above articles, and consequently
in the practice on them, then there is an Achan in the camp; and no
marvel that Israel hath, in all reformations, be troubled therewith.*[519]

As Paine had recognized, however, this was the Achilles heel
of all reformations. He did not consider infant baptism to warrant
separation. Backus directly identified *Achan* in a rhetorical fashion,
"And is not the assuming a power to act for others in religious matters
the *Achan* of the Christian church?" The Middleboro Baptist puts
the problem squarely in the middle of the New Testament church era
and justified Baptist *separatism* over the practice of infant baptism.
Backus clearly separates the "third church" model of Avis[520] from
John Robinson and the reformation tradition and, unlike Luther and
Calvin, repudiated the constitution of the Roman Church, including
Robinson's legitimization of its baptisms.

Secondly, this identification of baby sprinkling as the "Achan"
shifted the justification for separation from the *new birth* to the
practice of *believers' baptism*. Heretofore, the Separates and the
SBBM had walked together in a strained fellowship under their
mutual commitment to new birth preaching. The breaking point

---

519   Elisha Paine died five months later on October 25, 1756. The Separate cause
continued to decline and never recovered the numbers lost to the Separate-Baptist cause.
Those that did not reject infant baptism were eventually re-absorbed back into the Standing
Church. Found in Appendix 16 of 26 in McLoughlin, ed., *The Diary of Isaac Backus*, 3: 1580.
520   Avis demonstrated that the Anabaptists' position constituted a third-church view
which centered around the baptism of competent believers only. See Avis, *The Church in the
Theology of the Reformers*, 55, emphasis added.

having arrived, Backus now argued that *further union* was impossible because both groups understood their common principles in different ways, and those differences could no longer be overlooked or ignored without damage to the purity of the particular church.

Backus reasoned:
One great end of the visible Church and of practicing in outward ordinances is the edification of the saints, but to try to go together in these practices is so far from edifying [sic], that it has a natural tendency to offend and burden each other and to try to keep those who are so differently minded together is destroying the end to accomplish the means.[521]

In short, Backus had learned that union at the expense of doctrinal principles was no union at all. Herein is a lesson for all Baptists ancient and modern! Such conviction by Backus was not just empty rhetoric or denominational positioning. Backus makes this clear in DCM in his closing dialogue with Mr. Fish on what he calls the "two sorts of separation described in holy writ." Separation, he says first of all, is produced "by an exalting of self above others; the other by such an adherence to divine rule as to part with those who will not conform to it. Isaiah 65:5, Psalm 119:115."[522] In describing the second sort of separation, Backus directs his thoughts to his "pedobaptist fathers and brethren" who he clearly understood as being guilty of willful disobedience to Scripture. Backus asserted that if these two groups,

---

521   Found in Appendix 20 under the heading, "Reasons of My Withdrawing Communion From Pedobaptists, Which I Once Stood With." McLoughlin, ed., *The Diary of Isaac Backus*, 3:1593-1594.

522   Backus, *A Discourse, Concerning the Materials, the Manner of Building, and Power of Organizing the Church of Christ*, 143.

can convince us that HE who was faithful in his house, and worthy
of more glory than Moses, has yet left things at such loose ends,
as only to appoint the use of water in the sacred name, without
determining whether it should be by sprinkling, pouring or
burying, but has left that to be determined by men's consciences:
I say till they can convince us of this, all their noise about the evil
of re-baptizing and closed-communion, cannot satisfy our minds,
that we can duly regard the law of Christ, if we come to his table
with any who have not been buried with him in baptism.[523]

For the SBBM, fellowship in the visible church with those
who received infant baptism was no longer a tolerable option. If the
option for "further light" on such matters was Robinson's previous
justification for communion, that light was now a two-edged sword
capable only of division and ultimate separation from both the
Standing Church so constituted by the "founding fathers," and the
"brethren" who comprised the Separate churches. Backus, justifying
only adult believers' baptism, made this separation yet clearer in his
diary response to Congregational-Separatist Paine when he asked
rhetorically, "Is not baptism an ordinance of initiation into the
Christian church...?"[524] Consistently applying his own principles,
Backus would even withdraw fellowship from the Norton Baptist
Church for admitting members not properly baptized. In July of
1764, William Carpenter, pastor of the Norton Baptist Church, wrote
to the Middleboro Baptist Church asking forgiveness and requested a
restoration of mutual fellowship among their respective churches.[525]

---

523   Ibid.
524   McLoughlin, ed., *The Diary of Isaac Backus*, 3: 1585.
525   William Carpenter, "Backus Papers, Andover Newton Theo. School," in *Backus Microfilm Series* (1764). This letter notes the withdrawal of fellowship by Middleborough First Baptist Church from Norton Baptist Church. It further confesses admitting members improperly baptized and asks forgiveness from Backus. This is followed by a request for

According to Goen's chronology, this church had become a Baptist church en-bloc in 1761,[526] but had obviously remained ambivalent concerning receiving members upon a confession of faith in Christ and adult baptism. In 1769, this church merged en-bloc with the Taunton Baptist Church which held the same position.

Backus chronicles the example of the Separate church at Exeter, Rhode Island, founded by David Sprague in 1750 and continued as a Separate church until 1766 when it "was on the point of becoming a strict communion body."[527] By 1796, the Middleboro pastor confirmed that the Exeter church, now in the Baptist fold, had experienced greater blessings than at any other time in its history since abandoning their open-communion practices.[528] Situations such as this had become so commonplace that Backus claimed around the same year that none of the Separate churches continued to exist in Massachusetts.[529] Those Separate churches which had fully come over to the immersion side typically continued into the Baptist fold.[530] Those that did not generally returned to the parish church.[531]

---

restoration of fellowship.

526   Goen, *Revivalism and Separatism in New England, 1740-1800: Strict Congregationalist and Separate-Baptists in the Great Awakening*, 316.

527   Ibid, 242.

528   Backus, *A History of New England with Particular Reference to the Denomination of Christians Called Baptists*, 2: 509-510.

529   Ibid, 2: 508.

530   Ibid, 2: 414-15. Backus mentioned that a certain number of churches who wished to remain mixed-communion churches "began a yearly meeting in 1785, under the name of the Groton Conference. It was not in fellowship with either the remaining Strict Congregationalists or the Separate-Baptists in the Warren Baptist Association. It consisted of about seventeen churches at its inception and according to McLoughlin reached a peak of twenty churches in 1805, but by 1818 it had either dissolved or joined the closed-communion Baptist associations in their areas. See McLoughlin, *New England Dissent 1630-1833*, 1:435.

531   See the appendix provided by C.C. Goen regarding church separations in his seminal work on Separate-Congregationalism. The parish church in Raynham is a good example of the mixed situation. Several temporarily separated around 1749, but only "some" were immersed, and probably united with the First Baptist church in Middleboro after 1756. The pattern for those remaining after such baptisms would be to slowly creep back into the Standing Churches. After 1796 in Massachusetts, no neutral ground remained.

LOCAL CHURCH DISCIPLINE

Backus' experience in the Massachusetts ecclesiastical system was instrumental in the formation of his key opinions on church matters, particularly discipline. For the SBBM, the idea of any authority existing outside of the particular assembly was simply beyond the scope of Scripture. Backus expressed his fears in his response to Mr. Fish:

> *There are but a few who are convinced that the root of all this mischief lies in man's trying to model church affairs according to worldly rule. In civil states particular men are invested with authority to judge for the whole; but in Christ's kingdom each one has an equal right to judge for himself.*[532]

Of course, the pastor's fears were quite justified. The SBBM, while in its infancy, was a fragile David before a towering Goliath. Very few of them had fully inculcated the enormity of what they now opposed. The Standing Churches had known what was at stake in the challenge imposed on them by the fledgling Baptists, but did civil anarchy now loom in the distance if discipline for heresy and disobedience were removed entirely from the civil realm? Would the practice of church discipline to just visible churches produce a New England version of what had occurred at Munster? New England Puritans were convinced that as citizens of the theocracy, they "were obliged not to leave it to itself, but to identify the covenant of the people with the Covenant of Grace, to insert the terms of salvation into

---

532   McLoughlin, ed., *Isaac Backus on Church, State, and Calvinism: Pamphlets, 1754-1789*, 198.

the political incorporation and to unite the duties of civil obedience with the duties of Christian worship.[533]

What the Separate-Baptists had done with infant baptism, they were now willing to do with church discipline. They were not justifying change upon coercion or fiat but simply because biblical revelation appeared to be clear on the matter. Backus laid down the gauntlet saying, "In civil states particular men are invested with authority to judge for the whole; but in Christ's kingdom each one has a right to judge for himself."[534] The Middleboro pastor based his argument on Paul's admonition to the church in Corinth to expel the man guilty of fornication. Backus recognized the assembly's obedience to do that much:

> And after they had proceeded according to this direction, he calls
> it a punishment which was inflicted of many, I Cor. v, 12; 2 Cor.
> ii, 6. Now Christ's church is either particular or universal. All
> the churches that are described in the Bible as having the power
> of discipline are particular, in which each member has his right
> to judge, as in this at Corinth, another at Ephesus, etc.[535]

The "many" to which Backus refers are to be only those members of the Corinthian assembly administering the discipline. This is decisively noted by his next statement, "now Christ's church is either particular or universal."[536] It is very important to notice that he uses the word *universal* and not the word(s) *national* or *provincial* [emphasis added] as he does in the very next paragraph of his narrative to describe the contemporary view of the Standing Churches

---

533   Miller, *The New England Mind: The Seventeenth Century*, 412.
534   Quoted from FCN as cited in McLoughlin, ed., *Isaac Backus on Church, State, and Calvinism: Pamphlets, 1754-1789*, 198.
535   Ibid.
536   Ibid.

in Massachusetts. Why did he frame his point in the extremes of universal-particular terms rather than national-particular? It appears that he wanted to demonstrate the point of where God had placed ultimate authority for visible church issues. In a previous encounter between Fish and Backus, the former said concerning the locus of church authority, "Jesus Christ has but one church in the world, and that is the same as it always was." Backus replied, "I observed that the invisible church is so, but entered my exception against its being true of the visible church, which I took notice was what Mr. F. intended."[537] The context of this view is demonstrated in the common Puritan sentiment laid down first by William Ames and then John Cotton who said that the distribution of churches into the visible and the invisible "is not into divers kinds of Churches, nor into divers kindes [sic] of Members of the same Church, but into divers Adjuncts of the same Members of the same Church."[538] Samuel Hudson commented on Cotton's assessment declaring that Cotton's definition "seems to me to belong to an invisible Church and not to a visible."[539] Evidently, this is precisely how Mr. Fish's definition appeared to Backus. The argument, as evidenced by these combatants, was over emphasis. Emphasis alone determined for Backus which paradigm held real jurisdiction in a visible world. For discipline's sake, the paradigm would now be controlled by the demands of the particular church, while the universal body of the elect, which continued to exist in the mind of Backus, was being severely reduced in importance on very practical grounds.

However, the SBBM made a conscious doctrinal break from the traditional Puritan idea of a magisterial partnership or, as

---

537   Backus, *A Discourse, Concerning the Materials, the Manner of Building, and Power of Organizing the Church of Christ*, 15.
538   Cited from Samuel Hudson in "The Essence and Unitie of the Church Catholike" in Miller, *The New England Mind: The Seventeenth Century*, 442.
539   Ibid.

Cotton used the term "nursing fathers" to describe civil authorities. Backus said of them, "When men assume a power above particular churches, as they have neither divine rule to support their conduct nor earthly power to compel others to come to their bar...they are obliged to act contrary to Scripture and reason."[540] Such a decision by the SBBM, like their rejection of pedobaptism, was another flagrant repudiation of the Standing Order, New England Congregationalism, reformation principle, and Augustinian ecclesiasticism.[541] Luther and Calvin agreed with Augustine that there was no utilitarian manner in which ecclesiastical discipline could separate the elect from the hypocrites. Subsequently, the English Puritans and Separatists, in pursuit of the pure-church ideal, thought they had discovered in covenant relations a system whereby the elect could be identified, but unfortunately, not without inviting grave, doctrinal compromise.[542] Backus, however, operating on the same identical principle of *making visible what was before invisible*, was willing to jettison every point of obvious compromise. Stanley Grenz correctly pointed out, "Since his opponents continued to assume his premises, he was indeed more consistent than they, and his case against them was valid."[543] Backus made the ordinances constitutive for local-body life and its ongoing existence. The Puritans had assumed that they could advance Calvin's innocuous approach to discipline by clarifying elect status through the individual's testimony of a work of grace alone. At that point, the Puritans, like Calvin, were satisfied to make discipline the removal of *only* the openly scandalous or schismatic member. The premise of local-church discipline for the SBBM went beyond merely exposing

---

540   Backus, *A Discourse, Concerning the Materials, the Manner of Building, and Power of Organizing the Church of Christ*, 199.
541   Miller, *The New England Mind: The Seventeenth Century*, 4.
542   Tull, *Shapers of Baptist Thought*, 57.
543   Grenz, *Isaac Backus - Puritan and Baptist: His Place in History, His Thought, and Their Implications for Modern Baptist Theology*, 266.

hypocrites or the openly scandalous, it was essential for maintaining ecclesiological order (i.e., immersion and the Lord's Table) within congregational life for the purpose of experiencing the peace of Christ in His church.[544]

Secondly, and perhaps just as revolutionary, the SBBM believed that polity was no longer to be practiced from the *top* down but from the *center* out. Congregational government replaced elder rule and effectively placed the church officer on equal grounds with the most common member. Backus, in arguing this point against the Massachusetts authorities, stated in no uncertain terms that people under government authorities had more liberty in electing and deposing their leaders than did members of the Standing Churches their own ministers.[545] Backus described the newly discovered congregational unity and the Separate-Baptist plan:

Every church of Christ is a holy city, which has the right to censure and exclude all members and officers who break his laws, and refuse to manifest repentance therefore. And when they shall come to exercise this power faithfully, independently of all the powers of the world, such peace will be enjoyed as never has yet been upon earth.[546]

---

544   This congregational peace is something Backus observed as woefully lacking in his congregation at the Titicut Separatist church. Backus laid the blame directly on the practice of mixed-communion which in turn prohibited them from taking the Lord's Supper together.

545   Backus, *A History of New England with Particular Reference to the Denomination of Christians Called Baptists*, 2: 378. Backus' argument here is really a two-edged sword against the Standing Order in that his real contention is with a Dr. Lanthrop who had suggested that if every person in a church had equal claims upon the authority vested in the teacher or elder that there would be no order and unity. Backus' answer demonstrated that not only was the polity of the Standing Order under severe biblical scrutiny, but the tax-system which supported its ministers was equally unfair and without Biblical warrant. By 1794, Backus further noted that public sentiment was such in Boston that Baptists in Medfield, who had been jailed for refusing to pay a recently levied ministerial tax were released in a week without having to pay the Court.

546   Ibid, 2: 379.

In most Colonialists' minds, congregational discipline was ordained primarily for the maintenance of the greater good of the Commonwealth. Miller understood this elusive peace as the objective goal of local, ruling elders. He said, "If the clergy failed to control the internal affairs of their churches, then for all their attempts to maintain non-separation and unity, their parishes would inevitably drift apart, divergences and schisms appear, and popular frenzies break out."[547] Discipline seldom occurred except where it threatened the *greater good* of the body politic. It was not so much a question of where the authority for ecclesiastical activity existed but the effect such activity would have upon the populace at large. Miller suggested that unless the internal affairs of the churches were controlled "popular frenzies" could "break out" demonstrating this latent fear among the leaders of the Commonwealth. One such example of potential schism occurred during the Antinomian Controversy of 1636-1638. [548] In this case civil control was the primary issue. Backus wanted to demonstrate that the real concern was not the body politic but the local church as the body of Christ. He then gave in his history a list of fourteen beliefs held by Baptists which he said came nearest to "that of the first planters of New England, of any churches now in the land, excepting in the single article of sprinkling infants."[549] The ninth and tenth articles supported this claim:

547   Miller, *Orthodoxy in Massachusetts 1630-1650*, 176.
548   During the examination of Anne Hutchinson, its principal party, an Antinomian by the name of Steven Greensmyth was fined forty pounds and was ordered by the magistrate to apologize to every church for claiming (as did Hutchinson) that all the ministers with the exception of Mr. Cotton, Mr. Wheelwright, and Mr. Hooker, were all teaching a covenant of works. In this manner, the General Court manifested the reality that the Court, or the Massachusetts Commonwealth at large, could not suffer dissent with any greater tolerance than could individual churches, because in essence, they were merely the sum of all its parts. Discipline in New England was therefore a joint congregational and civil effort. See Hall, ed., *A Documentary History*, 8.
549   Backus, *A History of New England with Particular Reference to the Denomination*

That the whole power of governing and disciplining their
members is in each particular church; though advice and council
from other, in some cases, is becoming even necessary. That the
government of the church should be wholly by the laws of Christ,
enforced in his name, and not at all by the secular arm.[550]

This newly revitalized wing of the Separate-Baptists saw themselves "as instruments of a new reformation that would restore New England to its first foundation which earned them a sense of self-status as well as public respectability."[551] When the Separate-Baptists asserted that the reception or rejection of members was a prerogative belonging to a particular church's own membership, it proclaimed its belief that Christ had made the local body the pillar and ground of the truth reestablishing what they considered to be a valid pure-church ideal.

The SBBM clarified this position in "An Address to The Second Baptist Church in Middlborough Concerning the Importance of Gospel Discipline" (ASBC). The significance of this address was in the clarification of two principles which infuriated the Standing ministers. First, Backus placed all prerogatives for discipline within the jurisdiction of the particular church (He used Matt 18:3, 15, 18, and 2 Cor. 8:1) by affirming the church as the final arbiter and judge if personal confrontation proved insufficient.[552] Secondly, he derided the prevailing Congregational system for seeking support from the civil government in enforcing ecclesiastical measures by alluding to a previous pamphlet written in 1773.[553] Civil interference was to the

---

of Christians Called Baptists, 2: 232-233.
550   Ibid.
551   Wood, ed., *Baptists and the American Experience*, 30.
552   Isaac Backus, *An Address to the Second Baptist Church in Middleborough Concerning the Importance of Gospel Discipline* (Middleborough: Nathaniel Coverly, 1787), 3.
553   McLoughlin, ed., *Isaac Backus on Church, State, and Calvinism: Pamphlets,*

SBBM an unconscionable breech of one's individual rights given by the Creator:

> *According to its relation and connection to and with the*
> *Supreme Being and ourselves.... But the conceit that man*
> *could advance either his honor or happiness by disobedience*
> *instead of obedience was first injected by the father of lies,*
> *and all such conceits ever since are as false as he is.*[554]

Having placed ecclesiastical discipline back within the biblical perimeters of the particular church, the SBBM thought that their best protection was in a unified position of non-compliance by its member churches. Consequently, the Baptists who formed the Grievance Committee of the Warren Baptist Association in 1767 adopted a policy rejecting the certificate system in Massachusetts in May of 1773. Their mutual association as a group became the chief means of banding together the churches in mutual defiance of such things as the certificate laws of the Massachusetts General Court. Unfortunately, the SBBM had significant anxiety over the potential over-lording of the particular church by such organizations. As we will see in the following chapter, the most significant concern of the Separate-Baptists lay in expansion, and expansion would depend on continued evangelism.

1754-1789, 309-343. This work, entitled "An Appeal To The Public For Religious Liberty" (hereafter referred to as APRL), is based upon five arguments rejecting civil encroachment upon the religious liberties of the citizenry.
554   Ibid, 309-310.

SECTION THREE

Movement and Maturation

Chapter- Five
Separate-Baptists: From Revival to Disestablishment

INTRODUCTION

Although Backus died twenty-four years prior to the establishment of the New Hampshire confession, the SBBM should be recognized as having played a significant role in its evolution. Two primary factors emerged from the milieu of the Great Awakening and the development of the SBBM which directly affected both the confession itself and its eventual influence. The evangelical-Calvinism of Whitefield and other revivalists had introduced key changes in Puritan thought. The pre-layered conditioning for salvation which began with the process of infant baptism and the preparation doctrine had been subjected to the instantaneous and oftentimes emotional new birth experience. In real terms, this "direct experience of conversion was condensed from months or weeks to days and hours."[555] What had previously been thought of as something intended to occur within an orderly, planned, and predictable system was now displaced by uncontrollable forces.

As a strong proponent of revival firmly rooted in the Whitefieldian tradition, Backus still did not *formally* embrace the encroaching doctrinal variants in revivalism itself. With the theological perimeters of the old orthodoxy being pushed and challenged, Backus, in July of 1789, responded to the so-called *considerable errors* of Wesleyan Methodism in DPE. In this article the pastor, fearing the encroaching ideology of prevenient grace (God's

---

[555] McLoughlin, ed., *Isaac Backus on Church, State, and Calvinism: Pamphlets, 1754-1789*, 448.

grace which enables free-will choice of, or rejection of salvation), argues against what he considers to be the most flagrant of Wesley's doctrinal errors; freedom of the will, universal atonement, and the possibility of falling from grace.[556] Despite Backus' efforts to shore up the old orthodoxy, by 1790 the effort to maintain the extreme Calvinism of John Gill and others was confined primarily to the urban centers of Boston, Newport, and New Haven to the west.[557] The rural majority, especially in burgeoning New Hampshire, rallied around the banner of Whitefieldian revival with emphasis around immediate conversion, unfiltered Biblicism, the gathered church, and religious toleration. Pointing to the ultimate revival success in the four New England states, which in 1734 had only six Baptist churches, Backus claimed two hundred eighty-five by the time he finished his New England history and over twelve hundred among all Baptists in the country, most of which had begun in the "last forty years."[558] This ultimately favored the growth of the Separate-Baptists whose revivalist tendencies modified the election doctrine and made voluntarism[559] the door to all things ecclesiological.

The second primary factor emerging from the Second Reformation was the eventual demand for disestablishment of the

---

556   Ibid.

557   Marini, *Radical Sects of Revolutionary New England*, 22.

558   Backus, *Church History of New England from 1620 to 1804: Containing a View of the Principles and Practice, Declensions and Revivals, Oppression and Liberty of the Churches, and a Chronological Table. With a Memoir of the Author*, 237.

559   Technically, voluntarism is the free-will support of the church of one's choice. This was how the Baptists and other dissenters defined the support of their own churches in light of the demand by the Standing Order's policy of taxing an entire town's citizenry for the support of the local Congregational minister. However, the definition of voluntarism is really tied to the Baptists' view of the individual. "The institutional church became secondary, while the individual soul stood alone before God. The individual, it was held, might be unlettered, untutored, of lowly origin, of small ability, and of little worldly standing. This made no difference. Each person must have his own encounter with God in an experience of regeneration. Each could receive the immediate, direct leadership of the Holy Spirit." See Tull, *Shapers of Baptist Thought*, 75.

Standing Order. In Massachusetts, beside revival, no other single effort of Backus and his emerging denomination eclipsed the effort to bring toleration into the realm of government policy. Proving the Jewish theocracy was voluntaristic in its support of ministers,[560] Backus asserted that the right to affirm true ministers and reject false ones was "ever a matter between God and individuals," insisting that "no men can have any more right to support religious teachers by the sword, than they have power to pull down the Son of God from his throne in heaven."[561] It was this demand for disestablishment of the church from the state that drove Backus to demand that all powers of religious tests, ministerial taxes, or hereditary nobility be transferred to the individual, and that those powers, guaranteed by the Constitution,[562] be enshrined in the visible, particular church, presumably of course, Baptist. However, Backus knew better than most that such liberty would not grow the denomination by itself. For that, God would have to supernaturally move on the hearts of people to awaken them from their prevailing "stupidity" through revival.[563]

---

560   This "proof" of Backus concerning the OT people demonstrates Backus' inference of the Baptists leading the "new Reformation" not in terms of a theocracy, but rather a movement of voluntaristic, autonomous, churches committed to revival and the rights of all such persons to act in accordance with their private consciences.

561   Backus, *A History of New England with Particular Reference to the Denomination of Christians Called Baptists*, 2: 557.

562   Only nine Baptists voted for the new constitution on February 6, 1788. Backus was one of them, and he sincerely believed that the constitution was the best way to insure the ultimate disestablishment of the church in Massachusetts, which finally came in 1833. See Handlin, ed., *Isaac Backus and the American Pietistic Tradition*, 200.

563   From Backus' signing of the constitution, between 1788 and 1800, Backus' church and many Massachusetts Baptists had gone through an extremely dry period spiritually. Backus joyfully remarked that in 1801, several local Baptist churches in Boston and surrounding cities had experienced a powerful moving of God. At the same time he spoke approvingly of Lemuel Burkitt's revival account of the 6000 additions to the Kentucky Baptists, who along with the Methodists and Presbyterians, had participated together in camp meeting revivals. See Ibid, 225-226.

REVIVALS, AWAKENINGS, AND THE PROVIDENCE OF GOD

Like Backus, the evangelical revivals of both England and Colonial New England were considered by most as having been precipitated by God's Spirit through its notable evangelists. The divine factor, or that God played a "first cause" role, in the Awakening is a view held by the majority of Evangelical authors.[564] If we recognize that the revivals were providential events, this fact alone forces a dispassionate evaluation upon the revivals' ultimate results both theologically and socially. After all, if God's fingerprint could be observed as having affected the timing and results of the Awakening, then certainly, the Awakening's *doctrinal* influences should not be arbitrarily forced outside the realm of Providence.

In the recognition of God's involvement, it is also possible to mistakenly tie all of the contributing events together as being connected to only one common impetus, theological or otherwise.[565] However, despite the fact that the specific factors of the transatlantic Revival can be identified, no single one, or some combination of them account for "the emergence, the form, and the timing of the Revival."[566]

---

564   See David Bebbington, *Evangelicalism in Modern Britain* (Grand Rapids: Baker Book House, Publisher Name, 1992), 61-63, Gaustad, *The Great Awakening in New England*, 3, Arthur Skevington Wood, *Spiritual Renewal and Advance in the Eighteenth Century* (Grand Rapids: Wm. B. Eerdmans Publishing Co, 1960), 26-27.

565   Gaustad sees the movements on both continents as providential occurrences, and yet happening in such apparent unison, that he fails to recognize the movements occur on many fronts, and some of them were operating on entirely independent grounds, although parallel in nature and timing. For instance, the author says, "This Methodism in England, the Moravian Brethren on the Continent, and the Great Awakening in New England are part of a single broad, bold stroke of the brush." See this comment on page 3. Another Great Awakening historian draws a sharp distinction between the evangelicalism of the colonies and the pietism of Europe, suggesting that the former was based on Calvinistic preaching, while the latter was strictly Arminian in nature. This position ignores any and all middle ground between the two movements and unfortunately misses the fact that these two largely independent revivals had several parallel features not attributable to mere chance or a single theological mindset unique to itself. See Heimert, ed., *Religion and the American Mind: From the Great Awakening to the Revolution*, 3-4.

566   Crawford, "Origins of the Eighteenth-Century Evangelical Revival: England and New England Compared," 364.

The evangelists themselves oftentimes appeared to be conscious of being instruments in the hands of God.[567] Both Whitefield and Wesley, despite the fact they occupied opposite positions regarding free will and predestination, attributed their evangelistic successes to God's gracious blessings on both their ministries. In addition to this desire to credit God, Lambert pointed out that by the 1730s, and well into the 1740s, a well-formed literary correspondence was occurring by participants on both sides of the Atlantic, and men like Whitefield often advertised well in advance of their evangelistic appearances.[568] Providence, however, if truly seen as activity resting in the sovereign will of God, must be viewed outside the scope of both advertising campaigns and theological systems, regardless of the personalities behind them. While Whitefield and others decried the lack of piety and the woeful state of religion within the American colonies, English Methodists "attracted hearers because they provided what the Church of England did not," that being a vital experiential religious experience based on the doctrine of the new birth and the sense of sins forgiven.[569] Many of those reached in the context of the Methodist revival were in geographical areas and occupations "in which the traditional authority structure of English society did not operate."[570]

This same spiritual hunger may be observed of those colonists responding to Jonathan Edwards in 1734 followed by Whitefield in 1740. This "vital experiential religious experience" sought out by the

---

567   Whitefield saw the revivals and his participation in them as a great work of the Spirit of God. He felt as if God had bestowed a double portion of the Spirit upon him and was providentially leading and directing his evangelistic efforts. See Whitefield, ed., *Whitefield's Journals*, 201, 203, 330.

568   For a secular source documenting the transatlantic movement in terms of advertising and joint communication, see Lambert, "Subscribing for Profits and Piety: The Friendship of Benjamin Franklin and George Whitefield."

569   Crawford, "Origins of the Eighteenth-Century Evangelical Revival: England and New England Compared," 373.

570   Ibid, 367.

spiritually starving masses could be seen in any one of Whitefield's rural New England meetings usually announced just a few days, sometimes hours before his scheduled appearance, oftentimes bringing normal activities to a sudden halt.[571] However, prior to the well-known events after 1740, there were other significant factors which anticipated the British and American movements.

The first may be considered to be connected to the greater pietistic movement arising in Germany with Philip Spener in 1666 and spreading over Continental Europe. One small English manifestation of the movement was the Holy Club Society at Oxford in 1733, which brought together the personalities of John and Charles Wesley and George Whitefield. Although the Holy Club was never a factor in the revival itself, it did serve as a catalyst for what observers viewed God doing with both Wesleys and George Whitefield.[572] It was actually while Whitefield was practicing the austere disciplines of the Holy Club that he read the book, *The Life of God in the Soul of Man* by the Scottish pietist, Henry Scougal, leading to his experiencing the

---

[571]   One of the most noted of the evangelist's appearances was "George Whitefield comes to Middletown". This account vividly describes the incredible urgency for salvation experienced by those struggling to attend the sermon. One excerpt provides the following description given by Nathan Cole, a Connecticut farmer. "We went down in the stream but heard no man speak a word all the way for three miles but everyone pressing forward in great haste; and when we got to Middletown old meeting house, there was a great multitude, it was said to be 3 or 4,000 of people, assembled together. We dismounted and shook off our dust, and the ministers were then coming to the meeting house. I turned and looked towards the Great River and saw the ferry boats running swift backward and forward bringing over loads of people, and the oars rowed nimble and quick. Everything, men, horses, and boats seemed to be struggling for life. The land and the banks over the river looked black with people and horses; all along the 12 miles I saw no man at work in his field, but all seemed to be gone." Taken from Whitefield, ed., *Whitefield's Journals*, 2: 562.

[572]   Dallimore is correct in his assertion that the Holy Club played no direct role in the salvation of the Wesleys or Whitefield, or that it was an evangelical or a pre-revival movement. It did, however, serve to bring these three men together and ultimately to salvation through entirely unrelated means than the Club itself. See Arnold A. Dallimore, *George Whitefield: The Life and Times of the Great Evangelist of the 18th Century Revival.*, 2 vols., vol. 2 (Oxford: University Printing House, 1970), 1: 67-74.

new birth in the spring of 1735.[573] Wesley read deeply in the writings of Moravian leaders such as Zinzendorf, Peter Bohler, and Michael Linner before coming to his own experience of faith in Christ.[574] About the same time, future English evangelists Howell Harris and Daniel Rowland were experiencing the new birth in South Wales.[575] Just earlier in 1734, Jonathan Edwards, in Massachusetts, was in a powerful revival in his village of Northampton, but it was not until the period between Wesley's conversion in 1738 and the break-out of revival in Cambuslang, Scotland, in 1741 that Wesley even heard the news of Jonathan Edward's Northampton experience.[576]

Secondly, perceived in this great reformation of divine Providence, in which the Separate-Baptists saw themselves as participants, were notable doctrinal shifts. Brought on by a return to "the primitive purity and liberty of the Christian church," these changes challenged and overturned the doctrinal foibles of Puritanism and drove their ecclesiastical principles to their logical conclusions. Backus would later sum up all of these events under the premise that "a great and effectual door is now opened for terminating these disputes..." and which were now ameliorating "the effects of the apostasy...."[577] The First Baptist Church of Boston experienced a revival in 1803 which added one hundred thirty-five to the church by baptism. The Second Baptist Church had a larger number converted

---

573   Bebbington, *Evangelicalism in Modern Britain*, 20.
574   Bebbington, *Evangelicalism in Modern Britain*, 40, 45.
575   Bebbington, *Evangelicalism in Modern Britain*, 20.
576   Bebbington reported that Edward's "published analysis of the revival had impressed Wesley between his experience of trusting Christ and the inauguration of his traveling ministry...at Carbuslang." See the author's report in Ibid. After reflecting on Edwards revival account Wesley reported in his journal "Surely, this is the Lord's doing and it is marvelous in our eyes." See Nehemiah Curnock, ed., *The Journal of the Rev. John Wesley*, Standard ed. (New York: Eaton and Mains, 1909), I:83-84.
577   Backus, *A History of New England with Particular Reference to the Denomination of Christians Called Baptists*, 2: vi.

during the same period.[578] As the SBBM moved south under the leadership of Daniel Marshall and Shubal Stearns, Backus, the elder statesmen and historian of the movement, spoke glowingly of the southern revivals which had multiplied Baptist churches and several associations. Attributing the movement to the power of a sovereign God, Backus proclaimed, "If heavenly influence has not increased their churches, what cause can be assigned thereby?"[579] However, since Backus clearly believed that God had ordained the means, as well as the ends,[580] some of these other *means* between revival and disestablishment deserve mention.

ANDREW FULLER AND THE GENERAL ATONEMENT MOVEMENT

Benedict, who graduated from Brown University in 1806 (the year of Backus' death), offered several very clear assessments of Calvinism's decline in the midst of the burgeoning Baptist movement during the late eighteenth century in England and New England. This would include the early and middle periods of the nineteenth century, which would include the introduction of Andrew Fuller's theology. This development should be seen as part of the larger revival movement afoot on both continents and connected with the same moderating Calvinism that was articulated by Jonathan Edwards in Massachusetts. As an Edwardsean Calvinist, Backus followed the Evangelical model of his Northampton mentor but surprisingly, remained firm in his belief in a limited atonement. In contrast, Fuller did not "deny the sufficiency of Christ's death as atonement for the

---

578   Wood, *The History Of the First Baptist Church*, 294-296.
579   Backus, *A History of New England with Particular Reference to the Denomination of Christians Called Baptists*, 2: 558.
580   Backus, *Church History of New England from 1620 to 1804: Containing a View of the Principles and Practice, Declensions and Revivals, Oppression and Liberty of the Churches, and a Chronological Table. With a Memoir of the Author*, 231.

sins of the whole world and believed it the duty of all men who heard the gospel to believe it."[581]

Fuller was born into a Particular Baptist family whose soteriology was characterized by a refusal to offer gospel invitations and indeed, possessed a fear that indiscriminate invitations to all persons would actually reproach the sovereignty of God. Fuller began to question whether Gill's system was true to the biblical injunctions concerning world evangelism.[582] This was the initial breach in the door of the extreme Calvinist system. Benedict reported:

Those who espoused the views of Mr. Fuller were denominated Arminians by the Gillite men, while they, in their turn, styled their opponents Hyper-Calvinists. Both parties claimed to be orthodox and evangelical, and differed but little on any other points....[583]

As a Particular Baptist leader, Gill had been influenced toward extreme Calvinism by Tobias Crisp, an Anglican rector from Wiltshire, England. In 1690, Crisp's son published his father's written works which were the primary sources of English hyper-Calvinism. Crisp tended toward severe antinomianism (believing that no sin could threaten the status of believers), thus freeing them from any moral obligations to prescribed conduct.[584] There were several Particular Baptists who sponsored these publications, including Hanserd Knollys

---

581   Clipsham, "Andrew Fuller and Fullerism (1)," 104.
582   The prefix *hyper* or *high* represented a form of Calvinism which exceeded the traditional five-points of Calvinism such as saying that it was *Arminianism* to teach that the atonement was sufficient for the world, but efficient only for those in the covenant of election. This sort of hyper-Calvinism also thought it an affront to the sovereignty of God to offer invitations to sinners to believe on Christ indiscriminately, as if a natural man could effectively respond to such a presentation.
583   David Benedict, *Fifty Years among the Baptists* (New York: Sheldon and Company, 1860; reprint, The Baptist Standard Bearer, Inc.), 135-136.
584   From Tobias Crisp, *Christ Alone Exalted: Being the Compleat Works of Tobias Crisp* (London: 1690), 579, and cited in, McBeth, *The Baptist Heritage*, 173-174.

who had formerly been warmly evangelistic in tone.[585] The degree and emphasis placed upon election and perseverance by Crisp and his Baptist protégés had consequently become incredibly stifling to real evangelism.

John Gill probably imbibed his anti-invitation position from Joseph Hussey, a Cambridge pastor, who published his pamphlet entitled, "God's Operations of Grace: But No Offers of His Grace," wherein he concluded that to offer the gospel indiscriminately to all sinners would imply that the natural man had native ability to respond to the gospel. One of Hussey's members, John Skepp, who later converted to Baptist views had helped influence fellow Particular Baptists to this position from his pastorate at the Cripplegate Church.[586]

However, within the last quarter of the eighteenth century, the evangelical Calvinism of the Methodist revival had also influenced many of the Particular Baptists, particularly in western England, Wales, and in the Midlands. Some of Fuller's contemporaries had been affected and were beginning to spread their influence in preaching the gospel more freely. In 1775, Fuller visited London and was riveted by yet another pamphlet entitled, "A Modern Question Modestly Stated,"[587] written by a local independent pastor. Shortly thereafter he read a book written by Robert Hall, Sr., which had been expanded from a sermon entitled, *Help to Zion's Travellers* (1781). Concerning the impact of this particular volume, Fuller's Baptist contemporary William Carey proclaimed, "I do not remember to

---

585   McBeth, *The Baptist Heritage*, 171.
586   Ibid, 174.
587   This pamphlet was written by Mr. Maurice, the pastor of an Independent congregation at Rowell. He reaffirmed this by a second pamphlet in 1739 entitled, "The Modern Question Affirmed and Proved." The question concerned the "obligations of men to repent and believe the gospel." See Kirkby, "The Theology of Andrew Fuller and Its Relation to Calvinism", 50-51.

have read any book with such raptures."[588] Both Carey and Fuller were deeply affected by one of Hall's comments which declared that "the way to Jesus is graciously open for everyone who chooses to come to Him."[589] The twin ideas of salvation being "graciously open for everyone" and that offer being contingent upon the one who *chooses* were volatile theological ideas at the time. Robert Hall, Sr., then encouraged him to also read the published works of Jonathan Edwards. Fuller agreed and, in 1785, responded with a publication of his own. In GWA Fuller utilized quite extensively Edwards' work "Treatise on the Will"[590] which he adopted from Edwards.

In the preface to GWA, Fuller listed the influences behind his work as well as the criteria that formed the basis of his argument. First, he placed himself squarely in the camp of the evangelical Calvinists which provided him the theological platform from which to make his argument against the Hyper-Calvinist position. The second is in his articulation concerning the question of the sinner's *inability*. It is here that one author argues for a reappraisal of Fuller's original contention for "duty faith" (that it was the duty of all sinners to believe the gospel upon hearing it), suggesting that Fuller was guilty of understating the case for Adamic condemnation and the natural man's utter inability to respond to the claims of the gospel.[591]

---

588   Cited in Underwood, *A History of the English Baptists*, 161.

589   Ibid.

590   This concept first articulated as such by Jonathan Edwards was not a new one. This is the point which troubled Fuller in his earlier days while under the influence of John Gill. Gill expressed the concept as "the power of the hand," and "the power of the heart." Kirkby concluded that Fuller had not even read Edwards until 1777 and clearly demonstrates that Fuller had already formed his theological opinions prior to reading Edwards "Treatise on the Will." Technically Kirkby may have been correct in his finding, but Fuller certainly had been influenced by those who read Edwards and later articulated his own ideas within the construct of Edward's vocabulary. Kirkby's conclusion that Fuller was essentially articulating Calvin was shown to be based largely on evidentiary assumption. See Clipsham, "Andrew Fuller and Fullerism," Clipsham, "Andrew Fuller and Fullerism (1)," Clipsham, "Andrew Fuller and Fullerism (2)," Clipsham, "Andrew Fuller and Fullerism (3)."

591   In his article entitled, "Andrew Fuller's response to the 'Modern Question'- A

However, this charge hardly comes to grip with the overarching realities of the matter. Just two years later Fuller had to respond to Daniel Taylor, the leader of the *New Connexion* General Baptists, who agreed with Fuller concerning "duty faith," but believed Fuller to be inconsistent concerning the election doctrine suggesting that if God had "determined not to save" everyone, "why should they seek after salvation?"[592] In other words, what advancement does this new view bring to the table? In other words, Taylor might simply have asked, "If this does not constitute genuine autonomy on the part of man on some mitigating basis, is this nothing but a shell game?" Taylor argued that God, by offering salvation to all people, had made it possible for men to respond to the message.[593] This is ostensibly the teaching of *prevenient* grace, that is; grace which would *prevent* the effects of human depravity from disabling the sinner *entirely* in responding to God's offer of salvation. Taylor appeared to suggest that the ability to respond was not resident *before* the preaching of the gospel, but

---

Reappraisal of *The Gospel Worthy of All Acceptation*", Gerald Priest attempts to find in one of Fuller's "duty faith" explanations a justification for accusing Fuller of not fully comprehending the imputation of Adam's sin. Priest then suggests we are left with the question of "...how can sin be so interwoven and so deeply rooted in our souls as to be natural to us and yet allow us to have a motive to respond to the gospel independent of the disposition of our hearts?" Speaking of Gill's notion that no man is obligated to obey the gospel, Priest then replied that 'Fullerism' or moderate Calvinism countered with duty-faith: every man is obligated to accept Christ predicated on his ability to do so; the only reason he cannot is because he will not. Priest contends that "both of these views are unscriptural." Priest's position is predicated on the Calvinist dictum that total depravity precludes any *ability* on the part of a sinner to respond to God outside of God first regenerating the sinner to do so. Unfortunately, this offers little help in understanding how early moderate Calvinism evolved out of the views of Jonathan Edwards, Fuller's mentoring theologian. Most Baptists who accept a more moderate Calvinism believe that fallen man is enabled to believe by hearing the gospel coupled with the illuminating power of the Holy Spirit. For them, regeneration follows believing, but cannot theologically or practically precede it.

592   Quoted from Daniel Taylor, *Observations on the Rev. Andrew Fuller's Late Pamphlet, Entitled the Gospel Worthy of Christ Worthy of All Acceptation, in Nine Letters to a Friend* (London: n.p., 1786), 49 in Timothy George and David S. Dockery, ed., *Theologians of the Baptist Tradition* (Nashville: Broadman and Holman Publishers, 2001), 40.

593   George, ed., *Theologians of the Baptist Tradition*, 40.

became resident as the Holy Spirit empowered the Word in response to gospel preaching.

Fuller sought refuge from Taylor's argument, stating that given the *moral inability* of sinners to effectually respond to the gospel, only unconditional election could insure that grace would overcome the unbelief of some. This hardly sounds like Fuller's "duty faith" had succumbed to Pelagianism as Priest contended,[594] but it certainly does reveal that a reappraisal of human autonomy in salvation was underfoot among several of the Particular Baptists. Priest rightly asserts that it took human ability beyond "the bounds of orthodoxy" (or classic Calvinism),[595] but rather than accuse Fuller of Pelagianism or of a faulty definition of Adamic guilt, which Fuller adequately defended in his response to Daniel Taylor, he could have simply suggested he had adopted a form of *prevenient* or enabling grace. This may be why Dan Taylor, under the pseudonym *Philanthropos*, published his response to Fuller in "Observations on the Rev. Andrew Fuller's Late Pamphlet Entitled the GWA," in which he embraced the idea that Fuller had come to his own free-will position on the matter. Fuller *guardedly* responded back to Taylor by maintaining his distinction between *natural* ability and *moral* inability, and that the moral inability of men could only be overcome by elective grace.[596] Dan Taylor, as more of a free-will Baptist, was not in a theological position to convincingly argue that point. However, General Baptist turned Particular Baptist Abraham Booth in 1796 was, and he directly challenged Fuller's commitment to the *ordis salutis* of classic Calvinism in *Glad Tidings to Perishing Sinners or, The Genuine*

---

594   Gerald L. Priest, "Andrew Fuller's Response to the 'Modern Question'-a Reappraisal of the Gospel Worthy of All Acceptation," *Detroit Baptist Seminary Journal* 6 (Fall 2001): 66.
595   Ibid.
596   George, ed., *Theologians of the Baptist Tradition*, 40.

Gospel a Complete Warrant for the Ungodly to Believe in Jesus.[597]
Booth's contention was that the doctrine of justification by faith alone
was threatened by making regeneration *antecedent* to saving faith as it
appeared in the *ordis salutis* of Fuller's classic Calvinism. He felt that
by making regeneration a prerequisite for saving faith, the universality
of the gospel was being threatened.

This at least demonstrated that duty faith had indeed produced
a crack in the door of hyper-Calvinism and would continue to force
other door-widening revisions such as prevenient or assisting grace
for the sinner in order to be able to believe on Christ. Once the
atonement began to be interpreted in universal terms, the weight of
doctrinal concern essentially shifted back to the election doctrine. The
nineteenth-century theological question would no longer involve the
extent of the atonement but why God would limit salvation to a chosen
few, if in fact He had made it possible for all to be saved through
Christ's cross-work. Edwards and Fuller had, in fact, introduced an
ability which had in time become a "true ability, under which revival
preaching arose; and good practice in converting men and good
theology went together."[598] This raised the question of how this natural
ability began to usurp the place of moral inability thereby making it
the duty of all men to respond to the gospel. However, according to his
confession of faith, Fuller did not leave duty only in the hands of the
unregenerate. In giving the gospel and invitations for sinners to come
to Christ, he told his Kettering congregation, "I consider it as a part
of my duty which I could not omit without being guilty of the blood of
souls."[599] This, of course, begs the question of how a preacher could

---

597   Ibid, 41.
598   Frank H. Foster, *The Genetic History of New England Theology*, ed. Bruce Kuklick,
American Religious Thought of the 18th and 19th Centuries (Chicago: University of Chicago
Press, 1907; reprint, Garland Publishing , Inc. New York 1987), 78.
599   Kirkby, "The Theology of Andrew Fuller and Its Relation to Calvinism", 74.

be held guilty for the reprobation of sinners who ostensibly, were not elected.

James M'Gready, the frontier Presbyterian Calvinist, answered this question in 1790 by saying, like Fuller, the minister "must use every means to alarm and awaken Christ-less sinners from their security...though the world scorn us (as) Methodists - do this we must, or... the blood of sinners will be required at our hands - their damnation will lie at our door."[600] M'Gready's point demonstrates how in the passion and rhetoric of revival one could simultaneously preach a "free will" gospel while embracing a Calvinist creed.

THE ADVENT OF THE FREE-WILL MOVEMENT

Benjamin Randall started the Free-Will Baptist movement in 1780 particularly among New Hampshire Baptist congregations, many of which had been established by Separate-Baptist Samuel Shepherd. Randall had been converted after hearing Whitefield preach in Portsmouth on September 25 and 26, 1770. He rejected the Grand Itinerant's first message but was converted about three weeks later upon hearing of the evangelist's death in Newburyport, Massachusetts, on September 30.[601] Randall, a former Congregationalist, was therefore one of the last converts of the great evangelist and, like many others, had gone back to the Congregational church for spiritual sustenance. Later, like Backus, he determined that this was unacceptable. He then joined the Madbury Baptist Church in Madbury, New Hampshire and for the next ten years or so faced "familial challenges, political opposition, and ecclesiastical sanction

---

600   Taken from James M'Gready, *The Posthumous Works of the Reverend and Pious James M'Gready, Late Minister of the Gospel*, in Henderson, Kentucky. Edited by James Smith. 2 vols. Vol.1, Louisville, Ky., 1831; vol.2, Nashville, Tenn., 1833. Quoted in Boles, *The Great Revival*, 41.
601   Marini, *Radical Sects of Revolutionary New England*, 64.

for his faith."[602] During this time, Randall had become convinced
in the universal atonement of Christ resulting in his ejection from
Madbury shortly before 1779. This doctrine was the point of critical
departure from the bulwark of Calvinist entrenchment in New
England. Whitefield's vigorous response to Wesley and Backus' 1787
pamphlet both laid great emphasis on this doctrine as a precipitous
abandonment of Calvinistic orthodoxy. Randall's bold declaration of
this doctrine in the hill country, along with a strong open-communion
position, established them as obstinate competitors in the eyes of
Backus. For the SBBM, Randall's open-communion position was a
doctrinal throwback to the earlier struggle the SBBM had experienced
with the Congregational-Separates.

Conversely, the Free-Will Baptists fully cooperated with the
Methodists, a range of willing Baptists and, later, the Disciples of
Christ at the communion table.[603] Theologically, Randall's movement
had married elements of the Old Light Congregationalist tradition,
Whitefield's evangelical Calvinism, along with Baptist polity.[604]
Although not the first doctrinal challenge which served to soften
the stringent Calvinism of the Separate-Baptists, it was the first
major Baptist sect which openly reacted against determinism in New
England. Certainly, the leaven of the Free-Will Baptist movement[605]
must be considered in the overall declension of Westminster theology.
However, the advancement of the universal atonement doctrine
cannot be singularly blamed for its decline, and Randall's influence is

---

602   Ibid, 65-66.
603   William F. Davidson, *The Free Will Baptists in History* (Nashville: Randall House,
2001), 176.
604   Marini, *Radical Sects of Revolutionary New England*, 67.
605   Maring, *A Baptist Manual of Polity and Practice*, 173.

too tenuous to conclude that the theological views of the Calvinistic Baptists "had been greatly modified" purely on his account.[606] While Randall's theological views were at variance with Backus' Calvinism in PEV, the question remains as to how the SBBM and Randall had such similar revival results. The majority of Baptists, at least in New England, remained committed to the logic of Andrew Fuller's modifications through at least the fifth decade of the nineteenth century.[607] That does not suggest that questions were not continually raised concerning its inherent logic. The Calvinist defender could say with Fuller's dictum, "...if anyone perishes, it is not from the want of a full and free provision, but from his own willful perverseness." At the same time the defender would be forced to admit, "This does not, however, interfere with his gracious purpose to save by his sovereign mercy such as he may choose."[608] The logic of this soteriological double-speak continued to deteriorate under the frontier revivals because the sheer numbers of individuals being converted appeared to temporarily suspend limited atonement and the particular-election doctrine. Revival participants might wonder that if God had procured salvation as a universal provision with the duty of all men to believe, why did He arbitrarily limit the number who could come and partake, particularly when all who would not believe would suffer in Hell for their refusal? Does not *duty* involve responsibility? Or did they reject the gospel because they were not

---

606   Lumpkin, *Baptist Confessions of Faith*, 360.
607   Normally this meant that universal atonement was taught, as was particular election. The explanation was God's offer of mercy was perfectly honest and sincere because the provision was universal. This was held simultaneously with the doctrine that God had chosen only a certain number of those for whom the provision was offered. When the revivals in Kentucky and Tennessee began in 1799, even Calvinist Presbyterian preachers recognized that the "unprecedented size of the services simply relegated Calvinistic talk of particular election to the background; the immediate, convincing effectiveness of the revival spectacle pushed an emphasis on personal volition to the forefront." From Boles, *The Great Revival*, 68.
608   Wayland, *Notes on the Principles and Practices of Baptist Churches*, 20.

previously elected? Could both be true simultaneously?[609] Whatever these revival observers may have been asking themselves, or others, these modifying tendencies did pose serious questions regarding the stability of the former orthodoxy.

Within fifty years, Wayland reported that belief in the universal atonement of Christ "prevails almost universally" in New England and men that differ on the subject usually remain amicable, and "it is found that when their hearts are warmed with the love of God and desire for the salvation of souls, they all preach very much alike."[610] Here, two critical aspects of doctrinal change are broached: the love of God and the desire for the salvation of souls. In the sterile environment of the Westminster Confession and the Old Calvinist system, these two ideas were seldom considered.

Much of this influence had drifted over from the new missionary emphasis in England. Extreme Calvinism was being challenged by the kindred spirits of Robert Hall, Sr., Andrew Fuller, John Sutcliff, and William Carey.[611] Invitations and warnings taken to call sinners to an immediate salvation were being promoted as the divinely prescribed means for the salvation of His elect rather than presumptions upon the sovereign grace of God. All of these measures had formerly been considered unjustified in light of God's all-consuming sovereignty. Now they were the duty of all ministers which

---

609   These sorts of theological inquiry were demanding a "middle ground" among theologians which was philosophically positing the idea that God's sovereignty was grounded in something other than causal determinism as popularly articulated in standard Calvinist dictums. This "something other" was approaching the view that God's sovereign control of the universe was manifested through His omniscience rather than sheer determinism. This position was first proposed by Luis Molina, a sixteenth century Jesuit priest. Molina held to divine sovereignty and human freedom occurring simultaneously. For a theologically compelling discussion of Molinism, see Kevin Keathley, *Salvation and Sovereignty: A Molinist Approach* (Nashville, B & H Academic, 2010).
610   Wayland, *Notes on the Principles and Practices of Baptist Churches*, 19.
611   Hayden, *English Baptist History and Heritage*, 124.

they could not omit without "being guilty of the blood of souls."[612] Wayland noted that the movement toward the universal nature of the atonement during this period in New England[613] was also beginning to dominate in both the northern and eastern states.[614] Backus undoubtedly sensed that these ideas were no longer stable in the dynamic environment of revivalism and denominational expansion, especially as it moved from New England into the western territories.

These developments, brought on by revivalism and its inherent missionary spirit, diminished the influence of the Westminster Confession and helped foment the growing sense of need for the NHC which stood to become the first, truly American, Particular-Baptist Confession of note. In short, the choice between radical idealism and denominational pragmatism was now beginning to tilt toward the forces behind denominational proliferation. Consequently, growth and expansion, along with a modified Calvinism within the SBBM, had by the turn of the nineteenth century resulted in the demand for a modified confession of faith to accommodate its thought.

THE SHIFT: FROM WESTMINSTER TO NEW HAMPSHIRE

The idea that the radical Free-Will movements were the essential leavening agents to the weakening of the Calvinist doctrines at the close of the eighteenth century is not entirely justified. The Free-Will movement entered into decline nearly in direct proportion to the rate of decline of Orthodox Calvinism,[615] which suggests the

---

612   Taken from Fuller's "The Gospel Worthy of all Acceptation." Quoted in Ibid, 123.
613   Wayland, *Notes on the Principles and Practices of Baptist Churches*, 19.
614   Ibid, 20.
615   Baxter demonstrated that the Free-Will movement in New England prospered insofar as it participated in the overall decline of Calvinist orthodoxy. The author said, "Once this metamorphosis had seeped into Baptist thinking, the Freewill Baptist message lost its unique appeal." For an overview of his thesis, see Norman A. Baxter, "History of the Free-Will Baptists: A Study in New England Separatism," *Church History* 24, no. 2 (1955): 177.

movement shared common ground with other moderating forces and should not be blamed for single-handedly producing it. Randall's movement was produced in the pursuit of soteriological interests. By attacking limited atonement, he found a sympathetic populace, largely middle-class, ready to respond to a free gospel. Conversely, the SBBM had forged its revival interests upon believers' baptism preceding the Lord's Table in the local assembly. The mutual needs of survival and conformation so evident in eighteenth-century England and America were now beginning to transition into a period of both denominational expansion and freer doctrinal expression. Consequently, the New England Free-Will Baptists published their own "1834 Treatise" a year after the official publishing of the NHC in order to distinguish themselves from the rest of the Baptist majority. In the treatise, its delegates clarified at least three positions, among other lesser ones, which were unacceptable to Separate-Baptists. The first was open-communion. Davidson noted that their own records were full of "accounts of cooperation in worship with Methodists, other Baptist groups, and the Disciples of Christ."[616] He also admitted that the "lowering of the bars of access to the table allowed fellowship that would not have been possible otherwise."[617] This desire for fellowship via the Lord's Table was considered anathema by the majority of the SBBM. The second position in the Free-Will Treatise was their extended definition stating that the "Church of God, or members of the body of Christ, is the whole body of Christians throughout the whole world, and none but the regenerate are its members."[618] The SBBM never adopted such a view, particularly because it would have justified a form of *associationalism* which they ultimately came to reject in the WBA. A third position was the Free-Will view that the

---

616   Davidson, *The Free Will Baptists in History*, 176.
617   Ibid, 176-177.
618   Lumpkin, *Baptist Confessions of Faith*, 375.

"final salvation" of the regenerate is not "determined nor certain...."[619] These distinctions of the SBBM argue against the monolithic revivalist persona suggested by Mead.[620]

Unquestionably, the Westminster language, so clearly articulated in the Reformed-based PBC, is patently ignored in the NHC.[621] The NHC would articulate the typical Baptist view saying, "That such only are real believers as endure unto the end; that their persevering attachment to Christ is the grand mark which distinguishes them from mere professors; that...they are kept by the power of God through faith unto salvation."[622] In the PBC, the Calvinist idea of effectual calling for the elect is defined as from "God's free and special grace alone, not from anything foreseen in man, nor from any power or agency in the creature, co-working with his special grace, the creature being wholly passive ...is thereby enabled to answer this call...."[623] Conversely, the NHC declared that "nothing prevents the salvation of any sinner on earth except his own voluntary refusal to submit to the Lord Jesus Christ...."[624] In addition, the PBC unconditionally declared the universal Church consists of the whole number of the elect, that have been, are, or shall be gathered into one, under Christ, the head thereof...."[625] But no such connection between election and the universal Church exists in the NHC. Having made the election doctrine to be "perfectly consistent with the free agency of man," the NHC completely avoids any mention, and thereby any connection, of election to the universal Church.[626] Mentioning only the

---

619   Ibid.
620   Mead, *The Lively Experiment: The Shaping of Christianity in America*, 123.
621   Foster, *The Genetic History of New England Theology*, 78.
622   Lumpkin, *Baptist Confessions of Faith*, 365.
623   Broadus, *Baptist Confessions, Covenants, and Catechisms*, 69.
624   Ibid, 133.
625   Ibid, 84.
626   Ibid, 134.

visible church, it flatly declares that it is "a congregation of baptized believers...," without any further definition.

Clearly, ecclesiological tendencies observable in the SBBM had crystallized in Backus' twenty-five year absence. The question of import revolves around why so many Particular Baptists in New Hampshire, New England, and beyond were capable of accepting such a document which failed to clearly articulate Reformed doctrine on salvation and the church, if in fact Calvinism was not already in decline during this period.[627] O.C.S. Wallace pointed out in his description of the half century prior to the document's preparation that "the influence of this teaching had greatly modified the earlier New England Calvinism even when Arminianism was still rejected."[628] The question which immediately comes to mind with Wallace's then contemporary opinion is how Arminianism or any human volition in salvation, could directly affect any modification while being rejected at the same time. What he did not say, which he should have observed, was that both extremes of hyper-Calvinism and Randall's free-willism had been rejected by the vast majority of middle-class, revival-oriented Baptists of the period.[629] The fact remains that the articles in New

---

627   Daniel Walker Howe's work identifies this decline on the basis of social and political considerations. For instance, he says these changes in the larger context of Calvinism and Arminianism "should be seen as manifestations of varying social moods of fear and contentment. These changing moods were related, among other things, to international patterns of power politics. In the calmer days following the wars of religion and the revolution against the Stuarts, when the future of Protestantism no longer seemed in jeopardy, a rigid and uncompromising confession of faith no longer seemed necessary or appropriate." Although there is some truth in his argument, he fails to point out that all of Protestantism did not decline in Calvinist tenets either at the same time or in equal proportions Neither does he mention the role revivalism played in modifying Calvinism especially in New England with the eventuation of the New Hampshire Confession of Faith. Daniel Walker Howe, "The Decline of Calvinism: An Approach to Its Study," *Comparative Studies in Society and History* 14, no. 3 (1972): 322.
628   Terry Wolever, ed., *An Anthology of the Early Baptists in New Hampshire*, Anthology Series (Springfield, Mo.: Particular Baptist Press, 2001), 531.
629   Calvinist decline was more noticeable among the growing middle-class throughout New England, especially as the Separate-Baptists, who preferred the "warmer evangelism," began to migrate south-westward. See Lumpkin, *Baptist Confessions of Faith*, 360. The urban centers tended to maintain the old guard mentality, but by the end of the nineteenth century no

Hampshire were written to "reconstitute a theological consensus in *response* to views promoted by Free-Will Baptists" not as a consensus document.[630] The Treatise of the Free-Will Baptists of 1834 must be seen in turn as an equally *reactive* effort by Randall's followers to clarify distinctions unique to themselves and unacceptable to other contemporary Baptists, namely, open-communion and the possibility of apostasy for believers.

Two things then become evident. First, the mutual emphasis on revival in both *Baptist* camps which created a new theological environ had diminished. Second, both groups felt it necessary to inform constituents and observers of their doctrinal views at the point in which their mutual alliances had run their course. However, it is apparent that in the construct of revival, these doctrinal differences were seen as secondary to the harvesting of souls. By 1832, just a year before the official adoption of the NHC, a report was issued from an individual at the New Hampshire Baptist State Convention being held at Portsmouth:

God is doing great things for us as a denomination...so many added to our churches...new churches rising...qualified ministers increasing...sound in faith...warm with love...these and a thousand other things, combine to fill my soul with praise, and awaken the most precious hopes of good to come.[631]

One wonders how this sort of description of the Baptist denomination can be balanced with the negative descriptions by Wallace of the Free-Will Baptists, especially as the new churches and

---

strong consensus remained. See Crowell, *The Church Member's Manual*, 140.

630   Myron C. Noonkester, "'God for Its Author': John Locke as a Possible Source for the New Hampshire Confession," *The New England Quarterly* 66, no. 3 (1993): 449.

631   Wolever, ed., *An Anthology of the Early Baptists in New Hampshire*, 533.

qualified ministers are described as *sound* in the faith. The picture describing great unanimity and thankfulness for what "God is doing" fails to demonstrate great dissention or bitter infighting among Baptists on either side of the issues. Neither does it demonstrate a doctrinal capitulation by the Separate-Baptists to the doctrinal positions of the Free-Will Baptists. Stewart simply reported that in New Hampshire during this period "there seems to have been little said about the peculiar doctrines of *Calvinism*...,"[632] and that "Randall and his adjurors were acknowledged as sound on all the great questions of evangelical religion, Calvinism alone excepted...."[633] Both their agreement with the Separate-Baptists and their disagreements can be observed in what Stewart admits was their greatest secret. Among their "enterprise" and "efforts" he points to "the dissatisfaction of the people with extreme Calvinism, and their eagerness to hear and know a free and full salvation."[634] However, this also reveals significant differences with the SBBM.

No element of what Free-Will historian Stewart claims as their greatest secret involved a desire to clarify believers' baptism as requisite to the Lord's Table. Nor did they share with the SBBM the same level of indignation or determination to change the Standing Order's religious exploitation of the populace via infant baptism and the ministerial tax code. These issues were continuously raised by the Separate-Baptists in their efforts to elevate their evangelistic outreach.

REVIVAL: IDENTIFYING COMMON VALUES

One of the four things Sidney Mead listed as key in shaping American denominational Protestantism was revivalism. In describing

---

632   Stewart, *The History of the Freewill Baptists*, 45.
633   Ibid, 72.
634   Ibid, 471.

the gradual breakdown of uniformity within the civil jurisdiction, particularly in Massachusetts, Mead asserted that "revivalism soon emerged as the accepted technique of the voluntary churches."[635] This breakdown of uniformity was accompanied by the perception of doctrinal breakdown which became an inherent feature of the methodology of revival.[636] As the Separate-Baptists understood it, they were continuing what had been inherited from the first Great Awakening.[637] Despite his ardent Calvinist creed, the Grand Itinerant urgently preached the gospel as if every listener was one of the elect, and every person was capable of choosing life over death. It comes as no surprise that the decline of Calvinism noted among the revival-oriented Separate-Baptists was finally considered by Haller as a "heresy upon the doctrine of election itself."[638] In the final analysis, they concluded that revivalism "tends to lean theologically in an Arminian or even Pelagian direction with the implicit suggestion that man saves himself through choice."[639] Mead said that most

635   Mead, *The Lively Experiment: The Shaping of Christianity in America*, 121-122.
636   Revival is seldom attributed the emphasis it deserves in the decline of Calvinism in England and Colonial America with its advent, especially the period of revival in New England and the western frontier after the American Revolution. While the Great Awakening introduced a so-called Arminian vernacular in religious discourse, the ongoing revival movement eventually began to neutralize the election doctrine, and eventually, the Universal church concept.
637   Lumpkin, *Colonial Baptists and Southern Revivals*, 60.
638   This sentiment makes it almost certain that William Haller would not make any connection between the decline of Calvinism and the gradual disappearance of the universal-invisible church among the Separate-Baptists and other Baptists as seen in the noted New Hampshire Confession of Faith. His understanding of Puritan orthodoxy precluded the possibility in his mind that any moderating force on this element of Calvinist ideology could result in true reformation of the existing two-church model. See Haller, *The Rise of Puritanism*, 17.
639   Ibid.

Congregational church-men believed that revivalism "undercut the traditional churchly standards of doctrine and practice."[640] Despite these cynical reservations, revivalism became the means by which thousands of un-reached settlers in both the South and the western frontiers heard the gospel of God's grace for the very first time.

THE PRELUDE TO THE SECOND GREAT AWAKENING

Although, the post-revolutionary period had initially brought evangelistic success in New England and the Middle Atlantic states, there was a certain sense of spiritual malaise in many parts of the country throughout the 1790s. This malaise had several factors, some of which appeared to be confusion and malaise about what the future held for the nation recently united under a new constitution. Secondly, in the search for an answer to this depression, the collective leadership of the Presbyterians, Methodists, and Baptists recognized a spiritual decline. Some of this they blamed on the proliferation of deist literature, from men like Elihu Palmer and Ethan Allen,[641] which contributed to the moral apostasy.

In 1795, a Baptist by the name of David Barrows had toured throughout Kentucky and summed up his travels by saying, "Of all the denominations I can remember to have seen in this country, the

---

640   Mead, *The Lively Experiment: The Shaping of Christianity in America*, 123.
641   Boles, *The Great Revival*, 21. Boles' work encompasses the period from about 1787 to 1805. It is, without doubt, the best work demonstrating the background, components, and participants in the Second Great Awakening movement in the States of Virginia, North Carolina, South Carolina, Georgia, Kentucky, and Tennessee. The author drew from a variety of resources including church records, personal journals, memoirs, diaries, letters, and sermons. Concerning the manner of cooperation exemplified among the three major denominations (Presbyterians, Methodists, and Baptists), the author concluded, "Their theological differences were often subordinated in the midst of the revival. Again and again, sermons at a camp meeting purposely disregarded theological niceties." See the preface to the volume listed above.

Deists, Nothingarians and Anythingarians are the most numerous."[642] In 1801, Backus mentioned receiving a letter from a pastor Watkins in Virginia who said that "deism and irreligion abounded on every hand. Professing believers had become very carnal, many had apostatized... ."[643] Similarly, William Ellery Channing, then a tutor in Virginia, observed, "Christianity is here breathing its last. I cannot find a friend with whom I can even converse on religious subjects."[644] Others were quick to blame the rapid immigration of new settlers toward the ever-expanding western frontier, most without any organized religious connections and longstanding cultural conventions. Each of these intense social disruptions prevalent in the 1790s "intensified the deep longing for a strong, settled, secure religious life"[645] and opened the way for an equally intense revivalist tradition to provide the means. The Separate-Baptists were poised to fill the void.

THE QUEST FOR SOULS IN THE EAST

As early as 1781, Shepard wrote in a letter to Backus concerning these revivals in which he had participated in New Hampshire:

> Some hundreds of souls are hopefully converted in the counties of Rockingham, Strafford, and Grafton, in New Hampshire, within a year past.... I baptized seventy-two men, women.... I baptized forty-two in the town of Meredith in one day...there appears to be a general increase of the Baptist

---

642   Taken from Barrow, *"Diary,"* July 30, 1795, and quoted in Ibid., 10.
643   Backus, *Church History of New England from 1620 to 1804: Containing a View of the Principles and Practice, Declensions and Revivals, Oppression and Liberty of the Churches, and a Chronological Table. With a Memoir of the Author*, 220.
644   Taken from *Memoir of William Ellery Channing, With Extracts from His Correspondence and Manuscripts*, 2 vols. (Boston, 1848), 1:126, and quoted in Boles, *The Great Revival*, 10.
645   Ibid, 20.

principles through all the eastern parts of New England.[646]

Shepard's letter to Elder Backus reveals three important things. First, it demonstrates that Shepard wished to identify himself with Backus and the Separate-Baptist movement. Secondly, the physician-preacher recognized and clearly respected Backus' position among the Separate-Baptists by informing the pastor/historian of his activities. Thirdly, it reveals that he was extremely pleased in the results of the recent revivals in the state regardless of *who* may have been specifically responsible. Both Randall and Shepard had preached in Strafford, a former part of Barrington where it was reported that in Randall's visit "a most glorious revival had been in progress...for a time it swept almost everything before it, and the enemies of the cross gave up all hope of effectual opposition."[647] According to Stewart, Randall's visit came on the heels of Calvinist Shepard's, whose favorable results Backus had mentioned among the residents of the new towns occurring in 1780.[648] This may suggest that Randall's revival work was included in Shepard's assertion concerning the "general increase of Baptist principles through all the eastern parts of New England." If so, doctrinal exactness (and uniformity) was being relegated to lesser importance than the success of revival itself. Earlier, Backus even printed the letter wherein Shepard chronicled his own blessed revivals in Loudon and Canterbury:

Canterbury, in Rockingham county, has two Baptist churches gathered in the year past, one in the parish of Northfield: the number I cannot tell, but it is considerably large: I baptized thirty-one there, and a number have been baptized since by others:

---

646   Cathart, ed., *The Baptist Encyclopedia,* 1052.
647   Stewart, *The History of the Freewill Baptists,* 59.
648   Backus, *A History of New England with Particular Reference to the Denomination of Christians Called Baptists,* 2: 535.

the other is in the parish of Loudon, in said Canterbury....[649]

Free-Will historian Davidson assumed this meant they had broadened their fellowship to include Randall and his churches.[650] Stewart also reported that before the revivals, "The line of demarcation between the Calvinistic and Arminian Baptists was but faintly drawn for several years."[651] A good example of this cross-pollination involved Separate-Baptist preacher Joe Macomber. He had been greatly successful in bringing revival to the towns of New Gloucester and Lincoln and had written a personal letter describing the results of his meetings to Isaac Backus.[652] Because the Calvinist pastors at this time had no formal organization, Macomber went ahead and fellowshipped with the Free-Will Baptists at the second session of their Quarterly Meeting in New Gloucester, Maine, in 1784. He went on to be elected clerk and also preached on the Lord's Day during their March conclave.

In August of the same year, Backus recorded that Macomber was elected pastor of the new Separate-Baptist church established in Bowdoinham through the preaching ministry of Mr. Lock.[653] Backus likely was not aware of Macomber's association with Randall and, consequently, makes no mention of it. It is highly unlikely that he would have personally approved of such an association. This evidences quite a doctrinal tolerance by Macomber, not to mention his willingness to be discovered as having fellowshipped with Randall. However, the mingling of men operating under the auspices of such

---

649   Ibid, 2: 280, emphasis added.
650   Ibid, 132.
651   Stewart, *The History of the Freewill Baptists*, 72.
652   Backus, *A History of New England with Particular Reference to the Denomination of Christians Called Baptists*, 2: 484. Job Macomber was the son of a Congregationalist deacon in Middleboro. He joined Backus' church in 1772, and in 1774 he began to preach and itinerate around the New England area.
653   Ibid.

doctrinally diverse communions suggests that, at least practically for the sake of revival, doctrinal arguments among Baptists were being temporarily shelved. This passion for reaching the unconverted, undergirded by the sense of God's blessing and pleasure, seemed to assure men from both sides that fellowship was more vital than maintaining their own particular sense of orthodoxy. That following year, in 1785, the Calvinists began the New Hampshire Baptist Association, which also included the small number of Calvinist churches in Maine, and thereafter, cooperation essentially ceased among them.[654]

The primary point of contention for Randall was his belief that Jesus had satisfied God's requirement for the sins of the whole world rather than just a select few. However, Backus was not ambivalent regarding the Free-Will preachers and their churches. On one occasion Samuel Shepard, Separate-Baptist friend of Backus, ordained Pelatiah Tingley at the Baptist church in Sandford, Maine, in 1772. Not long afterwards, Tingley took a church in Waterborough where Backus noted, "He is pastor of a church that is not in *full* fellowship with *most* of our Baptist churches" suggesting that there were some of the Separate-Baptists who had refused to disassociate themselves from some who embraced the doctrine of general atonement.[655] But then, in a moment of unconscious inconsistency, Backus, in the same paragraph, lists Free-Will Baptist Tozier Lord as pastor "of a church in Shipleigh."[656] This church had started in 1781 as a result of a successful revival held by Lock where "about fifty were converted."[657] Consequently, it appears that avoiding Randall over doctrinal

---

654   Stewart, *The History of the Freewill Baptists*, 77.
655   Backus, *A History of New England with Particular Reference to the Denomination of Christians Called Baptists*, 2: 480, emphasis added.
656   Ibid, 2: 481.
657   Stewart, *The History of the Freewill Baptists*, 58.

differences appeared increasingly difficult as both groups struggled for souls in New England. Times were certainly changing. Earlier, Benedict reminded us that

> ...*all were set down as Arminians who did not come up to the highest point of Hyper-Calvinism. Our old ministers in this region, half a century since, would have denounced as unsound in the faith the great mass of our community of the present day, both in Europe and America, Fuller and Hall among the rest.*[658]

Revivalism had, in this instance, threatened the continued monopoly of a closed Calvinist system. With the greater emphasis upon granting greater autonomy to the individual inherent within revivalism, the election doctrine was being forced to shift in emphasis or simply remain a moot point among those interested in reaching more souls. The advancement of these modified principles in New Hampshire must be accounted for, especially as they relate to the formation of a new Baptist confession which was destined to soon emerge from the revival fires in this state.

A QUEST FOR SOULS: THE SOUTHERN REVIVALS

A convert of Whitefield in 1741, Shubal Stearns left New England Congregationalism in 1745 becoming a Baptist in 1751 (just five years before Isaac Backus). Backus confirmed that Stearns was ordained that same year in the Baptist church at Tolland, Connecticut, and in 1754 left the church shortly after baptizing Noah Alden, who the church called as their pastor in 1755.[659] Settling in Sandy Creek,

---

658   Benedict, *A General History of the Baptist Denomination in America*, 580.
659   Backus, *A History of New England with Particular Reference to the Denomination of Christians Called Baptists*, 2: 531.

Shubal Stearns established the Sandy Creek Church which, between 1755 and 1772, birthed forty-two more Separate-Baptist churches. Between 1755-1761 the Philadelphia Baptist Association made efforts to recruit new churches and pastors from the General Baptist groups primarily through an education program during the same period. Aimed at correcting their perceived Arminianism, the PBA sent Morgan Edwards and John Gano in 1755 to reorganize many of the old General Baptist churches in North Carolina for the Calvinist cause. Consequently, by 1761, only four of the General Baptist churches in the state remained.[660] Notably, during this reorganization in North Carolina, nine General Baptist pastors defected to Calvinist principles and no less than twelve churches migrated over.[661] However, Davidson quoted Paschal who asserted that in reality, no more than *five percent* of the General Baptist membership *actually* became a part of the new churches.[662] This re-orientation of church leaders toward the adoption of the Philadelphia doctrinal confession was clearly not the result of revival or evangelism.

Compare this effort with the accomplishments of the Separate-Baptists under the ministry of Shubal Stearns. Feeling the call of God to minister the gospel in the southern regions, Stearns largely divided his time between Virginia and North Carolina between 1755 and 1760. He reached and baptized hundreds of converts in both states.[663] This evangelistic activity among Stearns and his Baptist brother-in-law

---

660   Davidson, *The Free Will Baptists in History*, 66.
661   Ibid, 67-68. Davidson's numbers are taken directly from the sketches located in Edwards, "Furman MS"; "Tours"; Huggins, 'History'; Burkitt and Read, 'Concise History'; and Paschal; 'North Carolina. According to these tables, the defections of both preachers and churches occurred between 1755 and 1761.
662   Ibid, 66.
663   Torbet, *A History of the Baptists*, 228.

Daniel Marshall was highly effective and key to the growth of SBBM in the southern colonies.

This activity would prove to have an early and direct influence in the formation of both the Sandy Creek and Charleston associations, the two key Baptist organizations which would later lead to the formation of the Southern Baptist Convention in 1845. The Charleston Association, founded in 1751, adopted a predominately Calvinist confession which evolved directly from the Second London/ Philadelphia Baptist traditions.[664] Its origin can be traced to the 1749 session of the PBA, where Oliver Hart, who being recently called to preach, was encouraged by men present in that meeting to accept the pastorate of the First Baptist Church at Charleston.[665] Shortly thereafter, in 1751, Hart led his Charleston church along with the churches at Ashley River, Welsh Neck, and Euhaw into the Charleston Association (hereafter the CA).[666] Under Hart's leadership in the staunchly Calvinist PBA, this southern association took their confessional standard of the PBA as its model with the exception of the article regarding the laying on of hands.[667] Like the Philadelphia association, the CA offered its member churches assistance in resolving difficult church problems. In 1755 Hart also led the CA in the founding of an educational fund to aid young men preparing for ministry, the first of its kind among Baptists in the South.[668]

Earlier, in 1774, just a year before the Revolutionary War began, Hart met a young minister by the name of Richard Furman, who had been converted in revival services held by the Separate-

---

664   E. Ray Clendenen & Brad J. Waggoner, ed., *A Southern Baptist Dialogue: Calvinism*. (Nashville: B & H Academic, 2008), 81.
665   McBeth, *The Baptist Heritage*, 219.
666   Ibid.
667   Lumpkin, *Baptist Confessions of Faith*, 352.
668   McBeth, *The Baptist Heritage*, 220.

Baptists.[669] In 1780, when Hart was forced to leave Charleston and his church because of the Revolutionary War, young Furman was often asked to fill the pulpit of the demoralized and struggling congregation. After many attempts to restore Hart as their pastor, Furman finally was persuaded to accept a pastoral call in 1787.[670] Furman's subsequent place in history has since been recognized as having formed a bridge between the back-country Whitefieldian revivalist style and the orderly, stable style of the Regular Baptists. Having begun as an untrained Separate-Baptist, Furman eventually became an ardent educator. In 1821 he was the key leader in forming the Baptist Convention of South Carolina whose "grand objects" were missions and education.[671] Under Furman's leadership, South Carolina's first Baptist College was started in Edgefield in 1825, the year of Furman's death.[672] David Benedict said of Richard Furman, "I do not know of anyone in the Baptist ranks at that time who had a higher reputation among the American Baptists for wisdom in counsel, and a skill in management, in the affairs of the denomination."[673]

Just seven years after the beginning of the Charleston Association, nine Separate-Baptist churches in 1755 formed the Sandy Creek Baptist Association. Named after the original settlement of Stearns and Marshall at Sandy Creek, they formed the first Separate-Baptist Association in the South. Lumpkin noted that by the middle of the 1770s the Separates comprised over half the Baptists in South Carolina and probably equaled that number in the rest of the South.[674]

---

669   Timothy George and David S. Dockery, ed., *Baptist Theologians* (Nashville: Broadman Press, 1990), 140.

670   Ibid, 143.

671   McBeth, *The Baptist Heritage*, 442.

672   McBeth noted that this marks the date of the college movement in the South.

673   Benedict, *Fifty Years among the Baptists*, 48-49.

674   William Latane Lumpkin, *Baptist Foundations in the South: Tracing through the Separates the Influence of the Great Awakening, 1754-1787* (Nashville: Broadman Press, 1961), 54.

Although the original covenant of the Sandy Creek Church suggests a moderate form of Calvinism in holding to the doctrine of election, by 1845, their confession nearly exactly mirrored the wording of the New Hampshire Confession of Faith stating that "the blessings of salvation are made free to all by the gospel; that it is the immediate duty of all to accept them by a cordial and obedient faith; and that nothing prevents the salvation of the greatest sinner on earth, except his own voluntary refusal to submit to the Lord Jesus Christ." Clearly, southern revivals, as in New Hampshire, had served to soften both the Calvinistic and General Baptist trends toward doctrinal isolationism. In 1777, just twenty years after the Philadelphia Baptist Association's effort at bringing the General Baptists into the Regular fold, both groups began in eastern North Carolina to unite. The election doctrine was no longer a bar to their union under the banner of revival. Due to the desire for revival on both sides, by the close of the Revolutionary War, Baptists also united in the western part of the state.[675] Consequently, McBeth observed, "Both the order of Charleston and the ardor of Sandy Creek contributed to the synthesis that made up the Southern Baptist Convention."[676]

Revival was also the cause behind a similar union of Regular and Separate-Baptists which took place in Kentucky revivals between 1800 and 1803, led by Presbyterian evangelist James M'Gready.[677] Despite his orthodox Calvinist roots, M'Gready[678] did not allow the

---

675   Torbet, *A History of the Baptists*, 229.
676   McBeth, *The Baptist Heritage*, 234.
677   This union had been preceded by the great western revivals in Kentucky and Tennessee beginning with Hampton-Sydney revival in 1787 through 1805. During this time the Presbyterians, Methodists, and Baptists cooperated in a series of highly effective revivals where it was said that "Their theological differences were often subordinated in the midst of the revival." See Boles, *The Great Revival*, xvi.
678   M'Gready, a Calvinist Presbyterian by birth and training, was of Scotch-Irish stock, from the Ulster district, many of which poured into the Colonies in the eighteenth century. Many of these settled in the frontier areas. For more about the background of M'Gready and his influence, see Bernard Weisberger, *They Gathered at the River* (Boston: Little, Brown and

election doctrine to interfere in his methods or in how he exhorted his fellow Calvinists in reaching the vast numbers of irreligious people in North Carolina, Virginia, Tennessee, and particularly Kentucky. In an all-out effort to "awaken Christ-less sinners from their security, and bring them to a sense of their guilt," M'Gready exhorted self-respecting Presbyterian preachers to "use every argument to convince them of the horrors of an unconverted state," even if it meant the world "scorn and revile us...call us low preachers and madmen, Methodists - do this we must...."[679] The idea of using these means, or enduring such base criticisms for the purpose of awakening sinners, suggests that not only did ministers feel directly responsible for such efforts but also firmly believed that the gospel-enlightened unregenerate could respond to these arguments and, thereby, the gospel message. However, for orthodox Presbyterians, the election doctrine carried the idea that only a limited number would ever become God's elect constituting the true church. This Calvinist pre-disposition so concerned two of M'Gready's fellow evangelists that they thought the articulation of such doctrines could actually strengthen some of their potential converts in a state of unbelief.[680] This reveals the growing distance the revival wedge had driven between Orthodox confessions and actual practice. Timothy Smith concluded that the "Baptist endeavor to maintain the form of orthodoxy amidst revival efforts resulted in a practical nullification of the idea of unconditional election...."[681] Consequently, it was felt that if the individual's response to the gospel was legitimate in realizing his election/salvation, then this same individual type response to baptism

---

Company, 1958), 22-23.

679   Taken from James M'Gready, *The Posthumous Works of the Reverend and Pious James M'Gready, Late Minister of the Gospel, in Henderson, Kentucky.* Edited by James Smith. 2 vols. Vol. 1, Louisville, Ky., 1831; vol.2, Nashville, Tenn, 1833, and quoted in Boles, *The Great Revival*, 41.

680   Weisberger, *They Gathered at the River*, 40.

681   Timothy L. Smith, *Revivalism and Social Reform* (New York: Harper and Row, 1957), 25.

was necessary for realizing local church membership. The autonomy of the individual had effectually supplanted both election and its logical connection to any "True Church" concept. Evangelical passion had served to unite formerly disparate groups under the common banner of religious revival. The terms of one such union between the Elkhorn and South Kentucky associations in 1800 were flatly stated in their written agreement "that preaching Christ tasted death for every man shall be no bar to communion."[682]

Clearly revival, as it had been presented in highly individualistic terms by Whitefield, was now forcing rigid Calvinism to shift toward universal atonement coupled with the universal call for *all* sinners to respond to the gospel. Therefore, the softening produced under the preaching of largely *Calvinist-trained* men should not be categorized as Arminianism or worse.[683] The softening was produced not by a propitious *doctrinal* slide but by intentional lateral movements which attempted to strike a Scriptural balance between doctrinal emphasis and practical application. Under the motivation of winning the un-evangelized masses, Torbet was correct in saying that

---

682   William Warren Sweet, *Religion on the American Frontier: The Baptists 1783-1830* (New York: Cooper Square Publishers, Inc., 1964), 24.
683   Gerald L. Priest, "Revival and Revivalism: A Historical and Doctrinal Evaluation," *Detroit Baptist Seminary Journal* 1, no. 2 (1996): 240. In his article aimed at exposing the deficiencies of Finney's revival methods, the author attempts to categorize nearly everything that cannot be defined as orthodox Calvinism as rank Unitarian heresy. He suggests that the phrase "modified Calvinism" used by the majority of historians to show the adjustments of New England Calvinism to the forces of revival, came essentially from the same sources producing Unitarianism. This inferred connection of "modified Calvinism" to the Unitarian heresy is simply unjustified. Unitarianism was rooted in unbelief among unregenerate churchmen well before Edwards and the Great Awakening. Those attempting to moderate Calvinism were regenerate men, who coming later, were impassioned for the souls of men. The Separate-Baptists, both in the northern and southern frontiers, along with many staunch Presbyterian Calvinists, had rejected the limiting influence of the election doctrine for the more inclusive idea that all men could be saved, needed to hear the gospel, and thereafter respond to the message. This was especially true of the camp meetings associated with the Second Great Awakening. Therefore, Priest's inference that any modification of so-called orthodox Calvinism, naturally ends up in full-blown Pelagianism, or in the rejection of the "forensic atonement" doctrine of justification like Finney, is simply theological overstatement.

the "strict Calvinism of Baptists was being weakened by the evangelical trend which stressed a personal response of the individual...."[684] By asserting the preacher's responsibility to preach and the sinner's to believe, election had shifted from being the theological property belonging solely to the realm of God's sovereignty to the autonomy of the gospel-enlightened individual. As with Whitefield and others, the main idea of the revival messages was aimed at calling all sinners to repentance and faith in Jesus Christ. As the revivals moved west and south, particularly in the frontier states of Illinois, Kentucky, and Tennessee, clearer outlines of the revival culture emerged from the participants among competing denominational groups. For many, the participation in these great efforts to evangelize the masses transcended denominational identities and created a sort of temporary unity unparalleled in religious cooperation.[685]

At the heart of these mass efforts was the common vernacular of preaching and singing which had begun to characterize the meetings themselves. The significance of this common voice emerging within the sermon and the song of revival may be seen in how it differed from the settled creeds of the day, particularly among the Regular Baptists and the Presbyterians, who both held strong views on the invisible universal Church, election, predestination, and man's inability to respond to the offer of the gospel. No other evangelical phenomena contributed more to the decline of the election doctrine and its universal Church ideology. In revival and the quest for souls, written

---

684   Torbet identified the revival practice as the catalyst for both the soteriological and ecclesiological changes taking place among the Separate-Baptists in the post-Great Awakening era. He said they had "produced rapid growth and expansion," and were also "a disruptive influence upon older church patterns." See Torbet, *A History of the Baptists*, 255.

685   Before, during, and after the revivals had ceased, particular days were set aside for brethren from all the evangelical denominations to fast and pray for particular local or national needs. This practice evolved from the idea that mutual participation in meetings focused on reaching the lost could also be organized on less, yet important issues to individuals, churches, and to the country at large. See Sweet, *Religion on the American Frontier: The Baptists 1783-1830*.

creeds and confessions were temporally suspended for purposes which appeared to be more vital, more eternal than normal church-life demanded. From the sermons and songs came an "alternate means of objectifying belief corporately."[686] The revival sermons revealed the passionate desire of the revival preacher to win all of the souls for Christ he possibly could at any cost. The revival hymns of the period further perpetuated these objective beliefs and created a populist theology which contradicted the common Calvinist creed. These became the accurate markers of what the common folk in the pew truly believed.

James Smith, the editor of Presbyterian James M'Gready's sermons, excused the apparent contradictions between M'Gready's sermons and his orthodox creed:

Some have objected to these Sermons being published by a Cumberland Presbyterian minister, because, in a few particulars, the doctrines exhibited, differ from those taught in the Confession of Faith of the church of which he is a member. But it should be remembered, that this work is not published by the Cumberland Presbyterian body, nor do they view it as giving an exposition of all the doctrines believed and inculcated by them. The Editor... published the work on his own responsibility from a sense of duty to God and to his fellow men; and being personally acquainted with hundreds who were converted by their instrumentality....[687]

Therefore, it appears that orthodoxy, as the Cumberland Presbyterian body understood it, was a moot point on account of the

---

686   Harry Eskew and Hugh T. McElrath, *Sing with Understanding* (Nashville: Church Street Press, 1995), 63.
687   James Smith, ed., *Posthumous Works of the Reverend and Pious James M'Gready*, 2 vols. (Louisville: W.W. Worsley, 1831), iv.

sheer number of individuals being converted. In the course of the revival, there were two fundamental reasons why the doctrinal creed was being temporarily shelved: the revival message and the revival music.

THE REVIVAL SERMON

The revival message, unlike the Puritan New England "Jeremiad,"[688] was aimed predominantly at bringing the masses of the un-evangelized to Christ. The evangelist would most often present the gospel in the context of a fear of God/love of God juxtaposition.[689] This concept, merging the offer of free grace on the one hand with the judgment fires of hell on the other, was known among the Methodists as "striking fire."[690] In contrast, the Puritan sermon would often focus on the fact that God was angry about sin and judgment was imminently possible. Christ's provision would be outlined, but never would an unconverted man in a Puritan sermon be exhorted to immediately respond to the gospel openly. The doctrine of God's love was hidden and bound up in the doctrine of election and considered only in terms of God's unique care for those He had elected for salvation. For the reprobated sinner, who was the unfortunate object of God's wrath, God's glory, rather than His love, became the mitigating factor in the process. During the pre-salvation period in which the Word worked in the sinner's heart, the resultant conviction of sin could remain for weeks, months, sometimes even years before

---

688   This sermon form was often used a means of warning church members or communities of the expectation of judgment, or at the least, God's displeasure over the careless lives of God's people, coupled with their thoughtless disregard for God's laws. In the theocratic environ of Massachusetts, this sermon form was often heard at various seasons of church decline in order to awaken the faltering consciences of church members.
689   Boles, *The Great Revival*, 114.
690   Charles Coleman Sellers, *Lorenzo Dow: The Bearer of the Word* (New York: Minton, Balch & Company, 1928), 16.

the sinner would be able to pass from this *preparation* [691] stage to actual conversion.

Beginning with the preaching style of Whitefield and the early awakeners, the exhortation to convicted sinners to immediately turn to Christ took on a predominant role. Benedict also noted that after the introduction of Fuller's theology, a significant "change followed on the part of many of our ministers in their mode of addressing their unconverted hearers on the subjects of repentance and believing the gospel."[692] This change involved the use of "direct appeals and exhortations to those whose conversion they desired."[693] Many of those ministers maintained the stereotypical phraseology of their orthodox creed while preaching in "the style of reputed Arminians."[694] This fits the template of Whitefield, who was similarly accused of his "Arminian dialect" and "semi-Pelagian addresses"[695] in calling for sinners to personally respond to God's offer of salvation.

To this sense of immediacy, the Great Awakening revivalists believed that "the sinner had to feel in his very bones the smoldering of guilt, abasement, hope and assurance."[696] Stone testified in his autobiography that it was this very combination of the fear of God and the love of God that resulted in his own conversion.[697] This method

---

691   Conviction over sin was an integral part of the salvation schema of the Puritans. Although this process varied from person to person and church to church, it was considered necessary for determining who may have been elect, because only those who went beyond this stage could actually begin to consider the gospel message in light of their hopeless and helpless condition. "Closing with Christ" was the accepted Puritan (Calvinist) description of the human side of salvation. See Morgan, *Visible Saints: The History of a Puritan Idea*, 68-69.

692   Benedict, *Fifty Years among the Baptists*, 140.

693   Ibid.

694   Ibid, 141.

695   Cited in Underwood, *A History of the English Baptists*, 160.

696   Weisberger, *They Gathered at the River*, 39.

697   Barton W. Stone was converted in 1791 in Virginia. Boles tells his autobiographical story of how Stone had heard the Presbyterian M'Gready preach damnation and hell-fire at one meeting, but failed to point Stone, among others, to the love of God in Christ. This left Stone in a depressed state for weeks until he heard another sermon given by Presbyterian pastor William Hodge on the love of God. He was converted upon hearing the assuring news

of awakening the sinner with the emotional combination of these corollary Scriptural truths accounted for several anomalies among the Calvinist-minded Presbyterian and Baptist participants. The first involved disregarding the predestination of both the elect and the reprobate. The staunch Calvinist M'Gready confidently declared that God would pardon "innumerable millions,"[698] suggesting that God had placed no arbitrary number upon salvation in terms of any particular person not being able to come if he wanted. It was in this sense that the Presbyterian and Particular-minded Baptists gravitated toward the free-will position of the Methodists. The doctrine of particular election had, in the environment of an unlimited atonement of Christ and the indiscriminate calling of sinners to repentance, become a conditional election where every sinner under the sound of the gospel was called to repentance and considered capable of responding to God's grace. Salvation was now understood in terms of human choice, a personal decision under the direction and admonition of the preacher-revivalist. God was no longer seen as the official arbiter of the transaction within a limited election but only in providing the provision of salvation and the power in reaching and transforming the willing sinner. In his sermon, "The Young Invited to Come to Christ," M'Gready warned young people that the time to come to Christ was when they were young and impressionable. He urged them to be saved early because as they grew older they would become hardened in their hearts.[699] Urgency, coupled with the inferred implication of free-will to respond to such urgings, was decidedly opposite of the evangelist's theological

---

of Christ's dying love for him in the gospel and immediately converted. See Boles, *The Great Revival*, 114-115.

698   Smith, ed., *Posthumous Works of the Reverend and Pious James M'Gready*, 1: 137.
699   Ibid, 2: 268.

creed. Similar admonitions were also to be seen among the revival hymnody.

This kind of reasoning made election and its theological connections seem irrelevant in the prevailing revivalist milieu. However, for the participating Presbyterians, Methodists, and Baptists, this did not mean they had altered their view of the depravity of man. The denominational leaders of each branch "agreed that God had to initiate the process of repentance and faith—this was not just a rigid Presbyterian notion."[700] Any suggestion, resultant from the revival, that this modified Calvinism advanced the cause of Pelagianism or Universalism, is therefore, not tenable.[701]

Another of the salient features of this sermon form was the so-called *application* portion which parallels the modern invitation. After the sinner had been duly informed of sin, its awful consequences, followed by the love of God for the hopeless sinner, the exhortation became a powerful tool in bringing multitudes to Christ. In the printed sermons, this portion was never included, but its emphasis in the actual sermon was noteworthy, and so noted by the editor James Smith:

Many of the sermons, even to the ordinary reader, will seem
to close abruptly, owing to an omission of the author in

---

700   Boles, *The Great Revival*, 133.
701   There is no record which substantiates the idea that the modified Calvinism which, beginning in the Great Awakening and continuing in the Great Revival, directly produced either Universalism or various forms of Pelagianism. This modified Calvinism was noted for its diminished view of the election doctrine, which often had to be downplayed for the sake of revival continuing among participating denominations. The Presbyterian, Methodist, and Baptist bodies all subscribed to confessions which clearly articulated man's depravity and need for God to initiate the salvation of the sinner on account of such depravity. In respect to salvation and its relation to this diminished view of election held by all the groups, one Separate-Baptist minister firmly declared, "those who finally perish, are lost, not on account of God's decree, respecting partial election...but on account of their unbelief." Taken from an extract of a personal letter from John Waller to Robert Carter on April 20, 1789, in the Robert Carter Mss, and quoted in Ibid, 138.

writing out the applications— that being a part he almost
uniformly delivered extemporaneously, and according to the
circumstances of his audience...forcing the truth home upon the
consciences of his hearers with almost irresistible efficacy.[702]

Although not printed in the sermons themselves, they
constituted a primary element in the sermon. Oftentimes, the
preacher delivering the sermon would call on other preacher-exhorters
who would speak directly to the unconverted in an informal address.
This address could last for several minutes and would often turn an
unproductive service among a *vast crowd* into a *perfect uproar.*[703]
These sermon extensions brought by other preachers on hand were
sometimes provided by willing laymen. At the formal sermon's close,
"there might follow an exhortation or two from any so moved...."[704]
Frequently, these exhortations from laymen were nothing more
than brief personal testimonies of how Christ had saved them, but
these simple means just as frequently produced the desired results.
The evangelist would remind all participants not to make creed or
confession more important than Jesus Christ,[705] but ironically, by
1809, the Presbyterian revivalist had "reluctantly returned to the
orthodox fold."[706]

THE SONGS OF REVIVAL

Similar to the sermonizing, the songs of the revival had a
strong Calvinist precursor. The best known Baptist hymnal of the

---

702   Smith, ed., *Posthumous Works of the Reverend and Pious James M'Gready*, 1:
preface.
703   Boles, *The Great Revival*, 117.
704   Sellers, *Lorenzo Dow: The Bearer of the Word*, 19.
705   Smith, ed., *Posthumous Works of the Reverend and Pious James M'Gready*, 2: 39-
40.
706   Boles, *The Great Revival*, 163.

day, and the first hymnal both collected and published in America, originated in Newport, Rhode Island, in 1766, and was called "Hymns and Spiritual Songs," probably taken from the title of Isaac Watts' first congregational song book.[707] Consistent with the prevailing hymnody of the day, this hymnal reflected a rigid Calvinist theology and a typical emphasis on Baptism and the Lord's Supper.[708] In the course of "objectifying" practical theology, no other medium was more capable than that of the popular hymns written and used during the period. Boles asserted that revival "hymnology provided an extraordinarily effective means of popularizing and disseminating complex theological doctrine."[709] In these brief, yet potent melodies lies a theology that went beyond the strictures of the standard written creeds of the day. Many of the Philadelphia Baptists attempted to portray the suggestion that Christ dying for all men was in fact, Universalist heresy,[710] yet

---

707   David W. Music, "The Newport Collection (1766): The First Baptist Hymnal in America," *Baptist History and Heritage Journal* 38, no. 2 (2003): 3.

708   Ibid. Although the Baptists used a variety of hymns and metrical psalms from other traditions, their own distinctive views on the ordinances occupied a conspicuous place in the hymnal.

709   Boles, *The Great Revival*, 121.

710   Most Baptists at this time, with the exception of the numerically smaller General Baptists, accepted the predominant features of the Philadelphia Baptist Confession. Based on the 1689 London Baptist Confession and its Westminster exemplar, this Baptist confession carefully articulated the standard orthodoxy of the Reformed position. Any suggestion that Christ's death provided atonement for every individual of the human race was considered to be heresy (i.e., Universalism). In a circular letter, dated October 5th, 1790, Rev. Samuel Jones offered thanks that "peace and good order so generally prevail, and that the work of the Lord is carried on....however....there are appearances, in two or three of our churches, of the leprosy of universal salvation...." Jones proceeded then to take each text used to teach the universal nature of Christ's atonement and interpret them strictly as election texts referring only to those belonging to the election class. Limited atonement rejects any idea that Christ's atonement could have included the non-elect, because the atonement only makes certain the salvation of those God elected. Under this view, Christ could not have died, and would not have died for non-elect persons. As a breach of this orthodox view, two views of hell were held up by Jones as the only universalist options. One: no real hell existed; or two: hell would only last for a limited duration, after which all would go to heaven. Not mentioned is the mediate concept that despite the atonement being universally provided, only those who personally obeyed the gospel would ultimately be saved. For the entire contents of this polemic against the perceived Universalist threat, see Gillette, ed., *Minutes of the Philadelphia Baptist Association from A.D 1707 to A.D. 1807: Being the First One-Hundred Years of Its Existence.*, 257-260.

numbers of their constituencies were singing songs which celebrated
that very idea in revival meetings. Similar to the sermon's enlarged
view of God's love and desire to save all men, the hymn embraced
these ideas and forged them into memorable tunes.

The Kehukee Association,[711] a strong Calvinist association
in Kentucky prayed for several years for revival among its member
churches[712] when in 1801, Elder Lemuel Burkitt, upon returning
from Kentucky and Tennessee, shared the exciting news with the
association that over six thousand had been converted to Christ
there in about eight months. The news was immediately felt and the
desire and expectation for revival among the association churches
was heightened. As greater numbers among them began to come to
Christ, Burkitt "published two or three different pamphlets which
contained a small collection of spiritual songs, some of which he had
brought from the western countries."[713] Association compiler Biggs
thought as many as six thousand song booklets had been disseminated
among the churches and that they were responsible for assisting the
promotion of revival among them. One of these pamphlets discovered

---

711   This Baptist Association was founded by eleven ministers, and first convened
at Kehukee, North Carolina, in 1765. C.C. Goen puts the organization date at 1769, but
his reliance on Newman here is mistaken. Nothing of any significance took place in the
Association until 1772 when their offer to the Separate-Baptists was refused on account that
the Regulars were considered by Separate-Baptist standards to be in doctrinal error concerning
at least three things. The Regulars were accepting the membership of those baptized in
unbelief; the salvation experience of members was not thoroughly checked; and their manner
of dress was considered too ostentatious. The Regular Baptist ministers had mostly been
General Baptists formerly led by Elders Paul Palmer and Joseph Parker, and later became
Regular Baptists through the efforts of the Philadelphia Baptist Association. From 1787 to
1801, several Separate-Baptist churches were admitted to the Association beginning with the
terms that the Regular Baptist churches would stop accepting the baptisms of those baptized
"in unbelief...." All of the Regular and Separate-Baptist Churches finally and officially joined
together in 1801 thereby becoming the United Baptists. See Biggs, *A Concise History of the
Kehukee Association*, 31-36.
712   Revival had been desired and prayed for by the Association since 1778, but their
desires were not proactive like the Separate-Baptist practices. This all changed after hearing
the news from Burkitt in 1801.
713   Biggs, *A Concise History of the Kehukee Association*, 114.

in the archives at the University of North Carolina at Chapel Hill revealed forty-eight hymns, many of which were considered new by Burkitt at the time.[714] They offer significant insight into the popular theology being sung by a typically Calvinist association during the revival period.[715] Many of those being converted pointed to these song booklets as the first means of their conviction of sin and need of Christ. Oftentimes, at the close of a service, the minister would make his rounds among the congregants while they were singing one of these popular little songs. The result was often astounding, so much "that the party, with whom the minister shook hands, would often be melted in tears."[716]

Several notable features of this new genre of revival music emerge demonstrating a noticeable difference from the standard hymnals of the period reflecting the theology found in the Philadelphia Baptist Confession.[717] This populist perspective indicates that the forces and dynamics of the revival ethos had created a sense of expectation and hope beyond the realm of predictable and creed-directed church life. In reality, the expectations created by the sheer unpredictability of revival suggested that doctrinal perimeters which

714   The pamphlet used in this work is a second edition of Burkitt titled, Lemuel Burkitt, *A Collection of Hymns and Spiritual Songs: Intended for Public and Social Worship, Some of Which Are Entirely New*, 2 ed. (Halifax, NC: A. Hodge, 1802).

715   Boles' list does not mention Burkitt's collection of hymns, though ironically he mentions the revivals among the Kehukee Association churches where this collection was used. Another collection by Lorenzo Dow has a similar title, but was not published until 1816, fourteen years after Burkitt's. For Boles' list, see Boles, *The Great Revival*, 123. For the complete works of Lorenzo Dow including his work of camp-meeting hymns, see Sellers, *Lorenzo Dow: The Bearer of the Word*, 267-275.

716   Biggs, *A Concise History of the Kehukee Association*, 115.

717   This collection of songs by Burkitt was also not known to Leonard in his discussion of hymnody among the early Baptists. He did mention the hymnal under the title of *A Selection of Hymns and Spiritual Songs* (1809) by Parkinson. The preface to his hymnal mentioned the new brand of revival songs as being "so extremely unsound in doctrine, that no discerning Christian can sing or hear them without pain." Undoubtedly he is referring to the type of songs, perhaps the very songs found in the Burkitt collection of 1802. Leonard did mention that "they continued to gain popularity in many Baptist congregations." See Leonard, *Baptist Ways: A History*, 126.

hindered or attempted to limit the free demonstration of God's Spirit were being temporarily suspended. The size of the crowds and the vast numbers of those who responded to the gospel relegated the talk of particular election to the back-ground and individual choice to the front, along with a host of other unorthodox ideas.[718]

> There were several notable features:
> 1. God's salvation available to all sinners;
> 2. The love of God presented as boundless;
> 3. The atonement presented in universal terms;
> 4. The need to respond to salvation when young.

This initial feature of salvation's availability may be seen in the first line, "I long to see the happy time, When *sinners all* come flocking home." Here the image of the camp meeting is brought to mind with hundreds of attendants under deep conviction of sin responding to the invitation to believe on Christ and being saved from certain judgment. In this overwhelming display of God's free grace, no one was refused who came. The question no longer involved God's election as a pre-temporal Sovereign choice, but rather a divine privilege or status available to all who would repent and believe. The next to last line, "Take your companion by the hand," even encourages the dying sinner to bring someone else with him to Christ. After all, who could be refused who came? Did not Jesus provide salvation for all? Could a sinner be refused on any grounds?

In the hymn entitled, "Good News to Mourning Souls," the songwriter describes this free grace:

> *...And streams of grace for sinners flow,*
> *As free as when He bled.*

---

718   The word orthodox in the larger discussion means the Reformation doctrines associated with strict Calvinism as represented in the Westminster Confession, the London Confession of 1689, and the Philadelphia Baptist Confession.

All glory, glory to my king,
He's now upon his throne,
Inviting strangers home to God,
and claims them for His own.[719]

The two italicized lines note two complementary ideas which both promote the concept of the availability of God's salvation to all sinners whom the writer refers to as *strangers*. Being known and chosen of God in eternity past, the elect are seldom described in such terms. The invitation appears to be as a present offer with the promise that, if received, God will *claim* the strangers *for His own*. If claiming them as His own is comparable to their status as God's elect, then their election occurred after having received the offered salvation—an exact reversal of the orthodox position.

A hymn Biggs mentions in his history declared, with all the inclusiveness of revival lore, the second key feature of the revivals, along with their participants:

I long to see the happy time,
When sinners all come flocking home;
To taste the riches of his love,
And to enjoy the realms above.
Take your companion by the hand;
And all your children in the band[720]

This second feature, found in the next line reveals the great compulsion for coming to Christ: "To taste the riches of his love...." The judgment and/or fear of God motif of the salvation cycle may

---

719   Burkitt, *A Collection of Hymns and Spiritual Songs: Intended for Public and Social Worship, Some of Which Are Entirely New*, 11, emphasis added.
720   Biggs, *A Concise History of the Kehukee Association*, emphasis added.

have prepared them, but it was the love of Christ which completed the transaction. This latter aspect of the salvation cycle may be better understood in the testimony of a typical frontier preacher by the name of Jacob Bower, whose salvation and assurance had been clarified to him by potent descriptions of the incomparable love of God.[721] Bower said in the ensuing days, the following hymn expressed the sentiments of both his heart and feelings. This plea for sinners to come to his Savior was based on similar principles of the universality of Christ's provision and the open invitation to any sinner, no matter how wicked, to come and find that "Jesus' heart is full of love:"

But I freely all forgive;
I myself the debt have paid,
Now I bid thee rise and live.

Come my fellow sinners, try;
Jesus' heart is full of love;
O, that you, as well as I,
May his wondrous mercy prove
He has sent me to declare,
All is ready, all is free;

---

721   This testimony is found in "The Autobiography of Jacob Bower." Bower, born of German Dunker parentage, was converted on February 8, 1812. Months before, Bower had been brought under deep conviction of sin and a sense of impending judgment through the means of the admonitions of an acquaintance of his father, followed later by a local earthquake. About midnight of February 8th, he believed that what Christ had done on the cross, he had done for him, and he "believed it." Not understanding that he had been converted, the next day, his neighbor and wife came by to see him. Asking him for his experience of salvation, he said he had none. But Mrs. Dudley persisted by telling him that she thought, "You speak the language of a Christian...." Pouring forth tears Bower replied, "Can it be possible, that God is so holy, so just, so righteous, can have mercy on, and save so great a sinner as I am?" With a final convincing stroke, Mrs. Bowers replied, "God is love else we all would have been in hell long ago." And with this Bower was convinced that God had truly saved him the previous night, and he rejoiced in the assurance of God's saving grace. For the entire testimony, see Sweet, *Religion on the American Frontier: The Baptists 1783-1830*, 185-196.

Why should any soul despair,
When he saved a wretch like me?[722]

This love, spoken of in limitless terms, suggested that no sinner could possibly be turned away, regardless of their sinful state or level of moral despair. Hymn number eight in Burkitt's collection also reiterates this love theme:

Come mourning and afflicted souls,
Draw near to God by prayer,
Where Christ his boundless love unfolds
He says he'll meet us there;[723]

The third noted feature speaks of the atonement doctrine in universal terms. This posed a significant change from the prevailing doctrine of limited atonement among revival participating Presbyterians and Baptists. Most Baptists within the Philadelphia Baptist Association considered unlimited atonement to be the road to universalism. No hymn in this small collection better articulates an unlimited view of the atonement doctrine than hymn number fifteen. Entitled "Christ the Fountain Opened," the opening line begins by calling all of humanity to the provision of his grace:

The voice of free grace, cries escape to the mountains,
For Adams lost race, Christ hath open'd a fountain;
For sin and transgression and ev'ry pollution,
His blood it flows freely in plenteous redemption
Hallelujah to the Lamb who hath purchased our pardon,

---

722   Ibid, 196, emphasis added.
723   Burkitt, *A Collection of Hymns and Spiritual Songs: Intended for Public and Social Worship, Some of Which Are Entirely New*, 7, emphasis added.

We'll praise him again when we pass over Jordan. [724]

This plenteous redemption is then taken beyond the perimeters of limited atonement. Here the songwriter evokes the image of the revival service where countless hundreds converge at their respective altars to cry out to God for mercy. No one is excluded, and there is no conceivable limit *to whom* this mercy is directed or to *how many* may come:

This fountain so clear in which all may find pardon,
From Jesus's side flows plenteous redemption; [725]

The twin ideas of the plenteous redemption suggesting its inherent capability to cleanse every sinner who comes regardless of the number, along with the pardon being promised to all who come, completely ignores any idea of a limited atonement along with its provision being applied only to the pre-temporal elect.

A fourth feature, which finds its only corresponding idea in the preparation doctrine of Puritanism, is the injunction for children to come to Christ early. However, the preparation idea does not even approach the threat to the orthodox position as does this novel concern within revival hymnody. The Puritan concept, although later exploited beyond its original application to elect persons only, is sung here in the exclusive context of universal provision in the atonement! Hymn thirty-eight entitled "The Joyful News of Salvation," presents the revival's invitation:

Come, dear children don't reject it,
Come to Jesus in your prime;
Great salvation don't neglect it,

---

724   Ibid, 36, emphasis added.
725   Ibid.

Come receive it now's the time;
Now the Saviour is beginning,
to revive his work again.[726]

These lyrics, many of which Burkitt identified as new (meaning contemporary with the recent Kentucky revivals), represented theological thinking which had been carried directly out of the camp-meeting and revivalist ideologies. Personal religion was now something reduced from the sovereign design of effectual calling to one's own personal experience, and the immediacy of the Holy Spirit upon the willing individual played the *key* role in transforming theology.[727] Because it was accepted in the prevailing revival experience that Christ had provided salvation for all men, it was equally expected that the Holy Spirit would convict all men of their sin. Initially, Backus arrived at this idea by recognizing that "a state church was a disavowal of the competency of the individual to respond in faith to the gospel."[728] By this new emerging definition, children of an accountable age were urged to respond to the gospel message. The possibility of the child's heart becoming indifferent through their own neglect had essentially replaced the effectual calling of the elect and the irresistible grace accompanying it.

Hymn eighteen in Burkitt's collection called "Invitation to Youth" includes a personal exhortation from the hymn-writer:

And hear what I do say;
I want your souls with Christ to live,
In everlasting day...

---

726   Ibid, 37, emphasis added.
727   Torbet, *A History of the Baptists*, 255.
728   Robert G. Torbet, "Baptist Thought About the Church," *Foundations* 1, no. 1 (1958): 22-23.

Pray meditate before too late;
While in a gospel land;
Behold King Jesus at the gate,
Most lovingly doth stand.

In a second verse, the capacity of the young person to choose is enjoined:

Will you pursue the dangerous road?
It leads to death and hell;
Will you refuse all peace with God,
With devils for to dwell?[729]

As in Presbyterian evangelist M'Gready's sermon to the young to come to Christ early because of sin's hardening capability, the songwriter casts the salvation process in terms entirely outside the sovereign control of God. With two questions he infers that the destiny of the young person rests on what the person pursues and finally, on whether he chooses or refuses God's offer of peace in Christ. While sounding more like a Methodist doctrinaire, this music was being sung in the pews of Regular Baptists who ostensibly opposed theology which accommodated free-will in their written creeds!

In summary, some thought that in the sermon and songs of revival, theological purity along with the importance of doctrinal confessions were being disregarded.[730] However, Torbet traced these revivalist ideas to the declining influence of the Calvinist-oriented Philadelphia Baptist Confession as well as the general lack of revival among their constituent churches. For a period of about thirteen

---

729   Burkitt, *A Collection of Hymns and Spiritual Songs: Intended for Public and Social Worship, Some of Which Are Entirely New*, 23-24, emphasis added.
730   Torbet, *A History of the Baptists*, 255.

years from 1755, the Philadelphia Association did little more than
send pulpit supplies to associational churches with the bulk of their
attention going to "reorganizing, *indoctrinating*, or settling difficulties
in churches, not evangelizing."[731] Between 1740 and 1790, which marks
the relative beginning of the southern revivals, the Regular Baptists
under the PBA started only ten new churches in Virginia and one in
North Carolina. During the same period, the Separate-Baptists were
responsible for starting several hundred.[732] This ardent evangelism
among those Baptists originating in New England eventually resulted
in the demand for a Baptist confession which articulated a modified
Calvinism in strict local church terminology.

THE NEW HAMPSHIRE CONFESSION

By 1830, the New Hampshire Baptist Convention appointed a
committee to prepare a new Declaration of Faith and Practice which
"may be thought agreeable to and consistent with the views of all our
churches in this state."[733] Most of these Regular Baptist churches in
New Hampshire had yielded to the revivalist tendencies of the Backus
Separates since the 1780s, especially in the union of the Regulars
and Separates in Virginia in 1787. When the New Hampshire Baptist
Convention met in the village of New London in 1826, Baptists began
another "program of concerted evangelism and church growth."[734] Just
four years later, the convention, meeting for the fifth time, determined
it was time to form a declaration of faith and practice among their
constituent churches. John Newton Brown, pastor of the Baptist
Church in Exeter, New Hampshire, was its primary author. Because

---

731   Lumpkin, *Colonial Baptists and Southern Revivals*, 156, emphasis added.
732   Ibid, 157.
733   Wolever, ed., *An Anthology of the Early Baptists in New Hampshire*, 531.
734   Duane J. Squires, "How a Baptist Confession Was Born," *Baptist Leader* April
1955, 13.

of the effects of revival in the state, along with the prospect of the eventual disestablishment of the Standing Church in Massachusetts, Brown was asked by the Separate-Baptist community to compose a new Baptist confession which reflected the diminished Calvinism and exclusive local-church position held by the majority of American Baptists in the burgeoning middle-class. Baptist views on soteriology had been directly affected by the moderating tendencies of revivalism, the Free-Will Baptists, and the rapid escalation of Methodism (i.e., Arminianism) in the western frontier. Among the Baptist constituency were many former Regular Baptists who abandoned the Baptists because of what they considered to be paralyzing Calvinism. Essentially, the influence of the Free-Will Baptist movement can be identified in two ways. First of all, the NHC originated in the same area where anti-Calvinist tendencies were the strongest, especially among the Free -Will Baptists. Secondly, the NHC suggests that all human *means* are brought to bear in accomplishing the salvation of sinners, and unlike the PBC, ignores any mention of the universal, invisible aspect of church while offering only visible, local church tenets.[735]

Beside the intense spiritual pressure and significant change which revival brought to the churches, it also introduced new pressures to adjust to the new voluntarism of revival and the demand by the people for a fair distribution of their tax burdens in the civic realm.

DISESTABLISHMENT AND NEW HAMPSHIRE

This New Hampshire Standing Church tax system was slightly different than the Bay State. In 1803, the State constitution

---

735   Ibid, 13.

gave power to the various towns and parishes according to their particular religious majorities, to elect their own public teachers and support them by local taxation. The Congregational system was the greatest benefactor of this new law, but a few towns had two or more denominations represented. Like Massachusetts, those who dissented had to show proof by filing certificates of membership from their respective churches. However, the Congregational churches were not always easy to get along with. In 1802, a Baptist by the name of Isaac Smith was imprisoned for failing to pay a fifty-cent tax to the Congregational minister in his town while he was in attendance at a Baptist church.[736] The court found for the Congregational church because Smith had never had the initiatory rite of baptism (probably because he was unconverted and was attending the church out of conviction). In this sense, the Standing Order not only fined him, but had essentially determined *congregational* polity for the Baptist church as well as their own. Ironically, he would have been accepted within the Congregational parish church, even though unconverted, as long as he remained current with his ministerial tax! For New Hampshire, this all changed in July of 1819 when the state legislature passed the "Toleration Act," thus ending the state-supported church system. Unfortunately, Bay State residents would have to wait another fourteen years before dismantling their own intolerant tax code.

DISESTABLISHMENT AND THE MIDDLE-CLASS

Because of the sociological impact of new birth, the waves of new immigrants, and the diminishing of ministerial power, the middle-class had gone through a steady growth cycle.[737] In actuality,

---

736   McLoughlin, *Soul Liberty: The Baptists' Struggle in New England, 1630-1833*, 292.
737   Trinterud admitted that these waves of Scotch-Irish immigrants were "nominal Presbyterians" and "constituted a missionary responsibility." Many of them seeking the allure of cheap land and prosperity were reached through the evangelical revivals of the period. For

the continued impact of revivalism had in fact, accelerated the ongoing decline of ministerial control long before official disestablishment. James Cooper suggests that this process began decades prior to the Great Awakening. He is correct in pointing out that this loss of clerical power preceded the Awakening but appears to severely underestimate the ultimate religious, social, and political impact revivalism played up to and beyond the American Revolution.[738] By 1770, Evangelicals who composed this burgeoning middle-class were now in a position to openly resist the tax system. Formerly, the evangelically-driven Baptists played no significant role in the resistance movement,[739] precisely because these middle-class Evangelicals were more focused on fixing their tax woes than British imperialism.[740] Independence from British supremacy however, was not far removed in principle from the attempt by Colonial authorities to force Baptists to pay ministerial taxes to churches they did not even attend. Evangelical Baptists saw a direct connection between forced taxation in Massachusetts and British coercion to Anglican social and religious pressures in the south. Evangelicals ultimately saw British imperialism as the greater enemy by the time the revolution began and went on to fight valiantly for American independence.

By the end of the revolution bigoted trade policies made American goods undesirable in the British West Indies, Spain, and France, forcing an economic depression in the east.[741] The mass

---

Scotch-Irish immigration and the middle-class, see Trinterud, *The Forming of an American Tradition: A Re-Examination of Colonial Presbyterianism*, 226-227. For the desire of revival and attractive democratic nature of Baptist church life, see Boles, *The Great Revival*, 4.

738   See James F. Jr. Cooper, "Enthusiasts or Democrats? Separation, Church Government, and the Great Awakening in Massachusetts," *The New England Quarterly* 65, no. 2 (June 1992): 270.

739   For the full discussion, see John M. Murrin, "No Awakening, No Revolution? More Counterfactual Speculations," *Reviews in American History* 11, no. 2 (June 1983): 165, Sweet, *Religion on the American Frontier: The Baptists 1783-1830*, 19-20.

740   Murrin, "No Awakening, No Revolution? More Counterfactual Speculations," 165.

741   Sweet, *Religion on the American Frontier: The Baptists 1783-1830*, 19.

immigration which was precipitated by the downturn brought all classes of men to Kentucky and Tennessee, but generally speaking, these immigrants were largely of middle-class origins seeking cheap land.[742] In Virginia, when Jefferson's "Bill for Establishing Religious Freedom in Virginia" came into effect in 1796, many middle-class settlers expressed that freedom by heading west to escape the "supercilious airs and opprobrium" with which they had been treated by Virginia's upper-class families.[743] In Kentucky and Tennessee, these socially disfranchised immigrants seeking new democratic freedoms were equally attracted to the gospel and the "pure democracy" of Baptist church government.[744] The former aristocracy of the old Standing Order, along with its theological domination of its constituency, had no support here. Election was no longer believed to be only the arbitrary choice of the Sovereign but also of the individual. Here, Baptist preachers lived and worked like the common man in making their own living. Consequently, the Baptist preacher "was particularly well suited in his ideas of government, in his economic status, and in his form of church government to become the ideal western immigrant."[745] As a result, revivalism nearly became the universal practice among them in terms of local church ideology, a burgeoning middle-class society, and the free-enterprise system which stood to expand both constituencies.

DISESTABLISHMENT AND THE RISE OF VOLUNTARISM

After the Revolutionary War and the breakup of Anglican domination in the South, "localized, individual ecclesiology" became

---

742   Sweet, *Religion on the American Frontier: The Baptists 1783-1830*, 19-20.
743   Sweet, *Religion on the American Frontier: The Baptists 1783-1830*, 20-21.
744   Ibid, 21.
745   Ibid.

"intimately related to the prevalent evangelical theology."[746] The theology prevalent in the revivalist ideals of the Separate-Baptists had produced an ecclesiology born out of the individualistic nature of personal conversion. Therefore, membership had to be equally as *voluntary* as conversion. Converts in the South, like those of the Great Awakening, desired churches which represented their biblical ideals in the absence of a national church.

In the Northeast, Backus continually hammered out his demand for equality under law and the removal of the ministerial tax-system controlled by the Standing Order. Any Christian, in his mind, had the right and responsibility to voluntarily support the church of his choosing. In real terms, Backus' conception of religious liberty was based on ending compulsory taxation from churches not their own, and promoting the voluntary support of their own local Baptist assemblies.[747] Much of the opposition had been aimed at the notorious third article of the new Massachusetts constitution of 1779 which, despite promising religious equality to all as a basic right, meant that religious taxes of all inhabitants were still being collected to support public, protestant teachers of piety, religion, and morality.[748] Other related sections of the article "reserved to the people the right to elect their own ministers, prohibited the subordination of one religion to another, and guaranteed equal protection of the laws to all Christians."[749]

The first real test case for the Baptists was that concerning Elijah Balkcom, a member of the Baptist church in Attleboro, whose members, while practicing civil disobedience,[750] refused to pay

---

746   Boles, *The Great Revival*, 125.
747   McLoughlin, *Soul Liberty: The Baptists' Struggle in New England, 1630-1833*, 229.
748   John Cushing, "Notes on Disestablishment in Massachusetts, 1780-1833," *The William and Mary Quarterly* 26, no. 2 (April 1969): 172.
749   Ibid, 173.
750   Cushing unfortunately describes disestablishment almost solely from the perspective

religious taxes to the city. Balkcom was told that if he did not produce a certificate proving he was a true dissenter, he would be forced to pay the ministerial tax supporting the approved "teacher" of the Congregational church.[751] Surprisingly, the county court in Taunton rendered a decision for Balkcom on March 16, 1782.[752] By 1783, when Backus wrote *A Door Opened For Christian Liberty*, the Middleboro pastor and the New England Baptist community thought they were on the verge of victory for their anti-tax cause when he joyfully declared, "It may be of public benefit to lay open the prospect we now have of their [taxes] being happily terminated."[753] For Backus, this was not only a victory for Baptist toleration but also a breaking forth of further light which had eluded the previous reformers, and subsequent attempts at carrying it forward. Backus reminisced about the past saying,

And for twelve or thirteen centuries all colleges and places for superior learning were under the government of men who assumed the power to lay religious bands upon children before they could choose for themselves and to enforce the same by the sword of the magistrate all their days. But I congratulate my countrymen upon the arrival of more agreeable times, and upon the prospect of a much greater reformation before us.[754]

of the Unitarian-Universalist conflict. He says that the first "significant litigation" involving the notorious third article was brought by the Reverend John Murray, a Unitarian-Universalist minister who brought a suit against the First Parish in Gloucester. The main problem there, however, was not necessarily taxes, but the questioned orthodoxy of the professed "protestant teacher." Cushing goes on to say in a footnote that the results of the Balkcom case "were of local significance only." However, this case struck at the very heart of the misrepresented third article of the Massachusetts revised constitution of 1779. Backus was so sure of this fact he thought that victory over the "established church" was imminent.

751   Cushing, "Notes on Disestablishment in Massachusetts, 1780-1833," 177.

752   McLoughlin, ed., *Isaac Backus on Church, State, and Calvinism: Pamphlets, 1754-1789*, 428.

753   Ibid, 431, emphasis added.

754   Ibid, 436, emphasis added.

This *much greater* reformation was undoubtedly connected in Backus' mind to the dissemination of biblical truth because he said, "Christianity is a *voluntary* obedience to God's revealed will, and everything of a contrary nature is antichristian."[755] The proposition which arbitrarily suggests that ecclesiological voluntarism originated through the political positions of John Locke, Thomas Jefferson, or the emasculated orthodoxy of liberal Congregationalist Lyman Beecher, diminishes the ultimate social impact of the Separate-Baptists and their subsequent brand of evangelical theology as a stand-alone social phenomenon. Sydney Mead thought revival to have been working concurrently with Lockean ideas of personal ownership and Jeffersonian views on individual freedom in producing a pragmatic approach to Christianity in general. He thereby characterized revivalism (more the Finney brand) as a primary factor in contributing to competition among the sects. This resulted in the "general erosion of interest in the historical distinctions and definable theological differences between the religious sects"...and promoting "revivalism as a technique, voluntaryism as a cohesive base, and historylessness as a cast of mind."[756] This view unfortunately underestimates the spiritual dynamic of the period. Backus' use of Locke was more a political formulation than a religious justification for his position.[757] For him, validating Locke in his argument for disestablishment from the Standing Order was only a *supplement* to his biblical position.[758] After all, these new believers all shared a

---

755   Ibid, 438, emphasis added.

756   Mead pays too little attention to the ultimate impact of disestablishment and how this new religious equality enabled the sect-style Baptist churches to balloon in numerical growth. See chapters entitled "Thomas Jefferson's 'Fair Experiment—Religious Freedom,'" and "Denominationalism: The Shape of Protestantism in America" in Mead, *The Lively Experiment: The Shaping of Christianity in America*, 38-71.

757   Maston, *Isaac Backus: Pioneer of Religious Liberty*, 106.

758   Maston agrees that Backus did not slavishly use Locke in his defense of toleration for the dissenters. He points out the fact that Locke's writings were "part of the air people

special relationship to God, and this relationship transcended any denominational connection. To some, this presented the strongest argument for ecumenical unionism among the denominations sympathetic to revival. Had these revival-driven tendencies become the norm for the participating denominations, it is likely that local ecclesiological concepts would have embraced the universal church concept as a means of demonstrating their mutually shared salvation experiences.[759] However, those who held such a concept in the South were "faced with a ruling institution, however ineffective, that equated church and state...having special reason to define the church in voluntaristic terms."[760] Well known to those who had experienced the new birth through revival influences was the fact that many on the rolls of the State-Church in the Colonial South "never had intimated any converting knowledge of God."[761] Consequently, populist theology determined that it was only through the local congregation that the voluntary society of believers could find active and continuous expressions for theological individualism after being converted. Backus and other Great Awakening converts had discovered the same thing among the Colonial system in Congregational New England. For them, the discovery of unconverted ministers and church members in

---

breathed" surrounding Backus, and Backus wisely utilized the widely read Locke rather than Roger Williams, along with plenty of Biblical passages, to his own advantage in political discourse. See Ibid, 55, 105-106.

759   This ecumenical mindset encouraged by mutual cooperation of the groups in the Great Revival is discussed at some length by Boles in his chapter entitled, "Unity and Schism." He demonstrates two things: first, the collective evangelical mindset fostered by the common beliefs of all the participants, and second, how the revival exposed various viewpoints particularly among the Methodists and the Presbyterians which ultimately splintered both denominations. The point that he fails to discuss is how the Baptists (Separate-Baptists from Virginia), who were largely responsible for the origins of the revival, became the greatest beneficiaries in the post-revival era. Because revival converts recognized the Scriptural injunction of believers' baptism, Baptist churches grew rapidly from revival converts in Virginia, Kentucky, and Tennessee just like the Separate-Baptists had from revival converts in the New England Great Awakening. See Boles, *The Great Revival*, 143-164.

760   Ibid, 127.

761   Ibid.

their respective churches demanded that they separate and establish new congregations based upon consistent New Testament principles. Similarly, in the south, a significant portion of dissent was focused on the demand for disestablishment from the state-sponsored Anglican system. In their minds, this break would accomplish two things, both of which would directly feed denominational self-interests. The first was that of total religious equality under the law. This is where the Separate-Baptists considered Luther's reformation to have failed. Furthermore, they considered the Baptists as having taken up that great "sword of truth"[762] by favoring complete toleration under the civil law, something which Luther and the reformers had been unwilling to offer the Anabaptists. Secondly, religious freedom for all would then force each denomination to manage its own affairs and promote its expansion upon the basis of individual persuasion and the voluntary efforts of its own memberships versus forced taxation and state support. This coercion of denominational interests down to the level of the local congregation had not only identified Baptists with the Puritan ideal, but had taken them well beyond it. The civil-church concept rearranged in Protestant ecclesiology and transported intact to Colonial America could not long endure under the demand for legal toleration for every denomination. "In the South all but the Anglican Church were dissenting sects, as in New England were all but the Congregational churches."[763] As the Presbyterians, Methodists, and Baptists became the dominant populous force, "they fought for the right to promote their own point of view in their own way unmolested by traditional civil and ecclesiastical customs and laws."[764] In voluntarism, the church shared a similar value with the

---

762   McLoughlin, ed., *Isaac Backus on Church, State, and Calvinism: Pamphlets, 1754-1789,* 395.
763   Mead, *The Lively Experiment: The Shaping of Christianity in America,* 36.
764   Ibid, 34.

emerging matrix of limited autonomy and the personal conversion of the individual.

No longer just leveraging his denomination against the Puritan Congregational principle found in John Owen, Backus substantiated his view of the local congregation by using Locke's voluntarism and the Jeffersonian principle of the separation of church and state to fight for denominational equality and what he hoped would become denominational dominance.[765] Hatch suggests that this egalitarian movement toward voluntarism in the church was driven more by political change than religious sentiment because "a new and explicitly democratic revolution united many who were suspicious of power and many who were powerless in a common effort to pull down the cultural hegemony of a gentlemanly few."[766] What he fails to admit is that the revivalist new birth message, moderate Calvinism, and the democratic principles were inherent to both (civic and spiritual realms), and *were* the actual instruments which had begun *to pull down the cultural hegemony of a gentlemanly few.* Hatch goes on to couch both parallel movements in what he termed a "crisis of authority in popular culture that accompanied the birth of the American Republic."[767] Hiemert argues that it was the theology of the revivalists which "provided pre-revolutionary America with a radical,

---

765   What must be remembered here is the fact that Backus did not seek to justify his ecclesiological position on prevailing philosophical views (i.e. John Locke, Thomas Jefferson). In his already published works, Backus painstakingly built his case for purely independent churches of the Baptist order on a Biblical foundation. In doing so, he depended heavily upon the arguments of the massively respected John Owen who declared, "Hence a visible church needs be a separate congregation; separation is a proper and inseparable adjunct thereof....a gospel church is a company of faithful professing people, walking together by mutual consent or confederation to the Lord Jesus Christ and one to another, in subjection to and practice of all his gospel precepts and commands, whereby they are separate from all persons and things manifestly contrary or disagreeing thereunto." See John Owen, *The Works of John Owen*, 16 vols. (London: Johnstone and Hunter, 1850-1853), 16:6.

766   Hatch, "The Christian Movement and the Demand for a Theology of the People," 561.

767   Ibid.: 567.

even democratic, social and political ideology...."[768] Both Hiemert
and Miller trace this theology to the new-birth message of the Great
Awakening.[769] Even antagonist Harry Stout approved of the analysis
that the connection between revival and revolution were in the "modes
of persuasion" used by both systems, but in the end, Stout admits,
like Perry Miller, that the fountain of the "spirit of liberty" was first
"manifest in the revivals".[770] This connection to revivalism, whether
Stout intended it or not, is unavoidably linked to the doctrine of the
new birth, followed by the doctrinal adjustments it forced upon the
Standing Order, and the exclusive local church ideology it fostered.
Torbet surmised that Jackson's emphasis on states' rights and local
politics coincided perfectly with Backus' rejection of ecumenical
church-ism. Consequently, Torbet said this resulted in Backus,
among later Baptists, dropping the idea of the "universal church" and
any interdependence of congregations in favor of the local-church
view.[771] Therefore, the Baptists not only provided a *terminus ad quem*
for subsequent ecclesiological change but also became the greatest
beneficiaries of revival and their emerging ecclesiology. Furthermore,
their view of baptism ultimately came to be the means of defining
local-church membership and provided the only right believers had
to the Lord's Table. This ecclesiological conservatism propelled
them beyond both the Presbyterians and the Congregationalists in
numerical growth by 1829. The doctrinal exactness of the Baptists
also provided a natural exit point from the other evangelical groups
to the Baptist position but provided few back. Because baptism of

---

768   Heimert, ed., *Religion and the American Mind: From the Great Awakening to the
Revolution*, viii.
769   Heimert and Miller, *The Great Awakening: Documents Illustrating the Crisis and Its
Consequences*, xxiv.
770   Stout, "Religion, Communications, and the Ideological Origins of the American
Revolution," 541.
771   Torbet, *A History of the Baptists*, 255.

an adult believer carried as much weight in voluntary membership as a personal decision for Christ in salvation, many new converts in the Congregational system who wanted adult baptism saw this step as an irreversible break with the Standing Order. As for the Baptists, disestablishment not only meant religious equality, but their strong local-church ideology held the potential for denominational superiority.

SUMMARY

This story of the Separate-Baptists is a story rooted in dissent, a dissent which became invariably tied up with revival, including a religious piety driven by this singular impulse.[772] The Great Awakening of 1740-1741 had demonstrated to Backus and the Separate-Baptists that God had providentially begun a second reformation in America and, consequently, laid before New England Baptists an unmistakable opportunity for garnering innumerable souls and possibly even ushering in the new millennium of Jesus Christ. These opportunities would not come by some new civil-state arrangement but by the forces of revival along with the assertion of the individual's competence before God and visible church membership. Similarly, as New Englanders began their move toward the frontier states, the camp meetings held among the Presbyterians, Methodists, and Baptists swore off denominational self-interests in the hope of reaching more souls under the banner of revival.

---

772   John Mecklin recognized in the post-Great Awakening era that dissent was no longer to be understood solely in terms of the opposition party but in the new rationale of revival, particularly of the Baptists. Revival became the almost indisputable catalyst for the rapid demise of Calvinism and the singular influence it waged upon local-church theology formally recognized in the New Hampshire confession of faith. See John M. Mecklin, *The Story of American Dissent* (New York: Harcourt Brace Jovanovich, Inc, 1934).

Chapter Six

Tracing the Separate-Baptists into the Nineteenth Century

INTRODUCTION

Backus and the SBBM had now come to view their denomination as becoming the rightful heirs of the second reformation, displacing the Separatist-Puritan vision of *a city on a hill* and the ideal of an American-style *theocracy*. As previously noted, it is doubtful that Backus recognized the greater implications of his ardently localized ecclesiology. The battle he waged was too personally intense and far too encompassing for him to regard cooperative Christianity on larger terms than the visible church. He believed that the Separate-Baptists were the scions of the continuing reformation in New England. They had picked up the mantle of the first reformers right where they had surrendered their biblical authority: in the practice of infant baptism.[773] Backus identified the Puritan confusion on sprinkling infants as an initiation into a "catholic or in a particular church-state."[774] Despite his personal use of the universal Church concept, his ardent local-church emphasis ultimately produced an ecclesiology void of external connections beyond the local, visible

---

773   Backus went to great length to explain this rationale to Rev. Joseph Fish of Stonington, Connecticut, in 1773. In essence, Backus contended that had the first founders continued to follow the light which had ultimately led them out of England, they would have made the same discoveries he (Backus) began making with his conversion in 1741, his baptism in 1753, and his ultimate separation from those who continued the practice of infant baptism in 1756. Backus saw pedobaptism as the door to birthright membership into the national church which had become accustomed to harboring mere professors of religion, many of which had become ministers of religion! See Backus, *A Discourse, Concerning the Materials, the Manner of Building, and Power of Organizing the Church of Christ*, 107-130.

774   Ibid, 18.

church. The Middleboro pastor explained his theological evolution this way:

> *I was thirty-two years in learning a lesson of only six words, namely, "one Lord, one faith, one baptism." It took me ten years to get clear of the custom of putting baptism before faith [i.e., infant baptism], and near five more to learn not the contradict the same in practice [i.e., open-communion]; after which, above seventeen trying years rolled over us, before we could refrain from an implicit acknowledgment of more than "one Lord" in religious affairs [i.e., civil jurisdiction in religion].*[775]

This led to the question of whether the SBBM would have embraced a greater interaction of denominational self-interests at the expense of the visible church. Clearly, Backus did not entertain such notions because he thought the need of associations as pragmatic institutions. They were only useful if they served the individual churches which used them.

THE EXEGETICAL ROLE IN LIMITING THE BIBLICAL TEXTS

In Backus' mind, two axioms, operating almost simultaneously, governed his biblical exegetical principle. First, Backus believed that "the proper notion of visible is the making manifest of what was before invisible."[776] The second was the fact that any visible representation of the church on earth had to be local and particular, thus suggesting

---

775   Hudson, ed., *Baptist Concepts of the Church*, 121. The original reference for this Backus quote is found in Backus, *A History of New England with Particular Reference to the Denomination of Christians Called Baptists*, 2: 261.

776   Backus, *A Discourse, Concerning the Materials, the Manner of Building, and Power of Organizing the Church of Christ*, 6. In saying that the idea was to make visible that which was before invisible, Backus seems to suggest a one for one correspondence. Although he never explained it this way theologically, his exegetical tendency was to ignore any basic distinction between the universal and particular senses.

that any supra-church concept, such as a national church, did not carry biblical authority [777] Both ideas brought Backus to interpret the vast majority of New Testament texts on the church in a strictly local sense thereby reducing the available texts necessary for demonstrating any larger sense of *ecclesia* which could have led to some form of ecclesiastical unionism. With his sense of congregational authority and a deliberately weakened clergy-class, Backus inadvertently made the church exclusively local. In reaction to Backus' view, some have even suggested that the early church had raised up leaders for the universal church as well as the local church![778] Most contemporary Baptists who accept both local and universal concepts of the church would never admit the possibilities of officers for the latter. Despite the fact that Backus accepted the church in the universal sense, it is important to recognize how he diminished the use of texts traditionally used to frame universal Church ideology.

THE MATTHEAN PASSAGES

Two texts, both of which had important universal Church connections in Puritan theology were Matt 16:18 and Matt 18:15-18. James Usher used Matt 16:18 in the classic Reformed sense in a selection he penned on the incarnation of Christ. Usher compared the house of Israel over which Moses was placed with the house over which Christ was head:

---

777   Ibid, 17.

778   Stanley Grenz infers that because of the inclusion of apostle and prophet in the 1 Cor 12:22-31 passage, the early church recognized an authority beyond the local-church which could rightfully be interpreted as legitimizing officers of a universal, visible, church, thereby laying the ground for possible interdenominational ecclesiastical relationships opposing the Backus model. It is difficult to see how Backus could have ever drawn such conclusions, even if he could have personally breathed the air of disestablishment and the denominational liberties it produced. See Grenz, *Isaac Backus - Puritan and Baptist: His Place in History, His Thought, and Their Implications for Modern Baptist Theology*, 282-283.

This house of God is no other then the church of the living
God: whereof as hee is the onely Lord, so is hee also properly
the onely Builder of his church...why we finde all the severall
mansions of this great house to carry the title indifferently of
the Churches of God, and the Churches of Christ.[779] *[sic]*

For Christ's first mention of church in the New Testament,
Usher quotes Matt 16:18, stating that *"the onely [sic] Builder of his*
church, which houses the *several mansions* of churches." The twin
Augustinian ideas of universal/mystical and its logical priority over
the local/particular are present in Usher's view. In the Reformed
tradition, it is this true church,[780] of which Christ, as the builder,
promises perpetuity and protection saying, "Upon this rock, I will
build my church, and the gates of hell shall not prevail against it."[781]
However, Backus interprets the text in the local sense asking Fish,
"How can any souls be fit *materials* of the church which those gates
shall not *prevail against*, but such as *believe* Christ with *their* hearts,
and *confess* him with their *mouths*?"[782] In arguing his case, Backus
makes regenerate church membership the first line of defense against
Satan prevailing against the visible church. The Middleboro minister
explains this point:

Is any other visible church-state instituted in the gospel, but a
particular one? The church spoken of by our Lord in Matt. 18:15,-18,

---

779   Hindson, ed., *Introduction to Puritan Theology*, 129, emphasis added.
780   The true church in Augustinian and Calvinist theology is the body of Christ which
is made up of the elect saints of all the ages, chosen by God. It bears no imperfection or
blemish because unlike its visible counterpart, it contains only those who avoid "the deliberate
disavowal of the Lordship of Christ...." For an accurate discussion of Calvin's understanding
and extension of Augustinian thought, see Niesel, *The Theology of Calvin*, 182-210.
781   Matt 16:18.
782   In giving his three reasons for separation from pedobaptist churches, Backus
similarly uses Matt 16:17-18 to describe how Christ builds upon the particular church upon
Himself. See McLoughlin, ed., *The Diary of Isaac Backus*, 3:1527, emphasis added.

is such an one as a brother can tell his grievance to; and whoever
thought that could be to any other than a particular community?[783]

Backus makes no effort to suggest these verses regarded a universal-invisible church of the elect. In contrast, both the first and second London Baptist Confessions used both Matt16:18 and 18:15-18 as constituting the Universal/Invisible Church composed of elect saints.[784] When Backus wrote this article in 1754, no Baptist confession yet existed in America other than the Philadelphia model. Within twenty years of Backus' conversion to Baptist principles, the Separate-Baptists took a strikingly similar position when uniting in 1777 with the Kehukee Baptist Association. This joint effort was the first Baptist associational confession in America which did not even mention the universal Church although, like Backus, they officially believed in it.[785]

THE EPHESIAN PASSAGES

Paul's letter to the Ephesians traditionally constitutes the bulk of universal Church connections in the New Testament.[786] Puritan Richard Baxter (1615-1691) utilized the majority of these in his

---

783   Backus, *A Discourse, Concerning the Materials, the Manner of Building, and Power of Organizing the Church of Christ*, 17.

784   Here Backus goes beyond both the first and second London Baptist Confessions in terms of local church emphasis. The London Confession of 1644 and the Second London Confession of 1689 both articulate the Universal church and use the Matthean passages interchangeably to describe both universal and particular aspects of the church. The two London confessions, along with the Philadelphia Baptist Confession all had the Westminster Confession as their exemplar and strongly maintained Reformed ecclesiology.

785   In a sense, this associational confession prefigures the New Hampshire confession in its silence concerning the Universal church, but more importantly, its descriptions of local church polity are quite similar to the Warren Association which would allow absolutely no associational interference in local church autonomy. See Lumpkin, *Baptist Confessions of Faith*, 355-356. For a concise definition of *church*, including a description of how the Regular Baptists viewed Baptist history, see the preface written by Lemuel Burkitt in Biggs, *A Concise History of the Kehukee Association*.

786   Verses normally given Universal church usage are Eph 1:22; 2:19-22; 4:4-6 and 5:22-32.

excursus on the New Testament church. Of Eph 1:22 and 5:23 he states, "That it is the catholic (i.e., universal) church is apparent...he is oft called the Head of the catholic church."[787] "The catholic church consisteth...of all that have the 'one Spirit, one faith, one baptism, one God and Father of all', &c" (Eph 4:4-6, 20-24).[788] In contrast, Backus' interpretation of these passages focuses on a local-church emphasis. Refuting the catholic idea that a New Testament church contained the unconverted, Backus appears to identify the saved with the household of God who are then eligible for church membership by saying:

> All who by birth or purchase were incorporated into a
> Hebrew's family had a right to all the ordinances of that
> church. So all that by Christ's purchase and the new birth,
> are brought into the household of God have a right to all
> the privileges of The Gospel-Church, Eph ii, 19-22.[789]

There is a legitimate question here whether Backus wished to distinguish between the universal Church as the *household of God* and the local church as the *Gospel-Church* comprised of those who had experienced the new birth. In his *The Bondwoman and the Free*, Backus argued with Fish that the New Testament church was not to be confused with the Old Testament church in terms of place. The Jewish body was confined to a physical location, he said, while "we are confined to no place, John iv. 21, but the saints are God's house who are builded [*sic*] for his habitation through the Spirit, Eph ii, 20-22."[790] In this use of the term God's house, Backus uses the term as defining the New Testament saints in church capacity. Furthermore,

---

787   Hindson, ed., *Introduction to Puritan Theology*, 236.
788   Ibid, 237.
789   McLoughlin, ed., *Isaac Backus on Church, State, and Calvinism: Pamphlets, 1754-1789*, 181.
790   Ibid, 147.

he uses God's house to describe those who are built into a habitation through the Spirit, making no distinction between the two titles as representing both the universal and local aspects of the church. In contrast, Calvin distinguished between the *universal* and *local* by making the household of God refer to the resurrection-based salvation status of the elect in a mystical sense.[791] Calvin made no comment on the phrase found in verse twenty-two which reads, "In whom you also are being built together for a habitation of God in the Spirit," (Eph 2:22 KJV) which identifies these believers in a local capacity (in Ephesus). In his treatise, *On the Libertines' View of the Resurrection*, the reformer used the two references of Eph 2:19 and 2:22 to support the hope that resurrected saints are "citizens of the Kingdom" and "citizens of Paradise" in the universal and invisible sense.[792] Puritan commentators normally followed an identical pattern of exegesis.[793] Backus followed a different pattern:

> *All that by Christ's purchase and the new birth, are brought into the household of God have a right to all the privileges of the Gospel-Church, Eph ii, 19-22. And to vary a step from this leads men into a jumble, and rather than yield the case they will say that the Scriptures have left this matter in the dark, about the subjects of baptism, when in truth all the darkness is in their own minds.*[794]

Rather than distinguish between *household of God*, representing the realm of the mystical church of the elect, and the *Gospel-Church*, Backus makes the particular church ordinance of

791   McNeill, ed., *Calvin: Institutes of the Christian Religion*, 2: 987.
792   Farley, ed., *John Calvin: Treatises against the Anabaptists and against the Libertines*, 293.
793   See Hindson, ed., *Introduction to Puritan Theology*, 242-243.
794   McLoughlin, ed., *Isaac Backus on Church, State, and Calvinism: Pamphlets, 1754-1789*, 160.

baptism a critical issue *to both* by virtue of *Christ's purchase* and the *new birth.* By establishing the right to church ordinances on this basis, *the household of God* metaphor loses it immediate connection to pre-temporal election (i.e., a universal, invisible church), prefiguring a later designation for that metaphor as representing the *family of God.*[795] Later Baptist interpreters often employ this designation in the place of the *True Church* conception.[796] Backus' rendering of Eph 4:5 connects the one baptism unequivocally to water baptism and the initiatory rite into local church membership with admission to the Lord's Table.[797] By making water baptism of believing adults the primary and essential baptism in the New Testament, the Middleboro pastor separated the Baptists *doctrinally* from the Standing Order. He concluded the matter by saying, "If truth breaks up churches, it highly concerns all that belong to them, to awake and consider what churches they are."

Fish, having argued that infant baptism fulfilled New Testament obedience to the ordinance, questioned why separation on such grounds was even necessary. Backus retorted, "Because we will not meet such persons there, as we cannot believe in our conscience to be baptized according to our Lord's direction." He then ended the matter adding, "I say till they can convince us of this, all their noise

---

795   Boyce H. Taylor, *Why Be a Baptist*, Reprint ed. (Lexington: Ashland Avenue Publications, n.d.), 9.

796   Baptist academic institutions such as those at Newton and Andover fostered much of the theological argument which had its roots in Backus' ecclesiology. For a prime example of their seminal literature see Thomas, *The Church and the Kingdom.* The "family of God" metaphor noted above is discussed on page 267.

797   Backus, *A Discourse, Concerning the Materials, the Manner of Building, and Power of Organizing the Church of Christ*, 143.

about the evil of re-baptizing and closed-communion, cannot satisfy our minds...."[798]

Baptist literature published within fifty years of the death of Backus reveals both a clarification and a popularization of his own exegetical tradition. As the NHC bore the influential marks of the period's revivalism upon local-church exclusivity, Baptist literary output of the same period revealed similar local-church dominance sanctioned by the most influential minds among their academic institutions. In what William Crowell called the "first attempt to exhibit the Baptist church polity in systematic order,"[799] he acknowledges his indebtedness in his *Church Member's Manual* to several well-known Baptist scholars around Boston who put their full approval on his labor in providing this written help.[800] Explaining the immediate necessity of such a work, Crowell affirmed that the primary question under debate was, "What is the church?...this is the great question of the age."[801]

But why did he feel the Baptist denomination was in a better position to answer this question than all of the others? Crowell comments on the Baptists' contributions:

The bold advocates of spiritual Christianity in its primitive form, as faithful martyrs of religious freedom, as laborious

---

798   Ibid, 142-143.
799   Crowell, *The Church Member's Manual*, 7.
800   William Crowell was chosen by his peers, as well as the widow of professor James Knowles of Newton Seminary, to continue his work on the principles of church polity. Crowell sought the assistance of the best theological minds in Boston for their advice and direction. He mentions professors Henry Ripley and Barnas Sears of Newton Seminary. Dr. Sears was the agent for the Massachusetts Board of Education for several years and was elected president of Brown University in 1855. Crowell also mentions Baron Stow, the long-time pastor of the Baldwin Place Baptist Church in Boston. Stow was said to be "one of the most eloquent and successful ministers of the denomination...." See Ibid, 6-7, and Cathart, ed., *The Baptist Encyclopedia*, 1115.
801   Crowell, *The Church Member's Manual*, 6.

missionaries to the heathen, they have contributed to every other department of theological literature; but the organic principles of church constitution have received little of their attention.[802]

Why had this issue "received little of their attention" up to this point? What had changed to produce this new desire for clarification upon an issue which was, in Crowell's own terms, "the great question of the age"? Presumably, the answer involves the fact that Baptist attention up to this point in history had been aimed at *survival* and *assimilation* within an ecclesiastical culture hostile to their most basic interests. Now having won religious freedom, including the constitutional right to follow their consciences dictated solely by the Bible, they were now ready to "promote, in some small degree, the intelligence, the harmony, the spirituality, the beauty, the stability, the usefulness, of the *household of God*...."[803] Of this household, Crowell rejects any non-local interpretation saying, "...we find, v. 22, that it was not universal, but a particular church which he had in mind.... If the Ephesian church were one habitation of God, it follows that every other church is so."[804] Again Crowell affirms, "From this passage we learn that Christ is the head of each and every church, and that each resembles a household, or a city."[805] In this case, like Backus, Crowell is rejecting the idea of a universal, visible church composed of "several churches in a province" or a "diocesan church" usurping unjust authority over particular churches which should be "regarded as

---

802   Ibid, 7.
803   Ibid, 8, emphasis added.
804   Ibid, 34.
805   Ibid, 67.

separate distinct bodies...."[806] Actually, Crowell followed Archbishop Whately who held a similar view of the "household of God":

The many churches which the apostles founded were branches of one spiritual brotherhood, of which the Lord Jesus Christ is the heavenly Head, though there was 'one Lord, one Faith, one Baptism,' for all of them, yet they were each a distinct, independent community on earth, and...by their mutual agreement, affection, and respect; but not having any one recognized Head on earth, or acknowledging any sovereignty of one of these societies over others.[807]

Because Crowell was formulating his church position with the blessing of so many Boston Baptists constituting the theologically elite, the doctrine of election continued to maintain its urban influence.[808] However, election was decreasingly observed in its connection to a universal, invisible Church comprised of the elect of all the ages. Crowell admits only that the "holy catholic [i.e., universal] church is composed of all the truly regenerated on *earth*, who being known to Him only who searcheth the heart, it cannot be a visibly organized

---

806   Ibid, 38.
807   Ibid, 41. Crowell takes this material from the Archbishop's Essays on "The Kingdom of Christ" published in 1841. Richard Whately, the Archbishop of Dublin, was born in 1787. This may explain why Backus did not avail himself of Whately's argument on the nature of the church. But Crowell and others found great benefit in his work for their own use in defending their rejection of universal, national, and diocesan conglomerates of churches.
808   It has been noted that among the rural population, and particularly where revival had predominated, the election doctrine had diminished significantly in influence as a populist doctrinaire. The exceptions were primarily in the larger centers such as Providence, Boston, and New York. The first two cities housed three major Baptist seminaries; Brown University in Providence which was founded in 1865, Newton Seminary in Boston which was founded in 1825, and Andover Seminary which began in 1807. In New York, the Philadelphia Baptist Association held great influence under such men as John Gano, pastor of the First Baptist Church of New York City. With election existing in the urban statements of faith, the universal, invisible church of the elect survived, and found expression in their more detailed expressions of doctrine. However, it is clear that in Boston and New England in general, where the influence of the Separate-Baptists was greatest, the doctrine of the universal-invisible church of the elect had diminished in its Augustinian connection to personal election.

body."[809] However, it also cannot be a universal, mystical body of the redeemed of all the ages because the *eternal* model transcends *earthly* limitations. Without this authority of a universal-mystical church anchored to a pre-temporal election, Crowell asks and answers the next critical question, "Is the power of a particular church derived from the church universal?" He replies, "If so, it will be necessary to prove that such an institution exists, that is has the power to spare, and has a right to delegate it."[810] Such proof, the author states, has no biblical foundation, and as such, the Scriptures "have not left this truth to depend on even so plain an inference."[811] By this definition, Crowell divests *all authority* from the universal-visible church, placing the priority of ecclesiastical authority in the local assembly. Backus did the same by simply saying that the universal-mystical church is "the same which it always was,"[812] but when Christ the great Head spoke to his church, it was not "as one national or provincial church, but as so many distinct churches, who are commended, or reproved by him, according as their works were, in each particular community."[813] Under critical analysis, both Backus and Crowell, although rejecting the universal-visible and universal-mystical aspects of the church on earth respectively, concur that no inherent *authority* from the universal concept is attached to either by virtue of biblical inference

---

809   Crowell, *The Church Member's Manual*, 112, emphasis added.
810   It is interesting that Crowell couches the reality of the concept of a Universal church in the word institution. This is not consistent with Reformed thinking which understood the universal-invisible/mystical church of the elect as conceptual. This is consistent with the Platonic comparison of the actual with its ideal counterpart. Although Backus was satisfied to leave the universal-invisible church as it was, he repudiated any form of a visible church which transcended local perimeters. Within one generation of Backus, Crowell appears satisfied to use John Milton's definition of a universal-visible church (on earth) while not admitting any basis for a universal-invisible/mystical church of the elect. See Ibid, 112-113.
811   Ibid, 60.
812   Backus, *A Discourse, Concerning the Materials, the Manner of Building, and Power of Organizing the Church of Christ*, 15.
813   Ibid, 17.

from Paul's letter to the Ephesians.[814] Jesse Thomas,[815] isolating the local interpretation in the Ephesian passages yet further, denied that two different church models could be *simultaneously* discussed in the same passage without doing irreparable damage to the text.[816] By repudiating Augustine's theological use of Plato's dualism,[817] Thomas argues for Aristotle's position, claiming that "undue expansion of the limits of a thing, whereby it becomes incapable of performing its characteristic functions, may destroy the identity of the thing itself."[818] Unfortunately, such theological criticism of Plato and the influence of *dualism* in Christian theology is a largely ignored discussion by contemporary theologians.[819]

THE 1 COR 12:13 PASSAGE

---

814   Stanley Grenz suggests that the failure to see that the local church gained its meaning from the "total society" is attributable to Landmarkism. According to the assessments of Backus and later Crowell, this trend toward the rejection of authority which flowed out from the Augustinian ideal predates the Landmark movement. Landmarkism built its movement upon the error that baptismal authority in the local church could only be passed from one church to the next thereby forming an unbroken succession back to the apostolic period. See Grenz, *Isaac Backus - Puritan and Baptist: His Place in History, His Thought, and Their Implications for Modern Baptist Theology*, 269.

815   Dr. Jesse Thomas was trained at the Rochester Theological Seminary and led several churches, the most notable being the First Baptist Church of Brooklyn beginning in 1874. He was noted as a "scholar in the broadest sense" and by "nature an orator." His later career brought him as a professor to Newton Theological Seminary where he gathered lectures previously published in the Western Recorder (Louisville, Ky.) into a volume entitled, "The Church and the Kingdom." He used the material in this book to teach an elective class at the seminary. For a brief biography of his earlier career, see Cathart, ed., *The Baptist Encyclopedia*, 1148-1149.

816   Thomas, *The Church and the Kingdom*, 254-265.

817   Plato taught that every transient object had a transcendent, ideal counterpart. This ideal was its true, perfect representation from which its lower manifestation received derivative meaning. Hence, as Augustine made reference to the earthly visible church, he maintained that its true, perfect counterpart was both universal and invisible, consisting of the elect, chosen before the foundation of the world.

818   Thomas, *The Church and the Kingdom*, 274-275.

819   Contemporary theologians offer little critical analysis or comment upon Augustine and his Platonic dualism along with its theological influence. On the contrary, nineteenth century scholars like Jesse Thomas repudiated Plato, by the use of his protégé Aristotle, and normally rejected Augustine, whom he saw as the progenitor of Roman Catholicism. For the contemporary use of Plato, see Erickson, *Christian Theology*, 1033. For an excellent survey of how Baptists critically analyzed Plato, Augustine, and Universal church theology, see

Working from the premise that the "one baptism" in Eph 4 is "Spirit" baptism, the Reformed tradition is fairly consistent that 1 Cor 12:13 represents a watershed doctrine based in universal/mystical interpretation.[820] Baxter provided four reasons for the Reformed position as supporting the unity of the universal or catholic body. First he says the universal Church "is more fitly denominated from Christ as the Head, than a particular church...it is not easy to find any text of Scripture that calleth Christ the Head of a particular congregation...." Second, it is called the "body of Christ" which is a title "not given to any" local assembly. Third he says it was given numerous gifts which were not to all be associated with any particular assembly, and fourth, the Spirit baptized Jews and Gentiles only into the "catholic" church, and this baptism was never to be understood as first being in water either "always, nor primarily."[821] The majority of modern, Baptist opinions would be at odds with at least the first three points. The fourth point is highly debated depending on one's sympathy with certain dispensational views. Early Anabaptist and Baptist interpretation is somewhat divided, although the earliest recognized English General Baptist Confession uses 1 Cor 12:13 in reference to water baptism.[822] The key Particular Baptist treatise of western

---

Thomas, *The Church and the Kingdom*. Regarding the influence of Platonic thought among the Alexandrian theologians and the conflict between Platonism and Aristotelianism, see Shedd, *A History of Christian Doctrine*, 62-74.

820   In the KJV, the verse reads, "For by one Spirit were we all baptized into one body, whether Jews or Greeks, whether slaves or free, and have all been made to drink into one Spirit." By attaching such a baptism to the ordinances, this verse was traditionally understood by Baptists as referring to water baptism. The Schleitheim Confession of 1527 uses the local sense by saying that baptism unites the believer "in one body of Christ which is the church of God and whose head is Christ." However, such a conclusion is doubtful in the Anabaptist Waterland Confession of 1580, which expresses that *the* body of 1 Cor 12:13 refers to a universal body of Christ, of which "every believer is a member of the body of Christ...." See Lumpkin, *Baptist Confessions of Faith*, 58.

821   Hindson, ed., *Introduction to Puritan Theology*, 236.

822   The 1611 "Declaration of Faith of English People Remaining at Amsterdam" is a prime example of the Anabaptist tradition which connected 1 Corinthians 12:13 to water baptism. It should be noted that election is played down in the confession and any Augustinian

England was the Somerset Baptist Confession of 1656.[823] Written by Thomas Collier, along with the probable help of other associational leaders, this confession identifies with the London Confession of 1644 and also seeks to articulate the Baptist principles of regenerate church membership, the right of churches to call out and ordain their own ministers, and the obligation to send out gospel representatives all over the world.[824] This confessional effort was also aimed at repressing any Quaker influence taking place among the Baptists within the association.[825] Article forty-three words this concept:

...it is the duty and privilege of the church of Christ (till his coming again) in their fellowship together in the ordinances of Christ, to enjoy, prize, and press after, fellowship through and in the Spirit with the Lord, and each with other (Acts 2:42; I Cor. 11:26; Eph 2:21, 22; Eph 4:3, 4, 5, 6; I Cor. 12:13; Eph 3:9; Col 2:2... "[826]

It remains unclear as to how the Spirit was involved. Such stated union was "through and in the Spirit." The word "through" first suggests *instrumentality.* In other words the union or fellowship was

---

connection to the mystical body of Christ is not clearly mentioned, "though in respect to Christ, the Church bee one". Conversely, the London Confession of 1644 in its only mention of the passage, references the unity of the Godhead out of which is one God, one Christ, one Spirit, one Faith, one Baptisme; on Rule of holinesse and obedience..." By not using the verse again in the confession relating to water baptism, it reveals an undercurrent of Reformed influence, understandable in the period. See Lumpkin, *Baptist Confessions of Faith*, 119-120. The Second London Confession does not utilize the reference at all in the section on the church or the ordinances of the church but only in reference to "all saints" in the opening paragraph. See Lumpkin, *Baptist Confessions of Faith*, 156. For the entire treatment of baptism in the London Confession of 1644, see 167.

823   This document is the first "earliest and important effort at bringing together the Particular and General Baptists" of the Western Association into "agreement and union." In article thirty-four, it sets forth the clearest statement on missionary obligation before the time of William Carey. See Ibid, 200-202.

824   Ibid.

825   There was a definite emphasis placed on their articulation of the ordinances which clearly distinguished them from the Quakers.

826   Lumpkin, *Baptist Confessions of Faith*, 214-215, emphasis added.

made possible by the means of, or through the medium, vehicle, or ministry of the Spirit. The second preposition "in" suggests the *sphere* or *location* of such fellowship. Since both are used together, the exact intended meaning of Spirit involvement remains ambiguous. However, since, the ordinances were the focal point of difference to which the Baptists alluded, it is likely that water baptism was the singular basis for such Spirit-fellowship. Kiffin, the opponent of Bunyan, translated 1 Cor 12:13 and Eph 4:5 both as belonging to water baptism into the local church.[827]

Interestingly, despite Backus' Separate-Baptist association and his ardent visible church hermeneutic, he never personally clarified a position on 1 Cor 12:13, but instead, utilized John Owen to clarify his position on what constituted the basis for church fellowship, and thereby what justified ecclesiastical separation.[828] In this use of Owen, Backus inadvertently supports this Reformed understanding, but apparently it is only in connection with his essential argument concerning church fellowship. Wayland, writing in the mid-nineteenth century narrowed this Spirit-produced fellowship among the saints at large to just the local church. Speaking of the local body as the *body of Christ*, he said the Christian "partakes at once of the communion of the saints. Every Christian receives him as a brother, and bestows upon

---

827   William Kiffin, *Some Serious Reflections on That Part of John Bunions's Confession of Faith: Touching Communion at the Lord's Supper* (London: Francis Smith, 1673), 13-15.

828   The Middleboro pastor, in his argument with Joseph Fish, deals with the accusation that the fellowship of Separate-Baptist churches was being based on mere feelings, etc., as a basis for church union. Backus turns to English Independent John Owen to spell out his own position. Owen, in speaking of being baptized by "one spirit" into the one body, said that this unites all believers into one body under one head, and added "so is Christ mystical." Backus' use of Owen supports his own residual universal "mystical" body, church of the elect view which ameliorated under revivalism and continual development of the local-church theology. It needs to be remembered, however, that Owen's explanation was used by Backus to only explain such issues under local church conditions. In a short time however, interpreters would completely ignore any implications concerning the larger church. For Backus' use of John Owen, see McLoughlin, ed., *Isaac Backus on Church, State, and Calvinism: Pamphlets, 1754-1789,* 222-223.

him more than a brother's love."[829] Winthrop Hudson's assessment
of Wayland allowed him only to say that although he "exhibited
some appreciation of the importance for nurture of a Christian
community, his extreme emphasis upon the individual prevented
him from perceiving the real dimensions of Christian fellowship."[830]
Crowell, his Boston contemporary, utilized the verse to support the
"supreme power of Christ in and over his churches."[831] The inherent
authority to which Crowell alluded was that "All offices, ordinary and
extraordinary, are established by him, and the authority belonging
to them (Eph 4:11; I Cor. 12:5-18), as well as all gifts of wisdom
and grace to discharge the duties of every station in the church...."
Rhetorically, Crowell asks of the apostolic church, "How did these
bodies of *christians* obtain the powers of *christian* churches? Or how
does a body of baptized believers now, obtain the right to exercise
those powers?" Answering he said, "Two things are necessary. First, a
mutual covenant, voluntarily entered into by all the members, to obey
and execute the commands of Christ; and second, a faithful adherence
to the obligations thus assumed."[832] There is no inference made of
any *derivative* authority coming from the universal church. Instead
Crowell asserted, "This power or privilege comes directly from Christ,
the supreme lawgiver, to each church as a body of brethren thus
united in covenant, and is not transmitted to them through any other
hands."[833]

    As Backus had already established, this centered all authority,
jurisdictional or ideal in the visible church, and made each local
body entirely independent, autonomous, and qualified by Christ to

---

829   Francis Wayland, *Sermons to the Churches* (New York: 1858), 93.

830   Hudson, ed., *Baptist Concepts of the Church*, 149.

831   Crowell, *The Church Member's Manual*, 61.

832   Ibid, 64-65, emphasis added.

833   Ibid, 66.

perform his entire earthly program.[834] By the middle of the nineteenth century, exclusive local-church authority predominated water-baptism over Spirit-baptism as "the most widely accepted position" in the interpretation of 1 Cor 12:13,[835] particularly among the Separate-Baptists as their influence continued to season their Baptist world.

Speaking for the majority of New England Baptists by his time, including Baptist academe in Boston, Thomas asserted, "The whole twelfth chapter of I Corinthians is so manifestly local in its drifts and statements that it would be incongruous to extend any part of it to a world-wide body."[836] Today, a significant number of contemporary Baptists would be far more comfortable with the visible church *coexisting* alongside its universal-invisible counterpart.

MASSACHUSETTS SEPARATE-BAPTISTS AND ASSOCIATIONALISM

The irony of the post-Backus era is the continuing and pervasive doubts Baptists in general continued to entertain about their relationship to each other and to other mainline denominations. This irony was based, in one instance, on the ongoing paranoia that formal education would ultimately produce a hireling ministry similar to that which the Baptists opposed in the Standing Order.[837] However, the

834   Backus, *A History of New England with Particular Reference to the Denomination of Christians Called Baptists*, 2: 340.
835   This position shifted with the rise of Darby and Dispensationalism which taught that believers are brought into the one "body of Christ" by the Holy Spirit who baptizes them into a invisible, universal body. For a discussion of the background of modern dispensational thought, see Clarence B. Bass, *Backgrounds to Dispensationalism* (Grand Rapids: Eerdmans Publishing Company, 1960). For a general discussion of the social and religious conditions prior to the rise of dispensational thought, see Robert Torbet's article "Dispensationalist Ecclesiology" in Hudson, ed., *Baptist Concepts of the Church*, 219-225. For a clear discussion of various dispensationalist views, see Charles C. Ryrie, ed., *Issues in Dispensationalism* (Chicago: Moody Press, 1994).
836   Thomas, *The Church and the Kingdom*, 231.
837   Leonard, *Baptist Ways: A History*, 128.

fear of an overeducated clergy paled in comparison to the concerns over associational connectionalism. Denominational growth had precipitated anxiety concerning denominational over-lording. What Backus had feared in the early years (1767-1770) of the Warren Association had become the collective concern of the Baptist majority as they continued to struggle for denominational identity into the nineteenth century.

Francis Wayland was the key Baptist representative who carried the ecclesiological views of Backus into the new century. He became president of Brown University in 1827 and continued there until 1855 (Rhode Island College became Brown University in 1805). During the 1820s, assuming the pseudonym *Backus*, Wayland defended a form of national connectionalism in the American Baptist Magazine which promoted local, state, and national associational meetings vesting considerable jurisdictional influence over constituent churches. The obvious intention was to expand Backus' original associational principles and powers under the assumption that Backus would have likely approved. In later life, Wayland published a series of letters under the pseudonym *Roger Williams* repudiating his former associational position, opting for complete local church independence from denominational connections, and of course, their possible control.[838] By the last quarter of the nineteenth century Wayland's latter position represented the *majority* position of Baptists. The author, admonishing his faithful followers, would say, "The more steadfastly we hold to the independence of the churches, and abjure everything in the form of a denominational corporation, the more truly shall we be united, and the greater will be our prosperity."[839] Wayland had arrived at his position affirming that whatever "the

---

838   McBeth, *A Sourcebook of Baptist Heritage*, 214-220.
839   Ibid, 220.

New Testament teaches, either by precept or through example, the church may require of its members, and the individual members may require of the church."[840] Everything beyond this he said "must be left to the judgment and conscience of the individual...being without [outside] the limit of church authority."[841] That being said for the nature of the church, Wayland could find no basis for how a church could "possibly be represented"[842] except by individuals exercising the rights of their own consciences. Individual autonomy, exercised through independent and democratic churches, became the inexorable pattern for Baptist growth and prosperity. Wayland continued to wage enormous influence over Baptists, so much so that he "became almost an oracle, a leader whose judgment on every subject was sought and usually followed."[843] Other key Baptist historians and writers such as Edward T. Hiscox[844] and John Newton Brown, [845] like Wayland, "contributed greatly to the Baptist molding of that which succeeding generations would regard as Baptist orthodoxy,"[846] which celebrated exclusive and independent local-church ideology. This American

---

840   Wayland, *Notes on the Principles and Practices of Baptist Churches*, 180.
841   Ibid.
842   Ibid.
843   McBeth, *A Sourcebook of Baptist Heritage*, 214.
844   Edward Hiscox was born in Westerly, RI, in 1814, educated at Madison University, and became pastor of the First Baptist Church of Westerly in 1844. In 1859 he published "The Baptist Church Directory" which by 1881 had sold over 30,000 copies. It had been translated into six languages, and it was used by missionaries worldwide. Norman Maring commented that Wayland and Hiscox did more to determine the direction Baptists took in the nineteenth century than any two leaders in the post-Backus era. For biographical information on Hiscox, see Cathart, ed., *The Baptist Encyclopedia*, 528. For Maring's comment, see his article on "The Individualism of Francis Wayland" in Hudson, ed., *Baptist Concepts of the Church*, 137.
845   John Newton Brown was the primary author of the New Hampshire Confession in 1830 which was published in 1833. He was the pastor of the Baptist Church in Exeter, New Hampshire, in 1829. The following year, because of the effects of revival in the state, along with the prospect of the eventual disestablishment of the Standing Church in Massachusetts, Brown composed—at the behest of the Separate-Baptist community—a new Baptist confession which reflected the diminished Calvinism and exclusive local-church position held by the majority of American Baptists.
846   Hudson, ed., *Baptist Concepts of the Church*, 135.

model bore little resemblance to the Philadelphia Baptist associational system, and even less to their English forebears, whose associational conception was inextricably linked to the *a priori* position of the universal church model.

ENGLISH BAPTIST ASSOCIATIONALISM

The Philadelphia Baptist Association, which had been based on the English system, set the early precedent for the American associational model. The Western or Philadelphia Baptist Association, constituted by five Calvinistic Baptist churches in the colonies of Pennsylvania and the Jerseys in 1707, had been established in the tradition of the long-standing English system which openly recognized the larger association of the universal Church. Torbet observed that Baptist associations reflected this during the seventeenth and eighteenth centuries because early English and Colonial Baptists had accepted this logical connection.[847] Shotwell listed at least five functions of early English associations. He affirmed that the following list suggests the basis for English associational life:

(1) To Stand on a Biblical Base
(2) To Affirm Beliefs and Action
(3) To Seek Counsel and Support
(4) To Affirm and Strengthen Ministry
(5) To Reach Out and Start New Churches[848]
(6)

However, he attested that beyond all the above reasons was the "ever present need and desire for Christian fellowship."[849] This

---

847   The Warren Association was the first American association that rejected all such connections. For the Baptist historian's statement above, see Torbet, *A History of the Baptists*, 255.

848   Shotwell, "Renewing the Baptist Principle of Associations," 94.

849   Ibid.

desire for fellowship also precipitated moderate fellowship in New Hampshire among the Separate-Baptists and Free-Will Baptists in their mutual efforts for revival.[850] This overarching passion for fellowship was echoed by E.A. Payne as the key to understanding English associationalism. "Earlier Baptists," he contended, "were much more committed to the *church universal* than to any atomistic conception of the church largely because they were of reformation stock, and more specifically, because of the influence of John Owen's 'The True Nature of a Gospel Church.'"[851] Although Owen's influence on Congregational associationalism was not fully evidenced until the nineteenth century,[852] his immediate influence is seen on English Baptists in their commitment to "fellowship and communion between churches," which he recognized as both an ecclesiastical necessity and obligation.[853] Payne commented on Owen and supervisory bodies:

[Owen] believed that it was by means of synods and councils that the churches should express their fellowship in the Church Catholick. These synods should consider questions of faith and order, questions of peace and unity...that even an individual had the right of appeal to a synod.[854]

---

850   This will be discussed in the section "The Theological Shift: From Westminster to New Hampshire." Fellowship became more attractive to various Baptist groups as revival spread despite sharp doctrinal differences between them.

851   E.A. Payne, *The Fellowship of Believers* (London: Carey Kingsgate Press, LTD, 1952), 15-16, emphasis added. It should be noted that Backus quoted liberally in his work "A Discourse Concerning the Materials, the Manner of Building, and Power of Organizing of the Church of Christ" from Owen's "The True Nature of the Gospel Church." However, Backus' use of Owen was strictly kept to his descriptions of the particular church and arguments related thereto. This further illustrates that the Puritan congregational system was Biblically consistent with the SBBM as far as its concerned local church ecclesiology and was implicitly used, primarily by Backus, as the model to which the Massachusetts Congregational system had been doctrinally unfaithful.

852   Hugh Wamble, "The Beginning of Associationalism among English Baptists," *The Review and Expositor* 55, no. 54 (1957): 544.

853   Payne, *The Fellowship of Believers*, 31.

854   Ibid, 32-33.

Believing that the local congregation was the visible expression of the *True Church*, an English association was understood doctrinally as its visible extension on earth. The Particular Baptists of London in 1644 prepared forty-seven articles about this very premise:

> *And although the particular congregations be distinct and*
> *several bodies, every one a compact and knit city in itself;*
> *yet are they all to walk by one and the same rule, and by all*
> *means convenient to have the counsel and help one of another*
> *in all needful affairs of the Church, as members of one body*
> *in the common faith under Christ her only Head.*[855]

To reject the free association of like-minded churches was, in effect, to reject the spiritual relationship of Christian brotherhood under Christ, the one common head of the universal Church of elect saints. It should be noted, as Wamble suggested, that there was a slight divergence of opinion among the General and Particular Baptists on this point. Owen's ecclesiological branch theory, best represented by the Particular Baptists, stated that local churches which failed to reach out to the larger universal Church in its particular duties were, in fact, guilty of schism.[856] Backus, despite his theoretical identification with Owen, clearly rejected all such notions as they related to associationalism.

General Baptists appeared to be highly inconsistent on the matter of all such visible church correlations. They were forced to reject the branch theory of the universal Church because they "affirmed that children dying in infancy are admitted into the

---

855   Broadus, *Baptist Confessions, Covenants, and Catechisms*, 47.
856   John Owen, *The True Nature of a Gospel Church and Its Government 1689*, ed. John Huxtable (London: James Clark and Company Ltd, 1947), 251.

spiritual church on the basis of God's mercy,"[857] and not because of a pre-temporal election. Therefore, babies were understood as being included within the True Church, yet, because of infancy, unassociated with any local body. With the exception of the Confession of 1679, General Baptists essentially ignored clarifying the doctrine of the universal concept after 1640.[858] Such a position suggests that the General Baptists possessed a utilitarian view of church concepts when they extended beyond the local congregation. As a result of rejecting the election of infants, this reduced the practical interplay between the visible and invisible church concepts. Lumpkin noted that it was also an attempt "at compromise between the two great systems of theology, thus anticipating the work of Andrew Fuller and others of the eighteenth-century."[859] This led to a looser methodology and more adaptive theology characteristic in the western expansion of the Baptists early in the nineteenth century. The General Baptists' original intention was to doctrinally align as many of the disparate Protestant groups as possible at the time.[860] It included a typical definition of the "one holy catholick church, consisting of, or made up of the whole number of the elect...."[861] Under the following statement in article thirty concerning "the catholic church as visible," the writer states, "Nevertheless, we believe the visible church of Christ on earth, is made up of several distinct congregations, which make up that one catholic church, or mystical body of Christ."[862] No written confession makes a clearer representation of the branch theory of a universal, visible

---

857   Wamble, "The Beginning of Associationalism among English Baptists," 544.
858   Ibid, 545.
859   Lumpkin, *Baptist Confessions of Faith*, 296.
860   Ibid, 297. The full title of the Creed reads, "An Orthodox Creed Or A Protestant Confession of Faith, Being An Essay To Unite and Confirm All True Protestants In The Fundamental Articles Of The Christian Religion, / Against The Errors and Heresies Of Rome."
861   Ibid.
862   Ibid, 319.

body of Christ. This is followed by Article thirty-nine which includes a strong associational statement on the power of the general assembly:

...it being of divine authority, and is the best means under heaven to preserve unity, to prevent heresy, and superintendency among, or in any congregation whatsoever within its own limits, or jurisdiction... and the decisive voice in such general assemblies...have lawful power to hear, and determine, as also to excommunicate.[863]

It should not go unnoticed that the General Baptists who wrote this confession used the Acts 15 passage no less than three times in this article, attributing to the association a similar authority relegated to the Jerusalem Council during the apostolic era. This attitude is in marked contrast to the founding of Philadelphia Baptist Association in 1707, which, while using Acts 15 in their associational confession, used it only as a precedent for the idea of association not in the sense of borrowing a similar authority.

This shifting and moderation among English Particular Baptists is notable because somewhat of a doctrinal parallel occurred in New England within the SBBM just before the turn of the nineteenth century. Backus' own assistant, Ezra Kendell, had changed his views concerning original sin and the damnation of non-elect infants creating a stir in the Middleboro Baptist Church. Backus, as the ardent Calvinist apologist,[864] came to the place where he simply called the vexing question a divine mystery which appeared to be a considerable softening from his former rigidness on the matter.

---

863   Ibid, 327.
864   McLoughlin, ed., *Isaac Backus on Church, State, and Calvinism: Pamphlets, 1754-1789*, 451-471.

THE PREDOMINANT ASSOCIATIONAL PRINCIPLE IN AMERICA

Despite the fact that Baptists in England had a rich associational life which had long preceded the Colonial experience, the ethos of the English associational system was not mutually shared in the American tradition:

> *The doctrine of the spiritual church provided the doctrinal basis of connectionalism. Baptists exercised certain informal relationships between churches, in keeping with their view of the spiritual church...involving scattered congregations, benevolence, church constitution and ordination, and cooperative discipline.*[865]

To some degree these principles were also apparent in the founding of the PBA, but the overarching principle which affected American associational life was to what degree, if any, the associational body extended its authority over the particular church. This issue was usually defined in terms of the "autonomy of the local church"[866] This general principle, as it worked out in the PBA, specified a clear distinction between church power and association power, but never at the expense of the underlying expressed obligation of churches to express their essential oneness in Christ. Sacks, in his massive work on church authority within the PBA, affirmed this principle:

> *Within the official documents of the P.B.A., one finds theological justifications for Baptist connectionalism. The major justifications are the nature of the Church as the Body of Christ,*

---

865   Wamble, "The Beginning of Associationalism among English Baptists," 547.
866   Winthrop Still Hudson, "Documents on the Associations of Churches," *Foundations* 4, no. 4 (1961): 333.

the universal Christian communion in His Spirit, the fellowship
in one Lord, one faith and one baptism, and, especially, the
obligations undertaken voluntarily in Christian covenants.[867]

Church power was understood as coming directly from Christ while association power came from the consent of delegates from the churches gathered in association. However, ambiguity still remained between the power of an association and the independency of the local church. In an attempt to clear up the confusion and allay concerns, the PBA used Benjamin Griffith's essay, entitled "Essay on the Power and Duty of an Association of Churches," as an official associational document to prevent the usurpation of local church authority by the association in the areas of church discipline, disorderly members, administering the ordinances, ordination of ministers, and other general local church concerns.[868]

For the SBBM, born out of Congregational oppression through the Massachusetts General Court, Connecticut Congregational law,[869] and the cauldron of Great Awakening piety, great anxiety governed their view of para-church organizations. Backus explained this general feeling among the Separate-Baptists:

Associations had been very cruel and oppressive in Connecticut,
as they were there established by law...and the abuse of them
which is very common.... When difficulties arise in churches,
few have the patience and wisdom which is necessary for the

---

867   Francis W. Sacks, *The Philadelphia Baptist Tradition of Church and Church Authority, 1707-1814*, vol. 48, Studies in American Religion (Lewiston/Lampeter/Queenston: The Edwin Mellen Press, 1989), 411.

868   Hudson, ed., *Baptist Concepts of the Church*, 47.

869   Lumpkin, *Colonial Baptists and Southern Revivals, 11*.Under the Saybrook Platform, the Connecticut Congregational system was as an oppressive a system to the dissent community as was the General Court in Massachusetts. The Saybrook Platform was supported by the Legislature of Connecticut.

carrying the laws of Christ into effect against offenders, without
looking to any earthly powers for help in such cases.[870]

This mindset was not universal among all Baptists beyond
Connecticut. Gillette's minutes show several references by delegates to
the larger spiritual fraternity. One such entry was found in 1756:

The elders and messengers of the several congregations,
baptized on profession of faith, in Pennsylvania, New Jersey,
and provinces adjacent, met in Association in Philadelphia,
October 5th, 1756. To the several churches we respectively relate
unto, do send our loving salutation. Dear Brethren - We your
messengers and fellow members of the same mystical body....[871]

This mystical definition of the church used here is drawn
from the Second London Confession of 1677 and 1688 and was
essentially the same as that found in the Westminster Confession.
At the time of the formation of the Second London Confession, the
intention was to offer a revision aimed at demonstrating doctrinal
alliances with both the Presbyterians and the Congregationalists.
Furthermore, its creation was predicated on the need for a "more full
and distinct expression of views than the confession offered" in the
London Confession of 1644.[872] Its expanded article on the church was
essentially appended from the Congregational Savoy Declaration.[873]

Although clearly Protestant in ecclesiological matters, it
omitted section seven of chapter three on Reprobation, chapter seven

---

870   Backus, *Church History of New England from 1620 to 1804: Containing a View*
of the Principles and Practice, Declensions and Revivals, Oppression and Liberty of the
Churches, and a Chronological Table. With a Memoir of the Author, 235.
871   Gillette, ed., *Minutes of the Philadelphia Baptist Association from A.D 1707 to A.D.*
1807: Being the First One-Hundred Years of Its Existence., 73.
872   Lumpkin, *Baptist Confessions of Faith,* 236-237.
873   Hudson, "Documents on the Associations of Churches," 332.

on Covenants, and a portion from chapter twenty-three on the duties of the civil magistrate to suppress heresy, corruption, and call church synods.[874] The original associational principle was founded within the many churches of the association:

> *[They] do by their messengers meet to consider and give their advice in or about that matter in difference, to be reported to all the churches concerned...howbeit these messengers assembled are not entrusted with any church-power properly so-called, or with any jurisdiction over the churches themselves, to exercise any censures either over any churches or persons; or to impose their determination on the churches or officers.*[875]

The founding of the WBA, on September 8, 1767, marked a new beginning for Baptists, particularly those in New England. By looking to their own ecclesiological needs, they were in effect responding to the policies of the Congregational system, especially in Massachusetts. The most powerful motivation for the new association was likely to expunge from public sentiment the idea that Baptists were opposed to higher learning.[876] The second overriding concern held by founder James Manning was to consolidate support for Rhode Island College, not only in America but in England.[877] The great preponderance of Manning's personal correspondence between the founding of the college and his death made various references to fundraising or endowment for the college.[878] The third great cause was

---

874   Lumpkin, *Baptist Confessions of Faith*, 237.

875   Benjamin Franklin, *A Confession of Faith* (Philadelphia: 1743), 96-98.

876   McLoughlin, *New England Dissent 1630-1833*, 1: 503.

877   Brackney, ed., *Baptist Life and Thought: 1600-1980*, 123.

878   Manning's tireless efforts in this area of personal correspondence are preserved in digital format at Brown University. His contacts in England proved to be of great benefit to the college in its early days and well beyond his death in 1791.

the determination by Separate-Baptists to create a better informed consensus among the New England churches for the purpose of working together for social change.[879] Over time, this probably became the most significant of the primary reasons justifying the association's existence. This became necessary for many reasons, but their common hatred of the ministerial tax system appeared to be paramount.

Manning also saw great value in keeping English Baptist leaders focused on the persecution of Baptists in New England in developing a broader base of opposition.[880] Just two years after its founding, the association adopted a plan to redress grievances for civil infractions against the non-conformist (Baptist) churches:

This is to inform all the oppressed Baptists in New England that the Association of Warren, (in conjunction with the Western or Philadelphia Association) is determined to seek remedy for their brethren where a speedy and effectual one may be had...by petition and memorial.[881]

There was a singular intensity felt among its founders that only under a unified voice could such petitions be both heard and felt among the ruling class. Independent voices had been summarily silenced in the collective colonial experience, and it was that collective memory to which one such advertisement from the Associational committee drew its ire:

To the Baptists in the Province of the Massachusetts Bay.... It would be needless to tell you that you have long felt the effects of

879   McLoughlin, *New England Dissent 1630-1833*, 1: 503.
880   Brackney, ed., *Baptist Life and Thought: 1600-1980*, 123.
881   Backus, *A History of New England with Particular Reference to the Denomination of Christians Called Baptists*, 2: 154-155.

the laws by which the religion of the government in which you
live is established. Your purses have felt the burden of ministerial
rates...such as, the taxes you have paid to build meetinghouses, to
settle ministers and support them, with all the time, money and
labor you have lost in waiting on courts, feeing lawyers...send
such cases to the Baptist Association to be held at Bellingham.[882]

Although Backus acted as the first clerk of the association,[883] he was reluctant to join over concerns that local church jurisdiction would be threatened by associational over-lording in two areas: first, that the association would receive no *complaints* against any local church, and secondly, that no complaint would be heard from any *censured* member of the churches.[884] These concerns resulted in Backus requesting founder James Manning on September 19, 1768, to revise the original plan with wording that would assure pastors "that this Association did not assume any jurisdiction over the churches...."[885]

However, these concerns of Backus should not be overemphasized in relation to other fears of association held by various Baptists and Independents of the day. The Second Church in Coventry voiced its opposition to the Association being justified on Acts 15,[886] which they saw as an unjustified effort to make the Jerusalem Council a jurisdictional body competing with the autonomy of the particular church. The Acts 15 principle had been traditionally used for years in England for qualifying Baptist associational life.[887] This sentiment did not prevail in New England. As clerk of the first

---

882   Ibid, 2: 155.
883   Goen, *Revivalism and Separatism in New England, 1740-1800: Strict Congregationalist and Separate-Baptists in the Great Awakening*, 279.
884   Ibid, 281.
885   Ibid.
886   Lumpkin, *Baptist Confessions of Faith*, 289.
887   E.A. Payne, *The Baptists of Berkshire* (London: Carey Kingsgate Press Ltd, 1951), 147-149.

meeting of the WBA, Backus simply referred to the opening sermon by New York Elder John Gano of the Philadelphia Association as "suitable."[888] Well aware of the Acts 15 tradition Gano utilized, Backus offered no further comment.

Shurden suggested that traditionally, *pragmatic* concerns were the primary motivations behind Baptist associations.[889] This was no truer than it was with the WBA. Consistent with this paradigm, the WBA, among other reasons, had been established to assist in the fight against the ministerial tax system. The New England Separate-Baptists knew that their ecclesiastical enemies were too formidable for any one church to stand alone. Backus, on the one hand, feared and detested synods and councils when in the threatening hands of the State, but on the other hand, embraced a para-church organization:

> ...in which the domination and control of the state could be frustrated; and as such, clearly it should be supported, strengthened, and used. In short, this association could properly be used to lengthen the arm of the local congregation, but never to shorten it; to add to its power and not to take away.[890]

This provides a clear window into Backus' theological feelings toward associations. Two things need to be mentioned here. First of all, he made no connection of associational life to *biblical* obligation. He never said that any overarching principle of fellowship prescribed by universal Church connections was being ignored prior to the

---

888   Backus, *A History of New England with Particular Reference to the Denomination of Christians Called Baptists*, 2: 154.
889   Walter B. Shurden, "Associationalism among Baptists in America, 1707-1814" (Th.D. diss., New Orleans Baptist Seminary, 1967), 5.
890   Hudson, ed., *Baptist Concepts of the Church*, 125.

founding of the Association. He himself had said concerning joining the new Warren Association in his own diary on September 8-9, 1767, "I did not see my way clear to join now if ever I do."[891] The "if ever I do" further suggests no conception on his part of Scriptural duty or obligation to join. For Backus and the majority of his New England brethren, fellowship through associational auspices was purely voluntary and justified only for pragmatic reasons. A recognized spiritual leader of Backus' caliber would likely never have consciously ignored personal obligation at the expense of clear Scriptural principle. This removes the SBBM and its view of associations from the PBA and its English forebears. English associational life had long been predicated on the branch theory in connection to the *mystical* body of Christ as articulated in the Orthodox Creed of 1679.[892] Shotwell attributes the branch theory to General Baptists, while Helwys and Smith called it "the branch of the Baptist tree."[893] This is decidedly narrower than the 1679 confession which makes the definition broad enough simply for participants to be in churches where the Word of God is rightly preached, "...And altho' there may be many errors in such a visible church...she is not thereby unchurched...and from such visible church, or congregations, no man ought by any pretence whatever, schismatically to separate."[894]

It should be noted that this confession made an unusually strong statement concerning associational authority over constituent

---

891   McLoughlin, ed., *The Diary of Isaac Backus*, 2: 671.
892   Lumpkin, *Baptist Confessions of Faith*, 319.
893   Shotwell, "Renewing the Baptist Principle of Associations", 152.
894   Lumpkin, *Baptist Confessions of Faith*, 319.

churches which, while often debated in English Baptist associational theory, was "sometimes observed in practice."[895]

Secondly, Backus tilted all para-church authority toward the local church suggesting that it ought to lengthen the arm of the local church and not shorten it because "a particular church of Christ is the highest judicature that he has established upon earth, to carry his laws into execution in his name."[896] His use of *highest judicature* was used in the context of Paul's apparent apology to the church at Corinth for any dishonor he had done to their assembly for not receiving money from them as he did from other church bodies. Backus' point is that there was, in Paul's mind, no *higher* or *greater* judicature than the Corinthian church itself to whom the apostle could have offered any meaningful apology.[897] This further suggests that Backus saw no latent authority in the Acts 15 council. This serves to illustrate Backus' unsettledness concerning the associational principle of the PBA. While the PBA carefully articulated the independency and autonomy of the local church, considerable ambiguity remained in the exact differences of confessional statements relating to churches and associational powers in the same documents. Sacks referred to the founding confessional statements by Griffith in 1743:

> *The churches' combined decisions have a considerable power ... to interpret their only infallible rule, the Scriptures. Thus, in Griffith's terms, a church council can both declare the mind of the Holy Ghost as well as decree the observation of things that are true and necessary because revealed in Scripture.... While Baptist assemblies possess no superior jurisdiction over member*

---

895   Wamble, "The Beginning of Associationalism among English Baptists," 555.
896   Backus, *A History of New England with Particular Reference to the Denomination of Christians Called Baptists*, 2: 563.
897   Ibid.

churches...they nevertheless exercise a crucial servant role...
of interpreting the mind of the Spirit in Holy Scripture.[898]

He asserted further that although the PBA technically
espoused that only the gathered church had authority as the seat of
Christ's power, the association accepted other levels of authorized
powers, namely, those which came from the church council who
deliberated the mind of the Spirit by assisting churches in settling
internal disputes.[899] Sacks thought that Griffith could have been
talking only of church councils here and not making reference to the
association acting as a church council in reference to "interpreting
the mind of the Spirit."[900] Manning had utilized this same argument
in the establishment of the Warren Association of 1767, failing to
convince the delegates. Because of Backus' opposition, this role of
the association as an "interpreter of the Spirit" was eliminated from
the original version. Sacks, despite Manning's use of the argument
from Griffith, believed that Griffith's expression was about the *council*
and not the *association*. It is likely that James Manning would not
have agreed with this assessment. Backus' primary argument against
the associational practice of hearing arguments from either offended
parties or churches was based on his interpretation of Matt 18:17-18.
For him, it appeared entirely sufficient for each party of the offence to
have "two opportunities to speak for himself, before the offence is told
to the church, whose sentence is to decide the case."[901]

Backus argued that such spiritual advice was exclusively
warranted by the particular church. First, because it puts the accuser

898   Sacks, *The Philadelphia Baptist Tradition of Church and Church Authority, 1707-
1814*, 420-421.
899   Ibid, 607.
900   Ibid, 396.
901   Backus, *A History of New England with Particular Reference to the Denomination
of Christians Called Baptists*, 2: 339.

and the accused face to face with the church as the final arbiter, both defended by Scripture and reason; secondly, because Scripture does not give authority to para-church councils over particular churches; finally, because such councils are a source of spiritual confusion among Christians in general.[902] As to Backus and others joining the WBA in 1770, he said that they had waited, "until they could be satisfied that this Association did not assume any jurisdiction over the church.... And... joined upon the express condition that no complaint should ever be received by the Association, nor from any censured member of any of our churches.[903] As we have been able to see regarding Backus and many of the Separate-Baptists concerning associationalism, two things are clear. First, he did not consider it a Scriptural necessity to join; and secondly, he was particularly jealous over the possibility of a threat to the autonomy of member churches. In his diary entry of September 11, 1770, he mentions that he had joined the association that gathered that year at Bellingham upon the conditions which the Middleboro Baptist Church had earlier submitted to James Manning in 1767. He reiterated these concerns in his explanation for not having joined three years earlier:

> *As ministers assuming a classical power and jurisdiction*
> *over the churches is contrary to the gospel, and has been*
> *found to be of pernicious tendency in all ages, of which this*
> *Land has had considerable experience; and as its rise...*
> *is generally in a gradual and imperceptible manner...you*
> *must not wonder at our not joining your association....*[904]

---

902   Ibid, 2: 338-39.
903   Ibid, 2: 209.
904   McLoughlin, ed., *The Diary of Isaac Backus*, 2: 774.

Backus saw danger inherent in para-church organizations, calling it a "pernicious tendency," and stating furthermore that such organizations gained power in "a gradual and imperceptible manner" which would result in giving them "the same power over the churches as a church has over its members."[905] In this sense, he saw all challenges to particular church autonomy as one and the same thing. For him, unguarded associationalism was an opportunity for unchecked power. He had witnessed these gradual encroachments by the Standing Order in Massachusetts and understood them as part of the context of greater church history back to the fall of the church under Constantine who he identifies in *The Testimony of Two Witnesses* (TTW) as "that man of sin" or the beast.[906] The sins to which Backus assigns this figure are both far-reaching and pervasive, but Backus' objective in the treatise is the establishment of the idea:

The Church of Christ is the only judicature upon earth, to carry his laws into execution in his name. But ever since the beast arose out of the bottomless pit, and the sword of the magistrate was employed to support deceitful teachers, the church of Christ hath never been fully governed by his laws, independent of the world.[907]

In TTW, Backus further identifies the "two horns" of Revelation as the joining of the officers of church and state which culminates in "uniting their influence in schemes of power and again, under the name of religion and government."[908] The Middleboro pastor, in the strongest possible language, calls all such magisterial churches "a

---

905   Ibid.
906   Isaac Backus, *The Testimony of the Two Witnesses, Explained and Vindicated with a Few Remarks Upon the Late Writings of Dr. Hemmenway and Dr. Lathrop*, 2d ed. (Boston: Printed by Samuel Hall, no. 53, 1793), 21.
907   Ibid, 13.
908   Ibid, 22.

damnable heresy" in which America too "hath followed her wicked ways."[909] For Backus, this scheming of those who were in the seats of power in the magisterial church, particularly in Massachusetts, like all of their Constantinian forebears including their Protestant daughters, were equally guilty for "suing to powers of the world for incorporations of societies to support religious ministers, which societies are not governed by the laws of Christ."[910]

This "pernicious tendency," which he observed in the magisterial system in Massachusetts, fueled latent fears of Baptist associations assuming similar "tendencies." To allow the new gospel freedom to be threatened by ecclesiological over-lording through church connectionalism was therefore as unconscionable as the uniting of church and state. To this end, Baptists have always struggled against the historical perception that their unwillingness to walk outside their Biblical convictions created *schism* in the *True Church*. Modern American Baptists, with a few exceptions, in their descent from their English and Separate-Baptist origins, are not immune from holding this opinion.

BACKUS AND THE ECUMENICAL SPIRIT

Grenz noted that in light of the Arminian revolt against Dutch Calvinism, individual participation in salvation is immediate "rather than being mediated through the eternal election of Christ.[911] He thereby asserted that Backus' ecclesiological model, in light of the prevailing theological mood, suffered a lack of ecumenical credibility. He claimed that "if this concept of the invisible church is found to be problematic, then its corollary, the pure church as a gathered church,

---

909   Ibid, 25.
910   Ibid.
911   Grenz, *Isaac Backus - Puritan and Baptist: His Place in History, His Thought, and Their Implications for Modern Baptist Theology*, 269.

must also be rejected."[912] Given that the invisible concept of the
Reformed doctrine holds the *a priori* position, this would be a logical
deduction. However, the author does not allow for the possibility
that this decline of the election doctrine actually helped promote an
exclusive localized ecclesiology which saw no practical necessity or
theological basis for a Platonic model. If, in fact, God's pre-temporal
election was the basis for the true church, then its *a priori* foundation
had been compromised by the mid-nineteenth century. In this light,
Grenz suggested that a new model would need to emerge in order to
enable continued ecumenical posturing. He concluded that for those
presuming the *a priori* position of the invisible/universal church, the
increasingly popular remedy for ecumenism was the process church
model.[913] Using this facsimile, and by exchanging a pre-temporal
election for the *Lordship of Christ* as constituting membership for "the
society" of God's people, the author surmised that we are all essentially
only waiting for the future realization of a present earthly reality,
namely, the rule of the eschatological king:

> *These persons are united by a bond stronger than any mere*
> *organizational structure.... However, the bond which unites*
> *all Christians is contradicted in practice whenever individual*
> *churches or persons refuse to cooperate and "fellowship" with*
> *others who likewise belong to the one church of Christ.*[914]

---

912   Ibid, 271.
913   This model, discussed by Riplinger, severs the visible church from the invisible
church defining the church in the future context by its "destiny to which it is continually
en route" (270) in the kingdom of God under the lordship of Christ. In essence, the only
difference with this view is that the tie to the universal, invisible church, rather than a pre-
temporal election, is the Lordship of Christ within the society of those who acknowledge
that rule. The primary difficulty with this new model suggested by Grenz is that it takes the
constitution of church fellowship outside of local-church life, something which Backus would
very likely have been unwilling to do. See Riplinger, *An American Vision of the Church*, 130-
132.
914   Grenz, *Isaac Backus - Puritan and Baptist: His Place in History, His Thought, and*

By taking the universal concept out of the Platonic realm and placing it in terms of a "historical society of men," Grenz surmised this strengthened ecumenism in two ways. "First, this movement has demanded that all Christian groups acknowledge a fundamental oneness"[915] which exists among all who are submitted to the Lordship of Christ. Secondly, the view demands that "Christian groups discuss together their theological and ecclesiological differences with the goal of emphasizing those things which they share in common."[916] He thought this would be possible by reconstituting the pure-church ideal of the Puritans.[917] But the author's position on how the Backus movement remains essentially misguided can be seen in his final re-evaluation of evangelical ecclesiology.[918] This re-evaluation or re-orientation of all the disparate elements of evangelical theology he thought would be possible by "renewing the center" through the means of a "generous orthodoxy."[919] Grenz defined this orthodoxy in:

> ... the renewal of the center of the one church...as focused
> on the gospel of convertive piety, oriented toward the
> doctrinal consensus of the church, motivated by a vision
> that is truly catholic, this is, a vision encompassing the

Their Implications for Modern Baptist Theology, 270.

915   Ibid, 271.

916   Ibid.

917   Grenz referred to the process concept of the church as necessitating "some formulation of the ideal...." However, this is clearly a *re-formulation* of a long-standing theological concept which Backus could not have accepted on its face, all latter repudiations of the universal idea notwithstanding.

918   The late Stanley Grenz passed away March 12th, 2005. His re-evaluation was the subject of a lengthy treatise entitled "Renewing the Center," Evangelical Theology in a Post-Theological Era."

919   In this work noted above, Grenz provided an excellent historical overview of Evangelicalism as a movement for the purpose of ultimately setting forth a basis for their advancement in the post-modern world. His ill-advised use of the term "generous orthodoxy" has since been seized upon by certain leaders of the "Emergent Church" movement to extend well beyond Grenz's earlier intentions.

whole church—and beyond the church, all creation.[920]

Grenz's conception was further seen as that which required a rediscovery of the sense of the church as community in the post-modern world.[921] D.A. Carson[922] expressed shock at Grenz's definition/question of community which he also extended to non-Christian religious groups. Dealing with the question of the absolute nature of Christian doctrine, Grenz's question was not "Which religion is true?" but "What end is most ultimate, even if many are real?" Carson suggested that this definition of an ecumenically-minded community undercuts the authority of Scripture to establish absolute truth. [923] Clearly, if Backus was so judicious with his interpretation of Scripture that he restricted fellowship among professing Christians in church context, it is highly unlikely he could have possibly entertained any ecumenical union which could have potentially *included* what he would have defined as pagans. Furthermore, it should be remembered that Backus' perception of "making visible that which was formerly invisible" was a limited concept, even after his era. The only historical *society of men* on earth the Middleboro pastor was willing to admit was the local church. What Backus had begun with his interpretation of the visible church, later pastors, evangelists, and theologians

---

920   Grenz, *Renewing the Center: Evangelical Theology in a Post-Theological Era*, 21.
921   Stanley Grenz introduces the word community in the broadest possible sense. Although he recognizes that the church is essentially local and yet it remains ultimately universal. He suggests that the mutually shared aspects of the Word and Sacrament should open the door for a communitarian ecclesiology which is achieved through a "renewed missional evangelical ecumenism.", 21. This concept of community has been dangerously exploited by other Emergent Church thinkers. Brian D. McLaren in his volume "A Generous Orthodoxy" takes his title from Grenz's argument for a generous orthodoxy and wildly expands it. The concept of a visible community is also exploited by editors Mark Husbands and Daniel Treier in *The Community of the Word: Toward an Evangelical Ecclesiology*.
922   D.A. Carson is a research professor of New Testament at Trinity Evangelical Divinity School in Deerfield, Illinois. He is the author of over 45 books, and offers both criticisms and commendation of the emergent church in a fair critique of the movement in D.A. Carson, *Becoming Conversant with the Emerging Church* (Grand Rapids: Zondervan, 2005).
923   See Ibid, 132-133.

finally disassociated from *any* connection to an invisible, mystical counterpart. Any contemporary effort at reinterpreting Backus forward into prevailing evangelical conceptions of ecclesiological ecumenism cannot therefore be maintained. Wayland, Crowell, and other Baptist seminarians throughout the nineteenth century made no serious attempts to find common ground with their denominational counterparts. By limiting local church theology, or accommodating it to a Christian ideal beyond what the SBBM considered its biblical scope, the local church emerged as the sole representative of the Greek *ecclesia*[924] in the New Testament.

Boston professor Jesse Thomas explained his difficulty with the coexistence of local and universal concepts:

> *The two ideas—that of a local organism on the one side, and that of a scattered and unaffiliated world-community on the other—are too incongruous to dwell harmoniously together under a common designation. To admit the idea of a Church universal, at all, is to... derogate from the importance of, and the honor due to, the local churches.*[925]

The reality for nineteenth-century Baptist churchmen was actually a reversal of the Protestant conception. The local, visible church became the basis for its heavenly counterpart. In his rendering

---

924   This New Testament term in nineteenth-century Baptist exegesis followed a decidedly local-church interpretation. Concerning the Matt 16:18 passage, Jesse Thomas, of the Newton Theological Seminary spoke in general terms for the anti-universal bias well established by his time. He asserted, "the universalization of the Church and its identification with the kingdom of heaven, with the prolonged Jewish *regime*, or with the elect of all ages, loads the passage with chronological and metaphorical incongruities of formidable character." See Thomas, *The Church and the Kingdom*, 250.

925   Ibid, 292.

of Heb 12:23, Thomas allowed only a local sense behind *paneguros*
(general assembly):

> *Either the "firstborn" gathered out of the earth at last into a*
> *single assembly, are set over against the hosts of the redeemed*
> *from the whole universe; or the local assemblies (ecclesia) of*
> *earth are represented as at last merging into and becoming a*
> *paneguros. In either case the same general implication once more*
> *returns, as to the primary individual meaning of ecclesia.*[926]

Thomas, among others, concluded that *ecclesia* had to be
representative of actual assemblies on earth, therefore the visible
concept was considered the only sustainable hermeneutic. To
reassemble the *a priori* position of a universal-invisible concept
in the post-Backus era without the recognition of the movement's
commitment to revival and local-particular church ideology is
therefore historically unsustainable. Historian Norman Maring
lamented that "under the impact of individualism, moralism, and
revivalism," the Baptists had rejected strict Calvinism, the construct
of the universal church, and the need for the traditional associational
dependence of local churches.[927] Beside Clarence Goen, Maring is one
of the few historians who intimate *Calvinism* and the *True Church*
concept diminishing simultaneously,[928] culminating in the practical
disappearance of the latter.

However, he offered little explanation explaining how the two
are connected. As discovered earlier, the only way Puritan theology
could include infants in covenant relations was by the insistence of

---

926   Ibid, 224-225.
927   See his article "The Individualism of Francis Wayland" in Hudson, ed., *Baptist*
Concepts of the Church, 136.
928   For Goen's reference see page 191.

infant baptism. In this way, infants were supposedly connected to the universal Church in the hope that they would, by their baptism, realize elect status by adulthood.[929] For Backus, rejecting infant baptism was the essence of rejecting the entire theocracy, inadvertently separating the elect from the universal Church. Despite any negative ecumenical implications, Backus concluded that separation from false churches was the only tenable solution because in the absence of repentance, the Lord had already promised to end the churches existence.[930]

BAPTISTS AND ECUMENISM

In light of the tightening of the etymology of *ecclesia* in the post-Backus period and Backus' predisposition toward the universal Church, it is difficult to see how Grenz could extrapolate Riplinger's process-model[931] as a working hypothesis for broadened ecumenical relations among the Separate-Baptists or their contemporary lineage for several reasons. First, Backus took an inexorable position concerning church fellowship based solely on mutual covenant relations among the members of each visible church. As the only judicature on earth which had the authority of Christ, ecclesiastical fellowship was governed by local parameters set forth in the New Testament. Secondly, he demanded agreement over the ordinance of baptism constituting visible church membership. Backus' own struggle over this issue, which culminated in his starting a close-communion Baptist church in 1756, sufficiently demonstrated his own principle. Thirdly, only those who had been baptized could actually

---

929   See the section regarding the preparation doctrine.
930   This was Backus' answer to Rev. Fish in his claim that the call to reformation did not include separation. See Backus, *A Discourse, Concerning the Materials, the Manner of Building, and Power of Organizing the Church of Christ*, 130.
931   Riplinger, *An American Vision of the Church*, 130-132.

gain access to the Lord's Table of the visible church fellowship.[932] Neither Backus, nor any other Baptist spokesman taught the universal application of believers' baptism to all denominations simultaneously. As noted earlier in DCM, Backus closed his one hundred fifty page discourse with Rev. Joseph Fish with this final ultimatum, "Till they can convince us of this, all their noise about the evil of re-baptizing and closed-communion, cannot satisfy our minds, that we can duly regard the law of Christ, if we come to his table with any who have not been buried with him in baptism."[933]

In effect, he reduced the requirements necessary for denominational fellowship to agreement on the ordinances for all covenant communities. This forced obedience to not hinge in the mutual submission to the Lordship of Christ as advanced by Riplinger but on observing the law of Christ as resident in the ordinances of the local church. For Backus, there was no observable distinction between the law of Christ resident in a proper administration of the ordinances and the Lordship of Christ, and Backus believed this deliberate breaking of Christ's law demanded *separation*.

Grenz's discussion of Backus' separation position as being invalid is established on two considerations. First, he says that most of the New Testament books dealt with "individuals falling into heresy, while being members of a local congregation."[934] Secondly, he asserts that the New Testament assumes that a local church by definition "is a body which is true to apostolic teaching. Therefore it would seem that any group which has departed from that teaching is not a

---

932   The majority of Baptist historiographers identify regenerate church membership, baptism as an initiatory rite of church connection, and the observance of the Lord's Table as traditional Baptist doctrines. For one of the best summations of what historical Baptists have generally believed see Leonard, *Baptist Ways: A History*, 2-7.
933   Backus, *A Discourse, Concerning the Materials, the Manner of Building, and Power of Organizing the Church of Christ*, 143.
934   Grenz, *Isaac Backus - Puritan and Baptist: His Place in History, His Thought, and Their Implications for Modern Baptist Theology*, 306.

church, i.e., not part of the one universal body."[935] Unfortunately, no definitive listing of doctrinal tenets is given to identify the composite of true apostolic teaching and Grenz immediately adds, "Failure of one such church to recognize the unity which it shares with all others and separation of an individual from any such congregation is schism."[936] Consequently, a disgruntled member, says the author, "should remain in the congregation of which he is a member, believing that God will remedy the situation by giving either the congregation or himself further light on the issues at stake."[937] Ironically, this further light in the eyes of Whitefield, Davenport, Tennant, and scores of Separatist pastors and churches since 1740 had already been amply provided, claiming that in many parish churches the new birth had never been preached nor had many of their ministers experienced it. Consequently, converted individuals needed to seek enlightened ministers and attend their meetinghouses.[938] Grenz suggests that this "undefendable [sic] error" could have been prevented:

It would have been better for them to continue attending public worship while meeting separately. Had this been the case, the church could not have censured them for withdrawing from worship, and any demand that these additional services be stopped would have constituted a violation of Christian freedom and have altered the situation.[939]

---

935   Ibid.
936   Grenz, *Isaac Backus - Puritan and Baptist: His Place in History, His Thought, and Their Implications for Modern Baptist Theology.*
937   Ibid.
938   As noted above, Whitefield advocated this practice in light of the loss of spiritual piety in the Standing Churches. See 185-186.
939   Grenz, *Isaac Backus - Puritan and Baptist: His Place in History, His Thought, and Their Implications for Modern Baptist Theology*, 306-307.

However, that is the very reason the dissenters separated themselves in the first place! Actually, they thought their Christian freedom to have been violated from the beginning of the Massachusetts Commonwealth. Those who refused to bring their infants to the Standing Order parishes to be baptized did so under direct threats of physical punishment, severe fines, or banishment from the colony, especially after the Massachusetts General Court decision of 1644. Those who met separately and continued in the Standing Church often met the same fate. Others were banished altogether from their Standing Churches for holding anti- pedobaptist opinions.[940] Backus would have likely rejected the notion that meeting separately or holding private assemblies was either doctrinally or practically indefensible. He had wrestled with this problem as a Separate-Congregationalist for five years from 1751-1756. Even infant baptizer Solomon Paine, and his Separate Church in Canterbury, "convinced the leading pedobaptist Separates that there would be no peace in the denomination until communion policies of *mutual rejection* were adopted by both the *sprinkling* Separates and the *immersionist* Separates.[941] Separation was the universal, not to mention, Scriptural answer.

ECUMENISM AND THE LORD'S TABLE

For Backus, this issue transcended any common agreement the Baptists had with the Standing Order in the realm of salvation epistemology (i.e., Lordship of Christ). He did not question the salvation of Congregational leaders to the degree that he questioned their obedience to the biblical pattern. In DCM, he clarified this point

---

940   For examples of these practices, see the section "Baptists, Communion, and Infant Baptism" in the second chapter.
941   McLoughlin, *New England Dissent 1630-1833*, 1:433.

all within the context of the Baptists' separation from those who had left to conscience that which they (the Baptists) had identified in Scripture. He said, "And unless our pedobaptist fathers and brethren can convince us that He who was faithful in his house, and worthy of more glory than Moses, has yet left things at such loose ends...that to be determined by men's consciences,"[942] the Word of God was being made null and void by such liberties. Backus appears careful here to distinguish between personal religion and visible church structure. In that light he said, "We have two sorts of separation described in Holy Writ: One is produced by the exalting of self above others; the other by such an adherence to divine rule as to part with those who will not conform to it."[943] For church union the critical issue then was clearly not Lordship predicated upon a common salvation or individual conscience but rather conformation to the biblical standard which Backus claimed precluded ecclesiastical fellowship.

In one sense this marks the point of departure for the Separate-Baptist movement from the Bunyan tradition of open-communion, including the free interaction from one local body to another based upon their emphasis of the invisible church over its visible counterpart. That is the perceived problem with Backus' ecclesiology. The *True Church*, although in Backus' words "is the same as it always was," bears no immediate connection to the *particular/visible church* except in both being constituted of redeemed saints. To the one who objects on grounds that unredeemed people sometimes get into local churches, Backus replied, "The only reason why any get into the visible church who are not born again, is not owing to the rule, but to the imperfection of men in acting upon it."[944] This suggests that

---

942   Ibid, 143.
943   Backus, *A Discourse, Concerning the Materials, the Manner of Building, and Power of Organizing the Church of Christ,* 143.
944   Ibid, 6.

Backus sees both church models on a single plane in terms of eternal importance, but he extends no *a priori* position to either one. Yet, when he speaks in the visible church context, he becomes entirely oblivious to any other ecclesiological reality outside of the particular/ visible church.

In this way, Backus inferred that baptism and the Lord's Table become constitutive of the visible church on earth wherever situate with the recognition that on earth there is no competing idiom. In Backus' mind then, obedience, measured by fidelity to the ordinances, marked the obedient Christian, including the church which practiced them. In a larger sense, it forces all Baptists to identify what shared values they have with other Christians outside their own ecclesiastical and denominational perimeters.

SUMMARY

From Backus to Wayland, Crowell, and Baptist academics like Thomas, all jurisdictional authority for church function was being exclusively understood as operating in and through the local church. Because the national church concept had been reacted against so vigorously, any perception of church authority which was not vested in the particular church was categorically rejected. Referring to Massachusetts disestablishment in 1833, which divested the Standing Order of exclusive power and granted "corporate powers to make by-laws and regulations, consistent with the laws of the Commonwealth, and for the due and orderly conducting of their affairs,"[945] along with

---

945   Crowell, *The Church Member's Manual*, 70.

the publication of their new confession, Baptists saw these events as the final cutting of the ecclesiastical apron string.

Responding to this novel and heady environment, Crowell resolutely proclaimed, "No bishop, no council of ministers, nor delegation from other churches, nor sanction of the church universal, can impart to them the least degree of church power."[946] Consequently, the Separate-Baptists' *ecumenical ethos* was nearly non-existent in his era, and likely would be today by Backus' own doctrinal standards.

---

946   Ibid, 69.

Conclusion

The Backus movement inaugurated an age when current doctrinal emphases trumped the possibility of so-called Christian unionism. For him, these principles were immutable—having led him to his discovery of particular church authority in the first place—and could not be improved upon or expanded to incorporate the mission of the local/particular church with that of *evangelical ecumenism* or the "one Body of Christ."[947] Consequently the ecumenical hopes, and the "larger social issues" connected with the contemporary concept of "Christendom," should not be forced upon Backus' own principles of further light and soul liberty.[948] For Backus and the Separate-Baptists, John Robinson's dictum of "further light" had culminated in the *sine qua non* of baptismal membership preceding the Lord's Table under the exclusive autonomy of the local, visible church of Christ."[949] Goen has told us that "All separatism is perforce based on a sectarian doctrine of the church which exalts local independency and autonomy at the expense of acknowledging the larger fellowship of catholic Christianity."[950] I will let the reader decide which of these

---

947   See Grenz, i.e., the ecumenical church in a universal sense. Ibid, 330.
948   See Stanley Grenz., 320.
949   Found in Goen, *Revivalism and Separatism in New England, 1740-1800: Strict Congregationalist and Separate-Baptists in the Great Awakening.*, 143. For comments suggesting Backus was shortsighted and immature in his ecclesiological views regarding ecumenism or the universal church see Gaustad in his article titled "The Backus-Leland Tradition" in Hudson, ed., *Baptist Concepts of the Church*, 134; Grenz, *Isaac Backus - Puritan and Baptist: His Place in History, His Thought, and Their Implications for Modern Baptist Theology*, 294-295; Hudson, ed., *Baptist Concepts of the Church*, 27; Maring, *A Baptist Manual of Polity and Practice*, 44; Marsden, *Religion and American Culture*, 77; Tull, *Shapers of Baptist Thought*, 77; Wood, ed., *Baptists and the American Experience*, 277.
950   See Goen, 288.

two emphases the Baptists of Colonial New England preferred and the direction to which that points their posterity.

In summary, the principles of the Separate-Baptist-Backus Movement were not new nor were they to be considered sectarian, but rather these principles were the final stage of the Second Reformation. Baptist ideology, as in earlier historical movements, *had been discovered in the Scriptures, recognized in the common strain of the ancient, dissent community, and leveraged against the original ideals* of the Puritan Commonwealth.

Despite the fact that Backus the historian devised intellectual arguments based in Puritan theology to justify the Baptists as *definitive Puritans* in New England, he ultimately identified himself with the people called Baptists whom he named the rightful heirs of the Puritans' visible church ideal. This hearty New England stock had, in effect, snatched the baton of the *new reformation* from certain Puritan failure, and had answered in full all of its doctrinal inquiries. Therein, the original reformation of Luther, Calvin, Zwingli, Bucer, and Henry had finally reached its consummate stage, and like its dissenting predecessors of earlier centuries, it had challenged in the New World its most virile doctrinal enemies, and won.

It remains the present challenge of our modern Baptist movement to keep these lessons fresh in our collective minds, so that, similar to Backus and his movement, we readily embrace our doctrinal identity and grand heritage *discovered in the Scriptures* for the generations yet to unfold.

Bibliography

Allen, J.W. *The History of Political Thought in the Sixteenth Century*. New York: Dial Publishers, 1928.

Armitage, Thomas. *A History of the Baptists: Traced by Their Vital Principles and Practices from the Time of Our Lord and Saviour Jesus Christ to the Year 1886*. New York: Bryan, Taylor, and Co., 1887.

Armstrong, Maurice Whitman. "Religious Enthusiasm and Separatism in Colonial New England." *Harvard Theological Review* 38 (1945): 111-140.

Avis, Paul D.L. *The Church in the Theology of the Reformers*. Atlanta: John Knox Press, 1981.

Backman, Milton Vaughn, Jr. "Isaac Backus- a Pioneer Champion of Religious Liberty." Ph.D. diss., University of Pennsylvania, 1959.

Backus, Isaac. *A History of New England, with Particular Reference to the Denomination of Christians Called Baptists*. Three volumes. 1777, 1784, 1796. (Second edition. Two volumes. Edited by David Weston. Newton, Massachusetts, 1871).

_____. *An Abridgment of the Church History of New-England from 1602 to 1804: Containing a View of Their Principles and Practices, Declensions and Revivals, Oppression and Liberty, with a Concise Account of the Baptists in the Southern Parts of America and a Chronological Table of the Whole*. Boston,

1804. (Second edition with a memoir of the author. Baptist Tract Depository, 1839).

Bass, Clarence B. *Backgrounds to Dispensationalism*. Grand Rapids: Eerdmans Publishing Company, 1960.

Baxter, Norman A. "History of the Free-Will Baptists: A Study in New England Separatism." *Church History* 24, no. 2 (1955).

Bebbington, David. *Evangelicalism in Modern Britain*. Grand Rapids: Baker Book House, 1992.

Belden, Albert D. *George Whitefield, the Awakener: A Modern Study of the Evangelical Revival*. London: S. Low, Marston & Co., 1930.

Best, Ernest. *One Body in Christ*. London: S.P.C.K., 1955.

Biggs, Joseph. *A Concise History of the Kehukee Association*. Tarborough: George Howard: Office of the Tarborough (N.C.) Free Press, 1834.
Boles, John B. *The Great Revival*. Lexington: The University Press of Kentucky, 1972.

Boardman, George Nye. *A History of New England Theology*. Edited by Bruce Kuklick.
32 vols, American Religious Thought of the 18th and 19th Centuries. New York, 1899. Reprint, Garland Publishing, Inc, 1987.

Brachlow, Stephen. *The Communion of Saints*. Oxford: Oxford University Press, 1988.

Briggs, J.H.Y. *The English Baptists of the Nineteenth Century*. Didcot: Baptist Historical Society, 1994.

Brackney, William H., ed. *Baptist Life and Thought: 1680-1980*. Valley Forge: Judson Press, 1983.

Broadus, John Albert. *Baptist Confessions, Covenants, and Catechisms*. Edited by Timothy and Denise George. Nashville: Broadman and Holman Publishers, 1996.

Burkitt, Lemuel. *A Collection of Hymns and Spiritual Songs: Intended for Public and Social Worship, Some of Which Are Entirely New*. 2 ed. Halifax, NC: A. Hodge, 1802.

Bushman, Richard L. *The Great Awakening, Documents on the Revival of Religion, 1740-1745*. Chapel Hill and London: University of North Carolina Press, 1969.

Cathart, William, ed. *The Baptist Encyclopedia*. Philadelphia: Louis H. Everts, 1881. Reprint, 1988, The Baptist Standard Bearer.

Christie, Francis Albert. "The Beginnings of Arminianism in New England." *Papers of the American Society of Church History*, series 2,3 (1912): 151-172.

Clendenen, E. Ray and Brad J. Waggoner, ed. *A Southern Baptist Dialogue: Calvinism*. Nashville, B & H Academic, 2008.

Clipsham, Earnest F. "Andrew Fuller and Fullerism." *The Baptist Quarterly* 20, no. 6 (April, 1964): 268-276.

_____. "Andrew Fuller and Fullerism (1)." *The Baptist Quarterly* 20, no. 3 (July, 1963): 99-114.

_____. "Andrew Fuller and Fullerism (2)." *The Baptist Quarterly* 20, no. 4 (October, 1963): 146-154.

_____."Andrew Fuller and Fullerism (3)." *The Baptist Quarterly* 20, no. 5 (January, 1964): 214-225.

Coolidge, John S. *The Pauline Renaissance*. Oxford: Clarendon Press, 1970.

Cooper, James F., Jr. "Enthusiasts or Democrats? Separation, Church Government, and the Great Awakening in Massachusetts." *The New England Quarterly* 65, no. 2 (June 1992): 265-283.

Crosby, Thomas. *The History of the English Baptists from the Reformation to the Beginning of the Reign of King George I*. 4 vols. London, 1738-1740.

Crowell, William. *The Church Member's Manual*. Boston: Gould, Kendall, & Lincoln, 1847.

Cushing, John. "Notes on Disestablishment in Massachusetts, 1780-1833." *The William and Mary Quarterly* 26, no. 2 (April 1969): 169-190.

Dallimore, Arnold A. *George Whitefield: The Life and Times of the Great Evangelist of the 18th Century Revival*. 2 vols. Oxford:

University Printing House, 1970.

D'Aubigne, Merle J.H. *Scenes from the Life of Martin Luther*.
Philadelphia: The Memorial Publishing Company, 1883.

Davidson, William F. *The Free Will Baptists in History*. Nashville:
Randall House, 2001.

Dawson, Joseph Martin. *Baptists and the American Republic*.
Nashville: Broadman Press, 1956.

De Jong, Peter Y. *The Covenant Idea in New England Theology*.
Grand Rapids: W.B. Eerdmans Publishing Co., 1945.

Deweese, Charles W. *Baptist Church Covenants*. Nashville: Broadman
Press, 1990.

Dockery, David S. *Southern Baptist: Consensus and Renewal*. B & H
Academic, 2008.

Elert, Werner. *The Structure of Lutheranism*. St. Louis: Publisher
Name, 1962.

Erickson, Millard J. *Christian Theology*. Grand Rapids: Baker Book
House, 1983.

Erikson, Kai T. *Wayward Puritans*. New York: John Wiley and Sons,
Inc., 1966.

Estep, William R. *The Anabaptist Story*. 3rd ed. Grand Rapids:

William B. Eerdmans Publishing Company, 1996.

Evans, Benjamin. *The Early English Baptists*. 2 vols: J. Heaton and Son, 1864. Reprint, The Baptist Standard Bearer, Inc.

Foster, Frank H. *The Genetic History of New England Theology*. Edited by Bruce Kuklick. American Religious Thought of the 18th and 19th Centuries. Chicago: University of Chicago Press, 1907. Reprint, Garland Publishing, Inc. New York, 1987.

Gaustad, Edwin S. *The Great Awakening in New England*. New York: Harper & Brothers, 1965.

George, Timothy. *John Robinson and the English Separatist Tradition*. Edited by Charles Talbert. Vol. 1, National Association of Baptist Professors of Religion Dissertation Series. Macon: Mercer University Press, 1982.

_____, David S. Dockery, ed. *Theologians of the Baptist Tradition*. Nashville: Broadman and Holman Publishers, 2001.

_____, Denise George, and John Albert Broadus. *Baptist Confessions, Covenants, and Catechisms*. Library of Baptist Classics. Nashville, Tenn.: Broadman & Holman Publishers, 1996.

Gill, John. *Infant Baptism: A Part and Pillar of Popery*. Philadelphia: American Baptist Publication Society, 1851.

Gillette, A.D., ed. *Minutes of the Philadelphia Baptist Association from A.D 1707 to A.D. 1807: Being the First One-Hundred Years of Its*

Existence. Philadelphia: American Baptist Publication Society, 1851. Reprint, Baptist Book Trust.

Goen, C. C. *Revivalism and Separatism in New England, 1740-1800: Strict Congregationalist and Separate-Baptists in the Great Awakening*. New Haven: Yale University Press, 1962.

Good, Kenneth, H. *Are Baptists Reformed?* Lorain: Regular Baptist Heritage Fellowship, 1986.

Goodwin, Gerald J. "The Myth of 'Arminian Calvinism' in Eighteenth-Century New England." *The New England Quarterly* 41, no. 2 (1968): 213-237.

Grenz, Stanley. *The Baptist Congregation*. Valley Forge: Judson Press, 1985.

_____. *Isaac Backus–Puritan and Baptist: His Place in History, His Thought, and Their Implications for Modern Baptist Theology*. Edited by Charles Talbert. Vol. 4,

National Association of Baptist Professors of Religion Dissertation Series. Macon: Mercer University Press, 1983.

_____. *Renewing the Center: Evangelical Theology in a Post-Theological Era*. Grand Rapids: Baker Academic, 2000.

Guelzo, Allen C. "An Heir or Rebel? Charles Grandison Finney and the New England Theology ." *The Journal of the Early Republic* 17, no. 1 (Spring 1997): 61-94.

Hall, David, ed. *The Antinomian Controversy 1636-1638*. Middletown: Wesleyan University Press, 1968.

Hall, Edwin. *The Puritans and Their Principles*. New York: Baker and Scribner, 1847.

Haller, William. *The Rise of Puritanism*. Philadelphia: University of Pennsylvania Press, 1938. Reprint, First Pennsylvania Paperback Edition, 1972.

Handlin, Oscar, ed. *Isaac Backus and the American Pietistic Tradition*. Boston: Little, Brown and Company, 1967.

Haroutunian, Joseph. *Piety Versus Moralism: The Passing of the New England Theology*. Hamden, CT: Archon Books, 1964.

Hatch, Nathan O. "The Christian Movement and the Demand for a Theology of the People." *The Journal of American History* 67, no. 3 (Dec 1980): 545-567.

Hayden, Roger. *English Baptist History and Heritage*. 2nd ed. Oxfordshire: Nigel Lynn Publishing and Marketing Ltd, 2005.

Haykin, Michael, A.G.. and Kenneth J. Stewart, eds. *The Advent of Evangelicalism: Exploring Historical Continuities*. Nashville: B&H Publications, 2008.

Heimert, Alan, and Perry Miller. *The Great Awakening: Documents Illustrating the Crisis and Its Consequences*. Indianapolis, IN: Bobbs-Merrill, 1967.

_____, Alan and Perry Miller, ed. *Religion and the American Mind: From the Great Awakening to the Revolution*. Cambridge: Harvard University Press, 1966.

Hovey, Alvah. *A Memoir of the Life and Times of the Rev. Isaac Backus, A.M.* Boston: Gould and Lincoln, 1858.

Howe, Daniel Walker. "The Decline of Calvinism: An Approach to Its Study." *Comparative Studies in Society and History* 14, no. 3 (1972): 306-327.

Hudson, Winthrop Still, ed. *Baptist Concepts of the Church*. Valley Forge: Judson Press, 1959.

_____, "Denominationalism as a Basis for Ecumenicity: A Seventeenth century Conception." *Church History* 55, no. 1 (1955): 32-50.

_____. "Documents on the Associations of Churches." *Foundations*

4, no. 4 (1961): 332-339.

_____. "The Ecumenical Spirit of English Baptists." *The Review and Expositor* 55, no. 2 (1958): 182-195.

_____. "Who Were the Baptists?" *The Baptist Quarterly* 16, no. 7 (1956): 303-312.

_____. ed. *The Lord's Free People in a Free Land*. Fort Worth: Evans Press, 1976.

Hulse, Erroll. *Introduction to the Baptists*. Sussex: Carey Publications Ltd., 1973.

Husbands, Mark and Daniel J. Treier, ed. *The Community of the Word: Toward an Evangelical Ecclesiology*. Downers Grove: Intervarsity Press, 2005.

Kenney III, William Howland. "Alexander Garden and George Whitefield: The Significance of Revivalism in South Carolina 1738-1741." *South Carolina Historical Society* 71 (1970): 1-16.

_____. "George Whitefield, Dissenter Priest of the Great Awakening, 1739-1741." *The William and Mary Quarterly* 26, no. 1 (1969): 75-93.

Leonard, Bill J. *Baptist Ways: A History*. Valley Forge: Judson Press, 2003.

Keathley, Kevin. *Salvation and Sovereignty: A Molinist Approach*. Nashville: B & H Academic, 2010.

Lambert, Frank. *Pedlar in Divinity: George Whitefield and the Transatlantic Revivals, 1737-1770*. Princeton, N.J.: Princeton University Press, 1994.

_____. "Subscribing for Profits and Piety: The Friendship of Benjamin Franklin and George Whitefield." *The William and Mary Quarterly* 50, no. No. 3 (1993): 529-554.

Littell, Franklin Hamlin. *The Anabaptist View of the Church*. Boston: Starr King Press, 1958.

Locke, John. *The Works of John Locke, in Ten Volumes*. 11th ed. London, 1812.
Lovejoy, David S. *Religious Enthusiasm and the Great Awakening*. Englewood Cliffs, N.J.: Prentice-Hall, 1969.

Lovelace, Richard F. *The American Pietism of Cotton Mather*. Grand Rapids: Eerdmans Publishing Co., 1979.

Lumpkin, William Latane. *Baptist Confessions of Faith*. Philadelphia: Judson Press, 1959.

_____. *Baptist Foundations in the South: Tracing through the Separates the Influence of the Great Awakening, 1754-1787*. Nashville: Broadman Press, 1961.

_____. *Colonial Baptists and Southern Revivals*. New York: Arno Press, 1980.

Maclear, J.F. "New England and Fifth Monarchy: The Quest for the Millennium in Early American Puritanism." *The William and Mary Quarterly* 32, no. 2 (April 1975): 223-260.

Maring, Norman H. and Winthrop S. Hudson *A Baptist Manual of Polity and Practice.* Valley Forge: Judson Press, 1963.

Marini, Stephen A. *Radical Sects of Revolutionary New England.* Cambridge: Harvard University Press, 1982.

Marsden, George, M. *Religion and American Culture.* Orlando: Harcourt Brace Jovanovich College Publishers, 1990.

Mather, Cotton. *Magnalia Christi Americana*, 1702; ed. by Kenneth B. Murdock. Cambridge, 1977.

McBeth, Leon H. *The Baptist Heritage.* Nashville: Broadman Press, 1987.

_____. *A Sourcebook of Baptist Heritage.* Nashville: Broadman Press, 1990.

McElrath, Hugh T. and Harry Eskew. *Sing with Understanding.* Nashville: Church Street Press, 1995.

McGoldrick, James Edward. *Baptist Successionism: A Crucial Question in Baptist History.* Atla Monograph Series, No. 32. Metuchen, N.J., & London: The Scarecrow Press, Inc., 1994.

McLaren, Michael D. *A Generous Orthodoxy.* Grand Rapids:

Zondervan, 2004.

McLoughlin, William G., ed. *Isaac Backus on Church, State, and Calvinism: Pamphlets, 1754-1789*. The John Harvard Library. Cambridge, Mass.: Belknap Press of Harvard University Press, 1968.

_____. *New England Dissent 1630-1833*. 2 vols. Cambridge: Harvard University Press, 1971.

_____. *Soul Liberty: The Baptists' Struggle in New England, 1630-1833*. Hanover and London: University Press of New England, 1991.

Maston, T.B. *Isaac Backus: Pioneer of Religious Liberty*. Plymouth: Latimer, Trend and Co. Ltd., 1962.

McNeill, John T. "The Church in Sixteenth-Century Reformed Theology." *Journal of Religion* 22 (1942): 251-269.

Mead, Sidney E. *The Lively Experiment: The Shaping of Christianity in America*. New York: Harper and Row Publishers, 1976.

Mecklin, John M. *The Story of American Dissent*. New York: Harcourt Brace Jovanovich, Inc, 1934.

Meyer, Jacob C. *Church and State in Massachusetts from 1740-1833*. New York: Russell and Russell, 1968.

Miller, Perry. "The Contribution of the Protestant Churches to Religious Liberty in Colonial America." *Church History*, 4 (March

1935): 57-66.

_____. *Jonathan Edwards*. New York: Meridian Books, Inc., 1959.

_____. *The Life of the Mind in America*. New York: Harcourt Brace, 1965.

_____. *The New England Mind: From Colony to Province*. Cambridge: Harvard University Press, 1953.

_____. *The New England Mind: The Seventeenth Century*. Cambridge: Harvard University Press, 1954.

_____. *Orthodoxy in Massachusetts 1630-1650*. Cambridge: Harvard University Press, 1933.

Milner, Benjamin Charles, Jr. *Calvin's Doctrine of the Church*. Edited by Heiko A. Oberman. 5 vols. Vol. V, Studies in the History of Christian Thought. Leiden: E.J. Brill, 1970.

Minear, Paul S. *Images of the Church in the New Testament*. Philadelphia: The Westminster Press, 1960.

Mitchell, Mary Hewitt. *The Great Awakening and Other Revivals*. New Haven, 1934.

Morgan, Edmund S. *The Gentle Puritan: A Life of Ezra Stiles 1727-1795*. New York: W.W. Norton and Company, 1962.

_____. *Visible Saints: The History of a Puritan Idea*. Ithaca:

Cornell University Press, 1963.

Mountfield, D. .M.A. *The Church and the Puritans*. London: James Clark and Company, 1881.

Murrin, John M. "No Awakening, No Revolution? More Counterfactual Speculations." *Reviews in American History* 11, no. 2 (June 1983): 161-171.

Music, David W. "The Newport Collection (1766): The First Baptist Hymnal in America." *Baptist History and Heritage Journal* 38, no. 2 (2003): 1-16.

Naylor, Peter. *Calvinism, Communion, and the Baptists*. Vol. 7. Studies in Baptist History and Thought. Nottingham: Paternoster Press, 2003.

Newman, A.H., ed. *A Century of Baptist Movement*. Philadelphia: American Baptist Publication Society, 1901.

_____. *A Manual of Church History*. 2 vols. Valley Forge: Judson Press, 1902.

Noonkester, Myron C. "'God for Its Author': John Locke as a Possible Source for the New Hampshire Confession." *The New England Quarterly* 66, no. 3 (1993): 448-450.

Nuttall, Geoffrey Fillingham. *The Holy Spirit in Puritan Faith and Experience*. Oxford: Basil Blackwell Publishers, 1947.

_____. *Reformation, Conformity, and Dissent*. London: Epworth Press, 1977.

_____. *Visible Saints: The Congregational Way, 1640-1660*. Oxford: B. Blackwell, 1957.

Owen, John. *The Works of John Owen*. 16 vols. London: Johnstone and Hunter, 1850-1853.

Payne, E.A. and N.S. Moon. *Baptists and 1662*. London: The Carey Kingsgate Press Limited, 1962.

_____. *The Baptists of Berkshire*. London: Carey Kingsgate Press Ltd., 1951.

_____."Contacts between Mennonites and Baptists." *Foundations* 4, no. 1 (1961): 39-55.

_____. *The Fellowship of Believers*. London: Carey Kingsgate Press, Ltd., 1952.

_____. "Who Were the Baptists?" *Baptist Quarterly* 16, no. 8 (1956): 339-42.

Pelikan, Jaroslav Jan, Hilton C. Oswald, and Helmut T. Lehmann, eds. *The Works of Martin Luther*. 55 vols. Saint Louis: Concordia Pub. House, 1955.

Pollock, John Charles. *George Whitefield and the Great Awakening*.

1st ed. Garden City, New York: Doubleday, 1972.

Priest, Gerald L. "Andrew Fuller's Response to the Modern Question: A Reappraisal of the Gospel Worthy of All Acceptation." *Detroit Baptist Seminary Journal* 6 (Fall 2001): 45-73.

_____. "Revival and Revivalism: A Historical and Doctrinal Evaluation." *Detroit Baptist Seminary Journal* 1, no. 2 (1996): 223-252.

Prince, Thomas. *The Christian History, Containing Accounts of the Revival and Propagation of Religion in Great-Britain & America* ...

No. 1-104; Mar. 5, 1743-Feb. 23, 1744,5. Boston, N.E: Printed by S. Kneeland and T. Green, 1744.

Pope, Robert G. *The Half-Way Covenant: Church Membership in Puritan New England.* Princeton: Princeton University Press, 1969.

Riplinger, Thomas. *An American Vision of the Church.* Frankfurt: Herbert Lang Bern, 1976.

Ryrie, Charles C. *Dispensationalism Today.* Chicago: Moody Press, 1965.

_____., ed. *Issues in Dispensationalism.* Chicago: Moody Press, 1994.

Scott, Earnest F. *The Kingdom of God in the New Testament.* New York: Macmillan Company, 1931.

Schaff, Philip. *The Creeds of Christendom.* 3 vols. New York: Harper and Brothers, Publishers, 1877.

Sellers, Charles Coleman. *Lorenzo Dow: The Bearer of the Word.* New York: Minton, Balch & Company, 1928.

Shedd, William G.T. *A History of Christian Doctrine.* 2 vols. New York: Charles Scribner and Sons, 1902. Reprint, Solid Ground Classic Reprints, 2006.

Shiels, Richard D. "The Scope of the Second Great Awakening: Andover, Massachusetts, as a Case Study." *Journal of the Early*

Republic 5, no. 2 (Summer 1985): 223-246.

Shotwell, Malcomb G. *Renewing the Baptist Principle of Associations.* Place of publication: Eastern Baptist Theological Seminary, 1990.

Shurden, Walter, B. "Associationalism among Baptists in America, 1707-1814." Th.D. diss., New Orleans Baptist Seminary, 1967.

Simpson, Alan. *Puritanism in Old and New England.* Chicago: University of Chicago Press, 1955.

Smith, James, ed. *Posthumous Works of the Reverend and Pious James M'Gready.* 2 vols. Louisville: W.W. Worsley, 1831.

Squires, Duane J. "How a Baptist Confession Was Born." *Baptist Leader* (April 1955).

Stewart, I.D. *The History of the Freewill Baptists.* Vol. 1: 1780-1830. Dover: Freewill Baptist Printing Establishment, 1862.

Stout, Harry S. "Religion, Communications, and the Ideological Origins of the American Revolution." *The William and Mary Quarterly* 34, no. 4 (Oct 1977): 519-541.

_____.. *The Divine Dramatist.* Grand Rapids: William B. Eerdmans Publishing Company, 1991.

Strong, A.H. *Systematic Theology.* Old Tappan, N.J.: Fleming H. Revell Company, 1907.

Sweeney, Douglas A. and Allen C. Guelzo, ed. *The New England Theology: From Jonathan Edwards to Edwards Amassa Park*. Grand Rapids: Baker Academic, 2006.

Sweet, William Warren. *Religion in Colonial America*. New York: Cooper Square Publishers, Inc., 1965.

Thomas, Jesse B. *The Church and the Kingdom*. Louisville: Baptist Book Concern, 1914.

Tolmie, Murrey. *The Triumph of the Saints: The Separate Churches of London, 1616-49*. Cambridge: Cambridge University Press, 1977.

Torbet, Robert G. *A History of the Baptists*. 3rd ed. Valley Forge: Judson Press, 1950.

Trinterud, Leonard J. *The Forming of an American Tradition: A Re-Examination of Colonial Presbyterianism*. Philadelphia: Westminster Press, 1949.

Troeltsch, Ernst. *The Social Teaching of the Christian Churches*. Translated by Olive Wyon. New York: The Macmillan Co., 1931.

Tull, James E. *Shapers of Baptist Thought*. Valley Forge: Judson Press, 1972.

Underwood, A.C. *A History of the English Baptists*. London: The Carey Kingsgate Press Limited, 1947.

_____. *Primitivism, Radicalism, and the Lamb's War*.

Oxford: Oxford University Press, 1997.

Vedder, Henry C. *A Short History of the Baptists.* Valley Forge: Judson Press, 1907.

Verduin, Leonard. *The Reformers and Their Stepchildren.* Grand Rapids: Baker Book House, 1964.

Walker, Williston. *The Creeds and Platforms of Congregationalism.* New York: Charles Scribner's Sons, 1893.

Wamble, Hugh. "The Beginning of Associationalism among English Baptists." *The Review and Expositor* 55, no. 54 (1957): 544-559.

_____. "A Case Study in Baptist Ecclesiology." *Foundations* 3, no. 3 (1960): 242-253.

_____. "Early English Baptist Sectarianism." *The Review and Expositor* 55, no. 1 (1958): 59-69.

_____."Landmarkism: Doctrinaire Ecclesiology among Baptists." *Church History* 33, no. 4 (1964): 429-447.

Wayland, Francis. *Notes on the Principles and Practices of Baptist Churches.* New York: Sheldon, Blakeman, and Co., 1857.

Whitefield, George. *Whitefield's Journals.* new ed. London: Banner of Truth Trust, 1960.

Williams, G.H. *The Radical Reformation.* Philadelphia: The

Westminster Press, 1962.

_____. and Angel M. Mergal, ed. *Spiritual and Anabaptist Writers*. Philadelphia: The Westminster Press, 1957.

Williams, Roger. *The Complete Writings of Roger Williams*. Seven volumes. Ed. Samuel L. Caldwell. New York: Russell and Russell, 1963.

Wright, Conrad. *The Beginnings of Unitarianism in America*. Boston: Starr King Press, 1955.

Wayland, Francis. "Letters on Associations." *American Baptist Magazine and Missionary Intelligencer*, no. 4 (1823): 198-203.

_____. "Letters on Associations." *American Baptist Magazine and Missionary Intelligencer*, no. 4 (1824): 242-244 and 324-348.

Walsh, J.D. *"Origins of the Evangelical Revival" in Essays in Modern Church History, in Memory of Norman Sykes*. Edited by G.V. Bennett and J.D. Walsh. New York: Oxford University Press, 1966.

White, Eugene E. "Decline of the Great Awakening in New England: 1741-1746." *The New England Quarterly* 24, no. 1 (1951): 35-52.

White, B.R. *The English Baptists of the Seventeenth Century*. Edited by Roger Hayden. 4 vols. Vol. 1, *A History of the English Baptists*. Oxford: The Baptist Historical Society, 1983.

_____. *The English Separatist Tradition from the Marian*

Martyrs to the Pilgrim Fathers. Oxford Theological Monographs. Oxford: Oxford University Press, 1971.

Wood, James Edward, ed. *Baptists and the American Experience.* Valley Forge: Judson Press, 1976.

Wood, Nathan E. *The History of the First Baptist Church.* Philadelphia: American Baptist Publication Society, 1899. Reprint, Arno Press 1980.

Ziff, Larzer. *Puritanism in America.* New York: The Viking Press, 1973.

Zuckert, Michael P. *Launching Liberalism: On Lockean Political Philosophy.* Lawrence: University Press of Kansas, 2002.

Pamphlets, Sermons, and Letters

All of the published pamphlets, sermons, and letters listed below are available in the Backus Collection at the Andover Newton Theological Seminary in Newton, Massachusetts. In addition, those pamphlets indicated below have been republished in one volume, *Isaac Backus on Church, State, and Calvinism: Pamphlets, 1754-1789,* edited by William G. McLoughlin.

All True Ministers of the Gospel Are Called into That Work by the Special Influences of the Holy Spirit : A Discourse Shewing the

Nature and Necessity of an Internal Call to Preach the Everlasting Gospel. Boston: Printed by Fowle, 1754. (Reprinted in McLoughlin)

A Short Description of the Difference between the Bondwoman and the Free. As they are the two covenants. with the characters and conditions of each of their children: considered in a Sermon delivered at Middleborough, wherein is particularly shewn, that none are proper subjects of the special ordinances of the Gospel-church but real Saints. Boston, 1756. (Reprinted in McLoughlin)

Spiritual Ignorance Causeth Men to Counter-Act Their Doctrinal Knowledge. A Discourse from Acts Xiii. 27. Providence, in New-England. Printed and sold by William Goddard, at the sign of Shakespeare's head, 1763.

True Faith Will Produce Good Works: A Discourse, Wherein Are Opened the Nature of Faith, and Its Powerful Influence on the Heart and Life, Together with the Contrary Nature and Effects of Unbelief, and Answers to Various Objections: To Which Are Perfixed [Sic] a Brief View of the Present State of the Protestant World, with Some Remarks on the Writings of Mr. Sandeman. Boston: Printed by D. Kneeland, for Philip Freeman, 1767.

A Fish Caught in His Own Net: An Examination of Nine Sermons, from Matt. 16. 18. Published Last Year, by Mr. Joseph Fish of Stonington : Wherein He Labours to Prove, That Those Called Standing Churches in New-England, Are Built Upon the Rock, and Upon the Same Principles with the First Fathers of This Country, and That Separates and Baptists Are Joining with the Gates of Hell against Them : In Answer to Which, Many of His Mistakes

Are Corrected, the Constitution of Those Churches Opened, the Testimonies of Prophets and Apostles, and Also of Many of Those Fathers Are Produced, Which as Plainly Condemn His Plan, as Any Separate or Baptist Can Do. Boston: Printed by Edes and Gill, in Queen-Street, 1768. (Reprinted in McLoughlin)

Gospel Comfort, under Heavy Tidings. Providence: Printed by John Carter, 1769.

A Short Description of the Difference between the Bondwoman and the Free. As they are the Two Covenants. With the characters and conditions of each of their children. The second edition corrected. To which is added an answer to Mr. Frothingham's late letter concerning Baptism. Boston, 1770.

A Seasonable Plea for Liberty of Conscience against Some Late Oppressive Proceedings, Particularly in the Town of Berwick in the County of York. Boston: Printed and sold by Philip Freeman, 1770.

The Doctrine of Sovereign Grace Opened and Vindicated. Providence, Rhode Island: Printed by John Carter, 1771.

A Reply to a Piece Wrote Last Year, by Mr. Israel Holly Pastor of a Church in Suffield; Entitled "the New Testament Interpretation of the Old, Relative to Infant Baptism." Newport. Printed, for the author, by Solomon Southwick, 1772.

Evangelical Ministers Described, and Distinguished from Legalists. A Sermon, the Substance of Which Was Delivered October 30, 1771, at the Ordination of Mr. Asa Hunt, to the Pastoral Charge of the Third Baptist Church in Middleborough. Boston, 1772.

A Discourse, Concerning the Materials, the Manner of Building, and Power of Organizing the Church of Christ. Boston: J. Boyles Publishing, 1773.

The Sovereign Decrees of God, Set in a Scriptural Light, and Vindicated against the Blasphemy contained in a late paper, entitled On Traditionary Zeal. In a letter to a Friend. Boston, 1773. (Reprinted in McLoughlin)

An Appeal to the Public for Religious Liberty against the Oppressions of the Present Day. Boston: Printed by John Boyle, 1773. (Reprinted in McLoughlin)

Government and Liberty Described; and Ecclesiastical Tyranny Exposed. Boston: Printed by Powers and Willis, and sold by Phillip Freeman, 1778. (Reprinted in McLoughlin)

Policy, as Well as Honesty, Forbids the Use of Secular Force in Religious Affairs. Massachusetts-state Boston: Printed by Draper and Folsom, and sold by Phillip Freeman, 1779. (Reprinted in McLoughlin)

An Appeal to the People of the Massachusetts State against Arbitrary Power. Boston, 1780. (Reprinted in McLoughlin)

The Substance of an Address to an Assembly in Bridgewater, March 10, 1779. Providence: Printed and sold by John Carter, at Shakespeare's Head, in Meeting-street, 1779.

Truth Is Great, and Will Prevail. [Boston]: Sold by Philip Freeman, 1781. (Reprinted in McLoughlin)

The Doctrine of Universal Salvation Examined and Refuted. Providence: Printed by John Carter, 1782.

Door Opened for Christian Liberty, and No Man Can Shut It. This proved by plain F-A-C-T-S. Boston, 1783. (Reprinted in McLoughlin)

An Address to the Second Baptist Church in Middleborough Concerning the Importance of Gospel Discipline. Middleborough: Nathaniel Coverly, 1787.

An Address to the Inhabitants of New England, concerning the present Bloody Controversy therein. Boston, 1787. (Reprinted in McLoughlin)

The Doctrine of Particular Election and Final Perseverance, Explained and Vindicated. Boston, 1789. (Reprinted in McLoughlin)

The Liberal Support of Gospel Ministers Opened and Inculcated.
Boston: Printed by Samuel Hall, 1790.

The Infinite Importance of the Obedience of Faith, and of a
Separation from the World, Opened and Demonstrated. 2d ed.
Boston: Printed and sold by Samuel Hall, no. 53, Cornhill, 1791.

The Testimony of the Two Witnesses, Explained and Vindicated with
a Few Remarks Upon the Late Writings of Dr. Hemmenway and Dr.
Lathrop. 2d ed. Boston: Printed by Samuel Hall, no. 53, 1793.

Gospel Comfort for Mourners: A Sermon, Delivered at
Middleborough, February 5, 1769, Upon Hearing of the Death of a

Godly Mother: To Which Is Added, Some Memoirs of Her Life. 2nd ed. Boston: Manning & Loring, 1803.

A Great Faith Described and Inculcated: A Sermon, on Luke vii. 9. Boston: Printed by E. Lincoln, Water-street, 1805.

Backus, Isaac, to David Sprague. In *Backus Papers, Andover Newton Theological School*, Middleborough, Mass., 1756.

_____, Isaac, to Peter Worden. In *Backus Papers, Andover Newton Theological Seminary*, 1769.

_____, Isaac, to *the Reverend Mr. Benjamin Lord, of Norwich*. Providence: William Goddard, 1764.

_____, Isaac, to *a Gentleman in the Massachusetts General Assembly, Concerning Taxes to Support Religious Worship*. [Boston: s.n.], 1771.

_____, Isaac, to Taunton Mass. Baptist Church. In *Backus Papers, Andover Newton Theological School*, Middleborough, Mass., 1772.

_____, Isaac, to Israel Holly. Middleborough, Mass.: Misc. Letters, Conn. Historical Society, 1778.

_____, Isaac to Jabez Brown, In *Backus Papers, Andover Newton Theological School*, Providence, 1802.

_____, Isaac, to Valentine W. Rathbun. In *American Baptist*

Historical Society, Middleborough, 1805.

_____, Isaac, to Mr. Butler. n.p.: Backus Papers, John Hay Library, 1788.

_____, Isaac. edited by n.p., "Reasons for Separation. An answer to 3. Questions concerning Church affairs proposed by a friend." Backus Papers, Andover Newton Theological School, 1756.

About the Author

Bruce Snavely is the founder and president of Global Baptist Training Foundation. He has spent 20 years doing church-planting work and 12 years in Christian higher education. He holds a Ph.D. in historical theology from Trinity College at the University of Bristol, UK. Bruce and his wife Grace have four children, and five grandchildren.